THE
STRATEGY
MACHINE

THE STRATEGY MACHINE

*Building Your Business
One Idea at a Time*

LARRY DOWNES

HarperBusiness
An Imprint of HarperCollins*Publishers*

HarperCollins books may be purchased for educational, business, or sales promotional use. For information please write: Special Markets Department, HarperCollins Publishers, Inc., 10 East 53rd Street, New York, NY 10022.

FIRST EDITION

Designed by Nancy Singer Olaguera

Library of Congress Cataloging-in-Publication Data has been filed for.

ISBN: 0-06-621129-8

02 03 04 05 06 QW 10 9 8 7 6 5 4 3 2 1

The dictionary said that inertia was a property of matter, by which matter tends, when at rest, to remain so, and when in motion, to move on in a straight line. Finding that his mind refused to imagine itself at rest or in a straight line, he was forced, as usual, to let it imagine something else; and since the question concerned his mind, and not matter, he decided from personal experience that his mind was never at rest, but moved—when normal—about something it called a motive, and never moved without motives to move it.

—*Henry Adams, "Vis Inertiae" (1903)*

CONTENTS

PART I

THE INFORMATION REVOLUTION
Why a Strategy Machine?

PART II

THE STRATEGY MACHINE

Putting the Pieces Together

PART III

THE EXECUTIONER'S SONG

Reinventing Your Business Every Day

PREFACE

Strange Tales of the New Economy

In the three years since I completed *Unleashing the Killer App: Digital Strategies for Market Dominance*, the mania for digital technology spread far beyond the modest world of business strategists and into private investing and the public markets. At the same time, it has leapt from start-ups and technology companies to the executive suites of the most staid businesses in the most stable of industries. By the beginning of 2000, even my retired Aunt Dorothy was writing to ask whether I thought she could make money by changing her last name to Com and claiming to be the original "Dot Com."

The festive mood changed abruptly in March 2000. That's when Judge Thomas Penfield Jackson issued his opinion in the ill-conceived antitrust suit against Microsoft, which was in many ways an indictment of the way high-technology companies had operated for 25 years. Jackson sounded a particularly loud wake-up call for investors, who began to wonder if Washington's efforts to help what was being called "the new economy" would instead kill the goose laying the silicon eggs. After two and a half years, boom turned to bust.

Ventures that had been launched with plans to reach profitability in five years were suddenly told to reach it in the next quarter. Strategies were scrapped, desperation set in, and companies failed. Day traders bailed out of public Internet companies and venture capitalists hunkered down with their existing portfolios to see which of their companies could be salvaged.

Like Captain Louis Renault, the character played by Claude Rains in *Casablanca*, investors were "shocked, shocked" to discover that they had sunk millions of dollars into companies that were little more than concepts hatched in first-year business school courses (more likely after class). They had given their money to kids who knew nothing about technology, let alone operating a business larger than a paper route.

Some ideas were just plain bad. Internet incubator E-Companies famously spent $7 million simply for the rights to the Internet *address* for "business.com."

The New York Times Magazine ran an admiring cover story in the fall of 1999 about the day-to-day activities of a group of entrepreneurs who had launched a company called "The Man," a dot-com focused on teaching affluent young men the fine points of manipulating women. The-Man.com was to be a "lifestyle Website" that would sell everything needed by a first-rate Lothario. "This could be a really, really major public company," the *Times* quoted twenty-something CEO Calvin Lui. The company ran through $17 million and shuttered its Website less than a year later, without ever posting the valuable "content" it had promised would draw shoppers.

A more sinister story was that of Pixelon, a Silicon Valley company that was building specialized software to compress and transmit high-quality video from its customers' Websites. The company received millions of dollars in venture funds from seasoned technology investors, based largely on the strength of patents held by the founder and CEO, Michael Fenne. The company, trying to establish its "brand" and build "buzz," spent nearly all of the proceeds of a $20 million round of financing on a "launch party" for Silicon Valley insiders which included live music from Kiss, Tony Bennett, the Dixie Chicks, and The Who.

The party was not their worst excess. It turned out there were no patents or even patentable ideas. The CEO, whose real name was David Stanley, was wanted in three states for various frauds, including bilking parishioners at the church where his father was the minister. Pixelon was run as a cult, with the CEO administering spankings to his senior executives. Only after the money was gone did the investors pay a visit, police in tow, to turn their entrepreneurial partner over to trial.

As the French say: "The more things change, the more they stay the same."

Disasters like the Internet calamity have happened many times before in Silicon Valley, though never on quite the same scale. In the mid-1980s, fueled by the work of a few leading computer science professors at Stanford, MIT, and Carnegie-Mellon, a similar mania developed for companies exploiting artificial intelligence (AI), the ability of computer software to learn and exhibit sentient behavior. Investors began to outnumber attendees at meetings of the American Association of Artificial Intelligence, and cover stories about "revolutions" appeared in *BusinessWeek, Forbes,* and *Fortune* magazines. Companies were founded and immediately began to jockey for position in establishing market dominance.

Few people remember Teknowledge, IntelliCorp, The Carnegie Group, Aion, Gold Hill, Symbolics, or Thinking Machines, Inc. They made the hardware and software, developed the "expert systems" and "blackboard architectures," and created the consulting firms to help traditional businesses learn how to transform themselves into early adopters. In their own more modest and less criminal way, they were TheMan.coms and Pixelons of their day. Venture-backed and run by eager young men and women with celebrity board members, most had inexperienced management, no business plan, and little sense of the difficulties of selling innovative new solutions to traditional companies.

And sure enough, all of them went bust. During the AI boom, I was working as a consultant at what was then Arthur Andersen & Co.'s consulting division, trying to help Fortune 500 clients find uses for the products of these companies. It became clear one day that this was a fool's errand. My colleagues and I were meeting with the CEO of IntelliCorp, the leading developer of software for expert systems—applications that used databases of rules to mimic human experts and make intelligent decisions and recommendations.

Up until then, IntelliCorp had written its software exclusively for high-end, specialized AI computers and sophisticated applications such as credit scoring (American Express) and diagnosing problems with oil drills (Schlumberger). If you simplify your product, we told the IntelliCorp management team, and make it work in conjunction with existing applications and databases, the range of uses would explode, and so would your market.

"We won't do that," the CEO told us. "Our engineers are only interested in solving hard problems."

Investors in Intellicorp and other AI companies must have been hearing a similar message, for just as quickly as the floodgates were opened, the money dried up. The AI companies closed their opulent palaces on El Camino Real in Palo Alto and Route 128 in Massachusetts, and the business press began to rail against the arrogance of the already-dying industry. The "AI Winter" had begun.

Aside from scale (no more than $1 billion was sunk into artificial intelligence), the AI Winter differs from the Internet bubble in one key respect.

The funding for companies like IntelliCorp was almost entirely private. Most never sold stock to the public, so public markets were not affected by their rise or fall. Individual investors shared neither the risk nor the potential reward. In large part, the failure of the AI companies was absorbed by the venture capitalists who simply offset their losses against other ideas that played out better—home computers, perhaps, or advanced video games—exactly what venture investors are supposed to do.

Combatants in the Internet revolution appear to have learned nothing from the example of AI, for they have repeated all of the same mistakes, and done so on a much more ambitious and expensive scale, with one important difference. For better and for worse, the public financed a significant portion of the Internet craze. In that regard, it is unique; indeed, it represents the first time in the history of capitalism that the basic development of a new technology has been funded in large part by public investors.

In previous waves of information technology, whether software, hardware, or services, the early stage (and therefore high-risk) investing was done by a combination of government, universities, and private investors. Only after a company had established its products, its distribution channels, and its markets—and nearly always *after* it became sustainably profitable—did it offer its shares to the public.

With Internet companies, the public jumped right in. Why? Both investors and the media became mesmerized by the stock price of the first Internet IPO, that of now-defunct Netscape Corp. The company offered a modest number of shares to the public in 1995, and the price was quickly driven up in multiples. The feeding frenzy began. The public demanded the opportunity to become, in effect, venture investors themselves, and the companies, investment banks, and lawyers fed them hundreds of offerings over the 24 months that followed.

So much money was flooding the markets that companies like The-Man.com, Pixelon, and dozens of others, equally ill-conceived, received funding, went public, and saw their stocks balloon into the stratosphere, yielding temporary values in the billions of dollars. When the first dominos fell, the investing, business, and popular media, which had fueled the riot for Internet stocks, turned an abrupt about-face, performing a second disservice by calling the new economy a bubble that had burst, inspiring another kind of panic in the hearts of the inexperienced investor.

I focus on the financial aspects of the Internet to make an important point about the actual state of the Internet revolution. The rise and fall of companies and their stock prices has largely dominated the public's understanding about what that revolution means. But it is only a part of the story and a part that has been misunderstood both on the way up and the way down. Even as each shuttering of a Website is reported with ghoulish fatalism, we should remember that in the same year that the Internet bubble "burst," worldwide Internet use tripled (from 6 to 18 million users) and U.S. Internet commerce grew to $250 billion, $45 billion in consumer purchases alone. America On-Line acquired Time-Warner (and not the other way around), and even at their 52-week lows Amazon was still worth over $5 billion, eBay nearly $20 billion. During the first three quarters of 2001, long after the bubble burst, venture capitalists invested over $25 billion in startups, far more than they spent in 1997 or 1998, when the Internet was first taking off.

The rest of the story is every bit as dramatic, and much more valuable for those who run businesses rather than simply invest in them. The rest of story is the subject of *The Strategy Machine*.

The Internet and related technologies really are part of a revolution in business and beyond. The "real" revolution is transforming industries and putting traditional assets at risk as it creates new ones. It is doing so not just for the benefit of entrepreneurs and startups, but for oil companies, insurance companies, grocery stores—even government agencies—in North America and around the world.

It is not the revolution of a stock market with violent mood swings. It is not a revolution that pits old economy against new economy, in which only one will win. Above all, it is not a technology revolution but a business revolution, perhaps the most serious expansion of and challenge to capitalism since James Watt perfected the steam engine and launched the Industrial Revolution.

This is a book about the real revolution, an Information Revolution, that continues—indeed accelerates—beyond the meltdown of stock prices and the failure of foolish investments. It is a story of managers in a range of industries using information technology strategically—that is, to make their business more profitable, in ways that can be sustained for years to come—learning sometimes painful lessons about how to implement new approaches to operating their companies. It is a story about how to overcome surprising internal as well as external obstacles.

If you are one of these managers—or if you would like to be—this book will help you succeed in the long run with a winning portfolio in the *next* economy. Regardless of the kind of business or the size of your company, whether you work in operations, sales, or finance, or whether you are the CEO or a manager in training, the tools in this book will teach you how to innovate on a daily basis, how to unlock value lost in your balance sheet, and how to profit from the transformation going on right now in your industry.

The artificial intelligence revolution ended, but much of the technology that it spawned lived on in new forms, and led to successful new products, services, and companies. It did change the world, though in far more subtle ways than its designers thought. The same will be said of the Internet revolution. It will not be the revolutionaries, but the students of their history, who will profit from the sacrifices.

INTRODUCTION

When machines determine your strategy, turn strategy into a machine.

Forget the Internet and the World Wide Web. They are only harbingers of the Information Revolution, dominated not by computers doing more things but by more things becoming computers, embedded into whatever you can think of, from clothing to food to the seats on the airplane where you are reading this book (which will also be an addressable object), intelligent products that can send and receive data across a global network—from the factory, from the store, or from your suitcase. Welcome to the age of disposable computers.

Today, an MIT consortium led by Procter & Gamble is testing intelligent product labels that can do just that for about $5 each. In 2002, the cost will fall to 5 cents. By the time you and I have retired—assuming that concept means anything by then—it will be cost-effective to turn each one of about a trillion items in commerce into computers, which will give us regular reports of their status from the moment they are made until they are finally consumed.

The Information Revolution won't be televised—it will beam its stories directly into our brains, where microchips the size of a molecule will live side-by-side with the rest of our gray matter, helping us see, move, and, if we're lucky, remember.

When machines determine your strategy, turn strategy into a machine.

The Strategy Machine describes a revolutionary approach to running a business, one that has been designed to work in the world of disposable computing. It is an approach being developed and used by companies in every industry. It is an approach that can work for you.

The book has three parts, each of which answers one important question:

Why do I need a strategy machine? How do I put it together? How do I keep it running?

WHY DO YOU NEED ONE?

To understand the future, we start with the past. The Industrial Revolution, which brought us factories, railroads, telephones and just about anything else you can think of, teaches us the folly of plans that assume the world will behave as you expect it to, even the plans of those who did the creating. The inventors of its greatest innovations often failed to find their markets or build companies that could continue to profit from their genius. The real winners were the machines, machines that made other machines, which in turn created and destroyed industries, and always in surprising ways.

The Information Revolution, dominated by disposable computers, is beginning that process anew. Now, however, the metamorphosis will be faster, fed by a tidal wave of new data. Its principal beneficiary and victim will be the supply chain, the integrated set of activities that produce, sell, and distribute products and services.

As companies piece together ever-clearer pictures of their markets, supply chains will be repeatedly dismantled and then put back together. The transformation happens in three distinct stages, just as it did 150 years ago, but with one important difference. All three stages are happening now. As Yogi Berra once said, "It's like *déjà vu* all over again."

In the course of industry transformation, the source of your profits will shift—sometimes subtly but more often in rude jolts—from products and services to information about products and services: Where they are, who is using them, how much they paid, and when they need more.

To answer these questions, a parallel structure, an *information supply chain,* will collect information about every sale, from producers to consumers and back again. The evolving information supply chain is the real source of productivity improvements today, but more important, it is the source of new value tomorrow—new products and services made up of information and sold as information.

HOW DO YOU PUT IT TOGETHER?

When the future is uncertain, as any good investment manager will tell you, hedge your bets. One strategy won't do it, even a good one. You need a portfolio of strategies, and you need to test all of them at the same time, shifting your focus and your resources as the environment inside the information supply chain stabilizes.

A strategy machine looks for ways to improve your business today, even as it tests new ideas that may destroy that business tomorrow. It scours your balance sheet searching for assets your current plans don't use and probably can't see. Information assets like brand, expertise, and market intelligence are the fuel of the strategy machine, a kind of invisible capital that increases in value the more it is used.

Load up the strategy machine with invisible capital, and it reinvents your business, creating more assets, which can be fed back in for still more capital. The strategy machine is an invisible capital engine, a perpetual motion machine.

The idea of a strategy machine is simple, but its impact on your business is profound. It is nothing less than the merger of planning and execution. The strategy machine is not just how you plan, it is how you run your business—not just once a year or once a quarter, but every day.

HOW DO YOU KEEP IT GOING?

The strategy machine is easy to build, but difficult to operate. It is a machine that creates change, and change may be difficult for some inside and outside your organization to handle, especially when it happens every day. The operation of your strategy machine will be challenged by a host of obstacles that suddenly appear the minute you turn it on. The obstacles take many forms, but in some sense they are just different names for the same force: inertia, the resistance to change.

Companies that can overcome inertia, as we will see, have done so not by eliminating it (that is impossible) but by stealing its power. From high school physics, you may remember that inertia keeps bodies that are not moving from moving, but it also helps bodies in motion keep going. Turn the obstacles around, use them to your advantage, and they transform into catalysts that make the strategy machine run faster.

First and foremost, this is a book about getting things done—constantly testing ideas, developing the ones that work, and discarding those that don't. The tools and techniques I describe have been distilled from real-world stories of managers at real companies—startups, incumbents, large and small, high tech and low, alone and in combinations.

There is one important word of warning about these examples. Over a hundred different companies appear in the pages that follow, some in leading roles and others in bit parts, some as examples of what to do and some as cautionary tales. None of them will have stopped moving. Even companies that build world-class strategy machines may abandon them later, fail to keep them running, or allow their invisible capital to degrade to the point of information bankruptcy. The stories in this book illustrate decisions that made sense (or didn't) at the time. Nothing more.

If you take one message from this book, understand that the strategy machine will change you along with your company. Reinventing your business is reinventing your career. As you build and maintain your company's machine, you fill the gaps in your own portfolio, find the hidden value of your private supply of invisible capital, and turn personal obstacles into personal strengths.

In the end, you won't recognize your business anymore; but then, your business won't recognize you either.

We start, as revolutionaries often do, with a walk through the desert.

PART I

THE INFORMATION REVOLUTION

Why a Strategy Machine?

A DISTANT MIRROR

Lessons of the Industrial Revolution

Why should we look to the past in order to prepare for the future?
Because there is nowhere else to look.

—James Burke, *Connections*

[THE REVEALING HISTORY OF THE SUEZ CANAL. REVOLUTIONARY
STRATEGIES: INNOVATING, PROFITING, REGULATING, PROMOTING, AND
FINANCING TRANSFORMATION. RULES FOR REVOLUTIONARIES.]

A PARABLE OF PORT SAID

Studying the past can teach you a lot about the future. Consider the story of a famous international effort to build new commercial infrastructure. Proponents of this massive project promised to eliminate time and distance as a constraint on commerce, reduce costs for everyone, and make investors fabulously wealthy. In its first years, the project raised millions of dollars, much of it from the public, and stock prices rocketed into the stratosphere. Minor setbacks and delays turned into years of stalled progress. As the project proved more difficult than expected, however, markets crashed just as dramatically as they had soared. A cottage industry of journalists devoted to tracking the failings, blunders, and arrogance of the project's promoters flourished.

That may sound like a synopsis of the last few years, but what I am describing is the construction of the Suez Canal, the 101-mile trench through Egypt's Sinai Peninsula, the brainchild of French engineer Ferdinand Marie de Lesseps. The Suez created a permanent passage from the Red Sea to the now-bustling town of Port Said on the Mediterranean—an engineering marvel on a global scale. It revolutionized the transportation business, making it possible to ship cargo between Europe and Asia without a long, dangerous detour around the southern tip of Africa.

The canal not only changed the nature of global commerce, but also played a starring role in the political fortunes of Britain, France, and the Middle East. After more than a century of operation, five owners and a seven-year war that temporarily shut it down, the canal is still in operation. Nearly 14,000 vessels will journey through the desert this year alone, carrying more than 400 million tons of cargo and generating nearly $2 billion in revenue for the government of Egypt.

The Suez Canal is characteristic of all great infrastructure projects. Because they attempt to do what has never been done, their design and construction is fraught with unknowns. Setbacks, accidents, and exasperating changes in strategy are frequent. They are often the obsessive dreams of visionaries who invariably come equipped with egos big enough to match their ideas, whose arrogance leads to startling turns of events. As a result, such projects become topics of never-ending fascination for the press, who cannot resist reporting on the folly of trying something new. Even when these projects are completed, stale traditions and rusty business processes resist adapting to their use, despite the obvious and immediate benefits of doing so.

Unfortunately, con men also find big projects irresistible, and as a result, the public is often drawn in too soon and given the worst financial terms. Project delays lead inexperienced investors to demand accelerated returns, which further delays profitability and threatens the project with collapse. Frequent panics, booms, and busts dog the effort from beginning to end. The media throws fuel on all the ups and downs, doting on each misstep and gleefully predicting total failure right up until the moment of victory.

REVOLUTIONARY STRATEGIES

The story of Ferdinand Marie de Lesseps is a fable for revolutionary technological change: an arrogant but brilliant engineer; an ambitious plan to change the nature of commerce; a fickle investing public demanding results before they can be delivered; high emotions fanned into flames by a sensational media first lionizing and later spurning the venture; and, finally, the belated realization of the plan and vindication of its creator well after his death.

De Lesseps was a leading figure in the Industrial Revolution, which began in the mid-18th century and continued for 150 years. It is no coincidence that his story echoes so closely our own age. It was, after all, the Industrial Revolution that created the original versions of the manufacturing, banking, retailing, and distribution industries we know—indeed, the concept of "industry" dates from this period. Even as information technology is remaking those industries, we should take a step back and understand the crucible in which they were formed.

We can go deeper still and observe the relationship between the technologies of the Industrial Revolution and the economic system that allowed them to flourish. It would be only a slight exaggeration, in fact, to say that industrial technology *created* the capitalist system. Capitalism's chief characteristics—public financing through debt and equity, asset-intensive global corporations, and infrastructures created and maintained at least in part by governments—are by-products of inventions like the steam engine, factories, and railroads, which created both the opportunity and the demand for such a system.

In particular, the Industrial Revolution required and produced strong national governments. Central banks maintain neutral and stable currency for the exchange of goods and services across borders. Courts provide a forum to enforce contracts as well as a strong deterrence against violating them. Public education takes a portion of the profits generated by industry and applies it to developing future generations of skilled labor who continue improving the system. Each of these institutions existed in some form before the Industrial Revolution, but it was the needs of a global industrial economy that expanded and shaped them into their highly evolved forms of today.

Even at the individual level, there is much we can learn from Ferdinand de Lesseps' example, and similar stories that can be told about nearly all major developments of the Industrial Revolution. Rather than repeat tales better told by others, however, I have distilled the most important lessons of the Industrial Revolution—specifically, the five different strategies employed by those who, we can say with the hindsight of history, won the revolution. As we will see in the chapters that follow, these five general responses to revolutionary change are as useful today as they were in the past.

1. Innovate Constantly

Larger factories meant more complex organizations, giving rise to the corporation and the "science" of management pioneered by Frederick Winslow Taylor in the early 20th century. The real winners of the Industrial Revolution were not owners who invested in one generation of machinery and then focused on getting the most from it, but those who *continuously* invested in technology, using whatever metrics they had for deciding which innovations showed the most promise and when the right moment might be to take the necessary leap of faith.

Not surprisingly, the names we remember are less those of brilliant inventors like James Watt and more the industrialists who invented processes for constant innovation and adaptation. These include inventors such as Thomas Edison and Alexander Graham Bell, who had the vision to build organizations around their creative genius, as well as industrialists whose competence was almost entirely in organizational and process management, like Andrew Carnegie, John D. Rockefeller, Henry Ford, and Alfred Sloan. The success of each of these executives took a career's worth of patience and an almost religious devotion to their individual strategies. Investors who wanted quick returns from these revolutionaries were doomed to disappointment.

2. Supply the Infrastructure

There were other winners who pursued indirect strategies for profiting from the revolution. As in any conflict, providing munitions to the combatants can generate exceptional returns. This is particularly true if the suppliers, by outfitting all sides with increasingly powerful arms, can extend the battle and increase its ferocity. Companies that provided dynamos for factories, steel for railroads, or copper wire for telephone networks often did far better than their customers, who were driven in part by the very same suppliers to ruinous competition with competitors.

In 1882, for example, the U.S. railroad industry consumed 75% of the nation's rolled-steel output, and redundant track was laid from one end of North America to the other. By the early 1890s, a third of American railroads were bankrupt while U.S. Steel became the world's first billion-dollar corporation. Providers of today's information infrastructure follow a similar strategy, making companies such as IBM, Cisco, Microsoft, and Intel among the wealthiest in history, even as hundreds of their high-flying startup customers burn up in the atmosphere.

3. Regulate and Support

Regulating the new markets that emerge from a revolution can be a source of profit, not only for elected government but for private organizations like trade associations, industry consortia, and standards-setting bodies. In the United States, industrialization gave rise to legislation such as the Sherman Antitrust Act, the Fair Labor Standards Act, and the Interstate Commerce Act. These laws created what has been called the "fourth branch" of American government (and, less charitably, the federal bureaucracy), whose own operation costs as much as 20% of U.S. economic output. It is in many senses the biggest corporation in the world, though its monopoly powers are being eroded by increased "competition" from global regulatory bodies such as NAFTA, GATT, and the WTO.

One of the most powerful forms of regulation for emerging markets is in establishing and maintaining support systems essential for new kinds of trade. Canals, railroads, bridges, telephones, telegraphs, the electricity grid, and the modern banking system were all creations of, and essential to, the Industrial Revolution. None could have been built at all, let alone quickly, without the direct involvement of government. In the United States, companies that built the industrial infrastructure achieved their vast power in part because it was granted to them through government subsidies, rights of way, free land, and the power to condemn property. For each new breakthrough in manufacturing, transportation, and communications, a new kind of public-private partnership evolved to develop and deploy it.

4. Promote Open Standards

Regulation more broadly includes the adoption of standards and protocols that benefit everyone by providing a common language and rules that reduce conflict. Railroad gauges, telephone interconnection protocols, voltage and socket standards for electricity, and the exchange of standardized financial instruments such as checks and other commercial paper all evolved to solve problems created by the expansion of commerce beyond preindustrial limits of time and distance.

The Great Exposition of 1851 in London, a trade fair celebrating the inventions of the Industrial Revolution, was the personal project of Britain's Prince Albert, who believed that by encouraging the rest of the world to learn first-hand about the fruits of England's free market economy (symbolically housed in the transparent Crystal Palace), other nations would follow suit, open their borders, and increase wealth for everyone. At the end of the 19th century, similarly, U.S. Secretary of State John Hay convinced world leaders not to restrict trade in China through colonization, but rather to keep an "open door."

The lesson of the Industrial Revolution is that open standards, whether imposed by governments or promoted by trade associations, almost always prevail in the long run over private ones, even those supported by powerful companies or countries.

5. Finance the Revolutionaries

Financing the revolution is still another source of revolutionary victory. In the 19th century, as the telegraph and railroad industries overdeveloped, waves of financial boom-and-bust invariably followed, including dramatic financial collapses in 1871 and 1893. Creative and often unscrupulous financiers engineered the consolidations, reorganizations, and bankruptcies that followed each contraction in the economy. The most notorious was Jay Gould, who took over Western Union in the 1870s and much of the railroad industry in the 1880s. Gould was principally a speculator, but his maneuverings did improve the profitability and long-term health of both industries, if only briefly.

Though the motives of Gould and his colleagues may not have been entirely admirable, their experiments in corporate and market manipulation mark the beginning of the modern and indispensable system of investment banking and venture capital that provides financial fuel for today's new technologies. Private and public markets for financing and risk management are essential for innovation of any kind. This is not a strategy limited to financial services companies. Increasingly, traditional organizations are learning to leverage not only their cash but also their networks of customers, suppliers, and other intellectual capital to become partners in technology startups.

RULES FOR REVOLUTIONARIES

The five strategies are a good beginning, but they tell only part of the story. The Industrial Revolution was a time not only of great technological change but also of dramatic and frequent change in the ways businesses interacted with each other and their customers. What was conventional wisdom became a recipe for disaster; what seemed daring or risky became the ante just to get into the game. Innovation was crucial, but lasting success came through superior execution. Then, as now, even mature businesses were suddenly forced to reconsider their most basic assumptions. It is not just the strategies that matter, in other words, but how the winners went about pursuing them.

The Industrial Revolution is a fertile source not only for strategy but also for new approaches to running a business—the operating rules for revolutionaries. Consider the application to your business of these hard-earned truths forged during the Industrial Revolution. Then get ready to apply them.

Early Ventures Often Fail

It is no easier to predict the consequences of a revolutionary technology today than it was 100 years ago. The most important inventions of the Industrial Revolution initially failed to perform as expected, were oversold and overhyped, or didn't find their true purpose until they were adapted for completely different uses than their inventors intended.

A relatively inefficient steam engine, for example, was first produced by Thomas Newcomen to drain water out of coal mines. Forty years later, James Watt added an external condenser to improve the engine's efficiency. Watt's contribution was an incremental change, but it was enough to transform the engine from a simple pump to a general engine with limitless uses, powering every other piece of equipment in factories, mills, and foundries. The steam engine became the symbol for the Industrial Revolution and it is Watt, not Newcomen, who is best remembered.

The development of the telegraph, starting in the 1830s with experiments by Samuel Morse and others, followed an even more uneven path. National governments began the construction of large-scale networks, but proved unable to hold off skeptics long enough to finish the job. When the private sector took up the task, promoters and speculators sparked investment frenzies. Many of the early companies sacrificed quality for speed, dooming their efforts.

As late as the early 1850s, for example, the idea of a transatlantic telegraph cable was considered ludicrous. But by 1857, after four attempts that failed because of inexperience, poor-quality cable, and shortcuts taken to meet promises of quick profits, a message was finally sent across the Atlantic. The London *Times* wrote, "Since the discovery of Columbus, nothing has been done in any degree comparable to the vast enlargement which has thus been given to the sphere of human activity." A month later, the fifth cable broke for good.

Don't write off high-potential technologies simply because they fail to live up to initial expectations. Instead, invest when disappointment is high.

Productivity Gains Are Hard to Measure, and Rarely Arrive on Schedule

When efficiency from new technology comes in sudden leaps after long periods when little seems to happen, justifying the initial investment is difficult if not impossible. Revolutionary change is not only hard to see, it is also hard to measure. Economists have taught managers to judge the success of new technologies conservatively, measuring the ability of new products to reduce the costs of doing business as we already know it. Industrial cable was first marketed as "wire rope," and the automobile as a "horseless carriage."

Productivity may arrive at unexpected destinations, however, as users take longer than expected to adapt old processes to new capabilities. Between 1857 and 1870, the price of steel fell to half its original price as demand grew and production became more efficient, but the improvements happened unevenly over time and varied dramatically between producers.

In one cotton mill in Lowell, Massachusetts, Professor Jeremy Underwood found that productivity increased steadily for 20 years after the installation of new machinery—*even though no additional investments were made.* It took the mill 20 years, in other words, to fully appreciate the potential of the equipment they had purchased, what is often called a "learning curve." Learning curves during the Industrial Revolution were long—new technology often took 20 years to deliver productivity improvements at the same pace as the previous generation of innovations, and twice that long before the earlier pace was actually exceeded.

A rational buyer might not acquire an individual technology or a single piece of equipment because the purchase won't yield dividends soon enough. Great improvements might come just outside the desired timeframe, or only if the technology is adopted along with other products. Looking out a little further than usual or evaluating products together not only improves your decision-making process but also exposes the obstacles that delay getting the best value from new technology as soon as possible.

What if the decision is not to buy a product but whether to invest in the company that developed it? Many of the standard ratios investors use to evaluate the value of stock use profit as their denominator. Some technologies can be made and sold profitably from the beginning, but revolutionary technologies often do not make money for their manufacturers until enough of them have been put to use for long periods of time. The customer's learning curve translates to delayed profits for the manufacturer. In the interim, the company looks like a bad investment. Waiting for profits, on the other hand, may mean waiting too long.

From 1973 to 1995, when companies were rapidly increasing their investments in information technology, standard measures of productivity increased only about 1% a year, leading economists to wonder where the promised gains had gone. Since 1995, however, these numbers have more than doubled, a phenomenon that has generated higher wages and stable prices, improving the standard of living for workers without triggering inflation—sustaining a "long boom" in the economies of most industrialized nations.

For new, unproven technologies, expand your definition of "return on investment" and learn to measure indirect benefits.

Productivity Is Not the True Source of Value

The steam engine and the cotton gin were created to reduce the hardship of manual labor, but the combination of the two revived the nearly dormant slave trade and introduced the horrors of child labor. While the cotton gin increased the productivity of handpicking by a factor of 50, the steam engine made it possible to increase textile outputs by a factor of 200. So even as cotton production increased, demand went up even faster, creating a need for more, not less, cheap labor. The result, according to Peter Drucker, was that slave breeding became America's most profitable industry for decades, until the industry was outlawed after the Civil War.

It is hard enough to assess the value of a new technology when its uses are obvious. So what happens when the real value of innovation comes not from improving existing processes but from creating new ones, with new sources of profits? In the Industrial Revolution, mechanizing the manufacture of previously handmade goods yielded tremendous gains, yet the biggest improvements in efficiency came from unexpected and unprecedented developments—moving groups of business operations closer together, for example, which multiplied the value. From 1830 to 1850, half of England's population moved into cities, creating the need for new industries.

In the 19th century, as now, there was no way to measure the potential value of new businesses, often leading to the erroneous conclusion that there was no benefit—or at least not one that would come quickly. As Sir William Preece, chief engineer for the British Post Office, told a House of Commons committee in 1876, "The Americans have need of the telephone, but we do not. We have plenty of messenger boys." Even IBM Chairman Thomas Watson predicted in 1943 that the world market for digital technology would be "maybe five computers."

Since the value of new processes and new kinds of businesses made possible by technology remains officially unmeasurable, revolutionary improvements are economically invisible until well after they have become part of everyday life. The railroads improved the efficiency of moving passengers and freight, but not for many years, and with economic results visible only in hindsight. More to the point, the true value of the vast rail networks constructed in the United States came from opening new markets and accelerating the settlement of the western frontier, which delivered economic benefits of a magnitude higher than those realized in reducing shipping costs, but which would never have shown up on a business plan. Railroads themselves relied on technology (again, Watt's engine) that was more than 50 years old.

Extraordinary returns come from unexpected uses of new technologies, but waiting for them to appear will forfeit much of the value to early

adopters. When uncertainty is high, consider making small investments, both to gain early access and to help shape the development of new technologies to your own needs.

Resistance Is Natural, but It Has a Major Impact on the Speed and Course of Change

Since the nature and course of change are as unknowable now as they were during the Industrial Revolution, it is not surprising to find social anxiety with the progress of transformation during both time periods, not only inside business organizations but among regulators, investors, and consumers. As with the Industrial Revolution, the outcome of the current revolution will seem inevitable only in retrospect.

That the Industrial Revolution was a force largely for good was certainly not clear while it was happening. Likewise, the complex interaction of markets, government, industry, and infrastructure we call the "free market" seems natural (or second nature, at least) to us today, but it did not to many who were there for its creation. Financial masterminds such as J. P. Morgan and Jay Gould, who threatened the civil and gentlemanly rules of the established and titled rich of 19th-century Europe and America, are still vilified as Robber Barons, and the new wealth they created in their lifetimes dismissed as unfortunate excesses during a Gilded Age. The laissez-faire relationship between industry and government proposed by economist Adam Smith and others, a cornerstone of modern capitalism, was initially considered heretical and unpatriotic.

Sometimes resistance to change even takes the form of armed conflict. In 1779, a farmer named Ned Ludd attacked a knitting machine in a fit of rage (or possibly epilepsy). Thirty years later, bands of laborers in northern England organized under Ludd's example to fight industrialization. The Luddites believed that machines were causing high unemployment among skilled workers and craftsmen, and attacked factories and destroyed equipment—what one historian referred to as "collective bargaining by riot." Later, Karl Marx and his followers criticized industrialization and its relationship to capitalism in subtler and ultimately more successful campaigns, posing a serious threat to the industrial economy for the better part of the 20th century.

While the resistance of the Luddites today seems quaint and Marx's radical conclusions have few remaining supporters, resistance to change is still a powerful determinant of both the speed and course of transformation. Industrialization was a revolution not just in a metaphoric sense. There are even modern Luddites, like Unabomber Ted Kaczynski, whose manifesto "Industrial Society and Its Future" concluded that modern technology was alienating human beings far beyond its value to them. Today, debates about the "digital divide" of rich and poor, lobbying over privacy rights for consumer data, and John Perry Barlow's libertarian "Declaration of Independence of Cyberspace" all dramatize the very real political consequences of the changing economy.

At a macroeconomic, corporate, and even personal level, the natural resistance to change must be factored in as a key contributor to the success or failure of a strategy. Find and eliminate the sources of resistance in your own organization first, then exploit the resistance of competitors.

First Movers Don't Always Win; Last Movers Don't Always Lose

If the Luddites and Communists were the losers of the Industrial Revolution, who were the winners? Today it is often said that the winners will be the "first movers," that is, those who enter emerging markets with both barrels blazing and capture the loyalty of new customers. The history of the Industrial Revolution suggests that may be true in some cases, but not always. Often the inventors and initial investors in new technology simply work out the bugs and develop the markets, leaving the real profits for companies that figure out ways to make the same products more cheaply or distribute them more quickly.

Of course, the riskiest strategy during a revolution is to do nothing at all—just keep making the highest-quality buggy whips as automobiles take over the roads or, more painfully, assume, as Western Union did, that new technology will take away only your lowest-margin business. After the U.S. Civil War, the telegraph giant carefully worked to gain monopoly power in both local and long-distance telegraph service. As local service slowly fell to the telephone, Western Union let it go, confident that local exchanges would never be able to offer long-distance service, its real source of profits. Rather than build an expensive long-distance network, however, AT&T simply established interconnection standards that made it possible to link the local exchanges which flourished under the telegraph company's nose. By 1908, Western Union was a subsidiary of AT&T.

Given the power of uncertainty, accidents of fate, and organized resistance to change demonstrated during the Industrial Revolution, the second most dangerous approach is to bet everything on one outcome or, even worse, on one technology. Monopolies, even so-called "natural" monopolies like railroads, telephone service, and power distribution, can be overcome by new technologies that eventually make the monopolists' technology obsolete without ever competing directly. Today's first mover's advantage is often tomorrow's handicap of a large customer base using old technology. The speed of successive revolutions increases as successive generations of information technology lower the costs of entering new markets of all kinds. So there is now less time to respond.

Entrepreneurs are often too emotionally involved with their inventions to recognize the difficulties of deploying them. Balance the enthusiasm of inventors with the pragmatism of executives trying to run a business today, but don't wait for the technology to become commonplace before making your move.

The hard-won lessons of the Industrial Revolution are far more than historical trivia. They provide a roadmap for companies trying to find their way during any time of great technological innovation, when rules are changing and developments that seemed unthinkable quickly become commonplace. As we will see in the chapters that follow, we are entering a new kind of Industrial Revolution, one powered not by steam engines but by integrated circuits and the information technologies they make possible.

The winning strategies of the Industrial Revolution will work just as well in the new revolution, but you will have to move faster. History will be repeated, not once, but every day.

2

DISPOSABLE COMPUTING

Drivers of the Information Revolution

Computers in the future may weigh no more than one and a half tons.

—*Popular Mechanics* (1949)

[DRIVERS OF THE INFORMATION REVOLUTION. THE ECONOMICS OF MOORE'S LAW AND METCALFE'S LAW. SONY'S TROJAN HORSE. THE AGE OF DISPOSABLE COMPUTING.]

WARNING SHOTS

In November 1952, Dwight D. Eisenhower was elected president of the United States, taking all but eight southern states. Though Eisenhower was expected to defeat Adlai Stevenson, no one imagined it would be so lopsided a victory. No one, that is, except a Census Bureau computer named Univac, which predicted an Eisenhower landslide after only 1% of the vote had been counted. Univac (an acronym for Universal Automatic Computer) weighed 16,000 pounds, performed about 1,000 calculations per second, and cost $750,000. It was the first commercially sold computer in the world, and the first to be used for business applications (General Electric programmed it to calculate its payroll in 1954). The Census Bureau's machine was the first; 46 had been sold by 1957.

Since 1952, advances in information technology have been characterized by computers like Univac adapting to perform tasks for which they were not initially designed. Fifty years after Eisenhower's election, there are now more computing devices in the world than people, and their numbers are growing geometrically, roughly doubling every few years (depending on how you define a computer, an exercise in philosophy we will no doubt soon abandon). The semiconductor, or "chip," the basic building block for computing power, was added to a calculator in 1967, to a toy in 1978 (the "Speak and Spell"), to a toaster in 1983, and to a wireless telephone in 1988. A "personal" computer was first sold in the early 1980s, and despite unfathomable advances in its power and its abilities, its price has dropped steadily for 20 years.

As chips have become cheaper and more prevalent, their impact has moved from the world of computers and high technology to nearly every aspect of our business and personal lives. Computers are the central driver

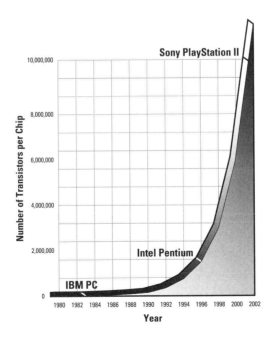

Figure 2.1 The Revolutionary Manifesto: Moore's Law

of productivity gains across industries, and software has become a key source of new products and services. As digitization accelerates, the impact of information technology has reached revolutionary proportions. While the Industrial Revolution created the modern capitalist system and the concept of "industry," computers are busily redefining the system and remaking industries as part of an Information Revolution.

Two driving principles are fueling that revolution: Moore's Law and Metcalfe's Law.

Moore's Law: Every 12 to 18 months, the number of circuits on a chip doubles, but cost holds constant.

Metcalfe's Law: The utility of any network is a square of the number of users attached to it.

I described Moore's Law and Metcalfe's Law in detail in *Unleashing the Killer App,* but these two principles are so central to the Information Revolution that some of that discussion bears repeating, even for those who already understand how they work. Even as markets for information technology expand and then shrink, and technology leaders rise and fall, Moore and Metcalfe are proceeding, quietly, to change the world.

MOORE'S LAW REENACTED

Gordon Moore, the founder and recently retired chairman of Intel, made an astonishing promise in 1965. He vowed to double the processing power of his chips every year or two without charging more for them. Neither Moore nor his competitors have yet reneged on this commitment, and there is every reason to believe they will continue to deliver on it for the rest of our working lives. Moore's Law works through a combination of improved design tools, better materials, economies of scale in manufacturing, and a relentless pursuit of miniaturization for components, which not only holds down cost but also improves performance by reducing the distance electronic signals need to travel.

All of this boils down to one remarkable fact: Computers continue to get faster, cheaper, and smaller, becoming more powerful by a factor of two with every succeeding generation. Since chips are the raw material of the Information Revolution, the implications of the faster-cheaper-smaller principle are profound, and many of them, while not contrary to the laws of economics, are nonetheless surprising. Consider a few examples:

1. *Price Inflation:* Basic commodities like oil, electricity, or cotton tend to become more expensive over time, with the increases working their way through the rest of the system.

   Computer prices have stayed the same, or gone down.

2. *Nonrenewable Resources:* Oil, natural gas, coal, and many of the sources of electricity, are nonrenewable—as they are used, they are also used up, raising prices and limiting further increases in productivity.

   The basic material of semiconductors is silicon, the second-most-abundant chemical on earth.

3. *Marginal Cost:* For most manufactured goods, such as automobiles, price is a function of three key elements: an allocation of the fixed cost of developing the goods (research and development, marketing); the marginal cost of producing each item (including raw materials, distribution, and customer service); and a profit margin.

   Software, the programming that tells computers what to do, can be marketed, manufactured, and distributed electronically, giving it a marginal cost that is close to zero.

When a basic commodity behaves not as a scarce good but as its opposite, a good that becomes more prevalent even as it becomes more powerful in a wider range of uses, revolutionary change follows. The more computer chips we make, the cheaper they become, increasing the range of useful applications—a kind of virtuous cycle.

Most of the key components of the digital computing environment exhibit the same unusual economic behaviors that chips do. Computer memory, data storage, and data communications have their own rough approximations of Moore's Law. Improvements in fiber optic cables (which transmit data at the speed of light) and the development of optical switches, for example, translate to data communications costs beyond the initial investment that are rapidly approaching zero. One fiber optic cable will soon be capable of carrying millions of simultaneous telephone calls. Total data storage, similarly, has been expanding geometrically, and is expected to triple again between 2001 and 2003. The average company in 2003 will have the capacity to store over 1,000 terabytes of data, enough for a library of over a billion books, roughly half of all the books at every research library in the United States today.

METCALFE'S LAW, STILL IN FORCE

While those numbers are settling in, consider the second key driver of the Information Revolution. Metcalfe's Law, formulated by networking pioneer Robert Metcalfe, is a mathematical expression of a phenomenon anyone with a telephone already understands: the more people you can reach, the more reasons you find to reach them. Networks—whether of railroad track, computers, or speakers of a particular language—exert a kind of gravitational pull, and the more nodes they have, the stronger the pull. Eventually, absent any economic or technical constraints, networks grow to the point where every possible connection is made and the system becomes so much a part of our lives that it becomes invisible. We assume that we can

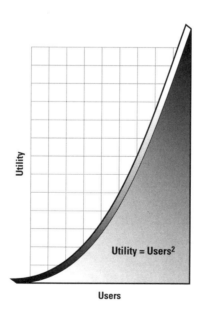

Figure 2.2 Manifesto, Part Two: Metcalfe's Law

call nearly anyone in the world. Urban dwellers are no longer amazed that water is always available, sewage disappears, and electricity and natural gas are always flowing.

The network of the Information Revolution is the Internet, a growing body of networking standards and other software that allows devices of all kinds to share information—not just data but video, voice, and someday perhaps taste and smell. Information is the basic fuel of the Information Revolution, and the Internet is its transportation network, an interlinked system of rail, road, and canal, moving information at ever-higher speeds along a nearly infinite set of pathways, shortening distances and eliminating borders. As the network's spread over the last ten years has demonstrated, the Internet is the *platform* on which businesses can be built.

The Internet became the dominant data communications network largely by following a principle that had proven itself with physical networks: the more open the network, the more quickly it spreads. Unlike proprietary networking standards that are now forgotten, such as IBM's SNA (which connected only IBM computers, and then in a strict hierarchy engineered to protect IBM's high-profit mainframe market), the Internet is available to any computer. It is a least common denominator standard, simple enough to be part of even the lowliest device—even PalmPilots, cell phones, and pagers can be full participants in the network. As Moore's Law gives intelligence to more and more things, each of them becomes part of the Internet, exchanging data with every other device already connected. Even as Internet stocks were melting down in 2000, the number of Web pages doubled to 2.7 billion and email traffic approached 10 billion messages a day.

The key to Metcalfe's Law is the inflection point in its curve, the point at which there are enough users so that the subsequent squaring functions add not a few but a few *million* new connections. Here's how it works: If you have a network of two telephones, the total number of possible connections is two (I call you, you call me). Add a third phone and we add not two but four additional circuits, still not very exciting. The millionth new phone, however, adds not two or even two hundred but a million new potential calls, making the network even more attractive for the next million users, and the millions after that. Reaching the inflection point (which varies depending on the kind of network) gives the network momentum, or what is sometimes called "critical mass."

In order to reach critical mass, it is crucial to attract as many users as quickly as possible, knowing that they will in turn draw the next wave. The best way to do that is to keep the cost of entry as low as possible, perhaps by giving away whatever equipment the user must have to connect and charging low prices for using the system.

Giving away free service was not an option for railroad, canal, telegraph, and telephone network builders, given the enormous debt they had incurred in building their service, debt that had to be serviced. Indeed, most U.S. railroads wrecked themselves trying to match the low freight charges of their equally self-destructive competitors, contributing to serious financial panics throughout the last half of the 19th century.

The additive value of standardization, or what economists call "network effects," was also poorly understood; railroads in the United States did not settle on a standard gauge until the 1880s, making interconnections between lines in the North and South complicated, slow, and expensive. Only in 1931 did dials appear on telephones, though the need for human switchboard operators had been a constraint on growth for some time. (Today's phone system, without self-dialing, would require more operators than there are human beings to operate it.)

Digital networks, however, are built on hardware that gets cheaper all the time and on software which can be copied indefinitely at almost zero cost for the additional units. As was amply demonstrated during the first wave of companies promoting software applications for the Internet, users can be attracted by offering low prices for digital services or—at least for a while—by giving free access to the company's reusable information.

The strategy for many startups in the late 1990s was to attract high-income users by offering them valuable content and low-cost services, then using the critical mass to sell advertising to producers of related goods. Once the system became indispensable to the users, access prices could also be raised. From its first day of operation, on-line auctioneer eBay has been profitable following precisely that approach (going it one better by having the users—as sellers—provide the content to other users—the buyers). After eBay reached critical mass, companies like Yahoo! and Amazon, despite their large user bases, found it difficult to break into the business despite offers of cheaper listing fees, and, later, no fees at all.

Even digital leaders can underestimate the power of Metcalfe's Law. When America Online began offering a flat rate for unlimited access to its chat rooms and other services, the company was amazed to find users increasing their time on-line by several hours per week, which swamped the network but ultimately fueled faster growth for the company. Similarly, when AT&T Wireless gave cellular customers the ability to call any-where in the United States for the same per-minute price in 1999, the response was a sudden leap in the Metcalfe curve of its network and, con-sequently, in revenues—once the company recovered from the surge. The president of AT&T Wireless admitted to the *Wall Street Journal* that "we underestimated how fast our Digital One Rate would catch on."

FROM IRON HORSE TO TROJAN HORSE

Double the power of computers every few years and keep expanding the reach of the Internet for as long as we have been and you have the recipe for revolution. Every new generation of chips brings dramatic improve-ments in the applications they support, applications which can be spread, shared, and used by an increasingly global network.

The most compelling example of the Information Revolution in action today is not a business application at all, but a toy, or more accu-rately, a supercomputer for 10-year-olds. From the moment in early 1999 when Sony announced its next-generation home video game console, the PlayStation II, powered by a custom-designed "Emotion Engine" chip, it was clear this would be no mere toy but the most stunning example yet of the power of Moore's and Metcalfe's Laws. Its games, which can be played against other PS2 owners over the Internet, provide three-dimensional graphics that are convincing enough to give many adults motion sickness.

To deliver that kind of performance, the Emotion Engine was built to execute over 6 billion instructions per second, making it the rough equiva-lent of 22 million Univac I's. To appreciate the comparison, consider that the PS2 is about the size of a small laptop computer and sells for $300. The comparable number of Univacs would fill an area larger than the city of Seattle and would have sold for over $16 trillion, almost double the cur-rent gross domestic product of the United States.

PlayStation II went on sale in the United States in October 2000, and immediately became the impossible-to-get Christmas gift of the year. After selling millions in Japan (2 million in the first *two days*), Sony had only 500,000 units available for the machine's U.S. debut. Throughout the Christ-mas season, while traditional PC sales proved sluggish or worse for Dell, Compaq, and Gateway, PS2's still in their box were selling on eBay for up to four times the list price (sellers who fear auctions as a price-leveling tool of buyers take note). Within a year, Sony had sold more than 8 million consoles.

Sony has been at pains to insist that the PS2 is not intended to replace PCs, but at the same time it is a computer with an operating system, a modem, and the potential to be used for more traditional applications than "Mortal Kombat." In late 2001, Microsoft released its own game console, the Xbox, not only to compete with Sony but also to establish a beachhead with the growing market for non-PC devices that require operating systems, application software, and network services. (The chip inside the Xbox, by the way, is more than twice as fast as the Emotion Engine, and its operating system is a variant of Windows.)

The PS2, Xbox, and other game consoles are at the very least Trojan horses—the first computer the next generation of customers, suppliers, and corporate executives will know—and their advanced user interface will set the bar for applications of the future. Our children, after all, can hardly be expected to dumb down to our level when they become adults. The Emotion Engine, like the steam engine of the Industrial Revolution, will power the imaginations of the true revolutionaries.

THE AGE OF DISPOSABLE COMPUTING

The PS2 is the first of a new class of computing devices more powerful than most computers yet sold as something else—in this case a toy. The console itself is sold at a subsidized cost to ensure that Sony benefits from the network effects of Metcalfe's Law. The *real* money is made by selling software in the form of game cartridges or, eventually, delivered over the Internet with other services that will enhance the user experience even further, such as playing host to leagues and tournaments. As Nicholas Negroponte first wrote in 1995 with his usual foresight, "Computing is not about computers anymore. It is about living."

Moore's Law and Metcalfe's Law are not the revolution. The revolution is what follows from them—the ability to put computing power into more and more things and to share data with an expanding world of other devices and users. The Information Revolution will be won when computing power is cheap enough to put into everything—into products, into packaging, into every piece of equipment involved in the manufacture and distribution of other goods . . . even in your body.

Put another way, the revolutionary aspect of Moore's Law is not that computers keep getting twice as powerful, but that price holds constant. Why does that make the difference? A new personal computer will not only be twice as powerful as its predecessor at the same price, but as soon as it goes on the market the earlier models get cheaper. *An important corollary to Moore's Law is that every 12 to 18 months the cost of today's chips decreases by 50%.* Not only do high-end computers get smarter, low-end computing gets cheaper at the same time, making it feasible to give rudimentary computing intelligence to an exploding range of devices—and non-devices.

In 1999, for example, University of Massachusetts graduate student Hariharasubrahmanian Shrikumar built a 49-cent computer that was smaller than the head of a match, which he attached to the University's network as an Internet server. The same year, a patent was granted for a process to make cellular phones that are almost entirely composed of the printed circuit itself. (Several companies are already selling pre-paid cell phones.) Once commercialized, this technique will lead to disposable telephones—indeed, phones that ultimately can be printed on your own printer. According to Andy Lippman, director of the Digital Life project at MIT's Media Lab, printed displays, keyboards, and computers themselves are not far behind. "You buy your printer," he says, "and it prints the rest of your computer for you."

These developments point clearly in the direction of the true revolution. At 49 cents for a computer, many new applications of information technology become cost-effective, but follow Moore and Metcalfe a few more generations (five to 10 years, perhaps) and instead of 49-cent servers we will have computers that cost .0049 cents, with built-in transmitters capable of sending data over short distances using the Internet. We will have, in short, disposable computing, the building block of the next generation of industries.

The process has already begun. In 2001, Procter & Gamble began testing wireless transmitters that will someday give every package of toothpaste enough intelligence to communicate. What does a tube of toothpaste have to say? More than you might think. It can tell you, for example, where it is—in a warehouse, on a truck, on the store shelf, in somebody's medicine cabinet, or in their suitcase. How much of it has been used? Is it almost gone? Is it being used as directed? What is it sitting next to? How many people are using it? What time of day do they use it?

All that information may be interesting, but may not be very useful, at least not for just one tube of toothpaste. When millions of tubes are all sending this tiny amount of data back up the supply chain, however—back to the retailer, the distributor, the manufacturer, even as far back as the suppliers of raw materials—that is when revolutionary change happens. If manufacturers had perfect information about consumer behavior, they could develop precisely those new products consumers wanted. Production scheduling for many goods today is based on very little data, but a complete information flow back up the supply chain would turn it from guesswork into a science. Theft and other "shrinkage," which estimates put at 2% or more of sales for fast-moving consumer goods, could be eliminated. Pricing and promotions, a major factor in determining profitability, could be made specific and appropriate down to the level of *individual* consumers.

In 1999, MIT joined with Procter & Gamble, the Gillette Company, and the Uniform Code Council (the people who brought you the now-ubiquitous UPC bar code) to form the Auto-ID Center. The Center's ambitious goal is to develop technology cheap enough to make every one of the billions of individual consumer products bought and sold every day into an intelligent device, a "smart product" capable of sending and receiving data. Over 100 companies are already participating in the project, including Coca-Cola, Wal-Mart, and IBM.

According to Kevin Ashton, the Center's director, the key to disposable computing will be an intelligent tag attached to each individual item. For the past 10 years most consumer goods have carried a prototype of such tags in the form of bar code labels that can be scanned at the retail check-out counter (5 billion bar codes are scanned every day in 140 countries). Bar codes, however, identify only the class of product (e.g., Panasonic Model PV-VS4821 VCR, 8-ounce can of StarKist chunk light tuna, or even this book), not each individual item.

Bar codes, moreover, cannot be updated to reflect a change in the item's location (in the warehouse, on a truck, on the shelf) or status (halfway used, used by four different people every day). Finally, because today's labels have no transmitter (no "intelligence"), they must be passed over a reader device in order to create data. Data is only generated when someone actively looks for it. Once the item leaves the retailer or the truck of a home delivery service, it ceases to provide any data at all.

Ashton and his team are working on tags that will solve these problems, using more sophisticated coding techniques and giving each tag the ability to communicate using wireless signals. The basic technology already exists. Radio frequency identification (RFID) has been in use for over 50 years in specialized roles such as tracking livestock and train cargo. RFID is the technology that lets you drive through tollbooths without stopping, with the receiver in your car tracking your tolls. RFID tags store data that can be read and updated, and at least one proposed data storage standard, the "electronic product code," has the capacity to distinguish between trillions of items, making it possible to give everything ever produced its own unique identifier. There will also be room for contextual data such as expiration dates, advertising, national language labels, and an area to keep track of consumption and other changes in status.

For tags with very short transmission range, RFIDs can already be produced for a little less than a dollar, making them feasible now for more expensive consumer items like electronics, furniture, or even perfume boxes (as International Paper is doing today to control against counterfeiting). Such tags use conductive ink to "print" an antenna right on the label, and use static electricity as a power source. When the tag comes close to a receiver, the proximity powers it on and starts the exchange.

According to Ashton, 5-cent tags will be ready in 2002, and tags costing 1 cent or less will be available within the next five years. That will require chips that are no wider than a human hair. One Auto-ID member, Alien Technology, has devised a method for making such chips using plastic sheets that are passed through a bath of tiny components, which assemble themselves by simply falling into place on the plastic.

Intelligent product labeling is only one of the new applications made possible by disposable computers. In medicine (where embedded chips are used to treat a variety of injuries and help those who are hearing- or vision-impaired) their potential to improve the lives of an aging population is immeasurable, while in media industries and consumer electronics, the power of Moore and Metcalfe leads to new formats and new forms of entertainment every year.

In fact, even if you cannot see it directly, the Information Revolution is already at work on your industry, transforming it from what it was—perhaps what it has been for many years—into something new. How you make money, how you add value, how you interact with suppliers, customers, employees, and investors are all changing, and the pace of change is likely to accelerate as more and more devices begin to generate and use more and more information.

The nature of that change, and the opportunity it creates for those who can adapt quickly, is the subject of the next chapter.

3

THE METAMORPHOSIS

The Stages of Transformation

He's not the finest character that ever lived, but he's a human being, and a terrible thing is happening to him. So attention must be paid.

—Arthur Miller, *Death of a Salesman*

[KAFKA'S *METAMORPHOSIS* AND THE TRANSFORMATION OF INDUSTRY. THREE STAGES OF INDUSTRY CHANGE. THE ECONOMICS OF EFFICIENCY IN THE SUPPLY CHAIN. THE RETURN OF EXCHANGES. THE EMERGENCE OF NAPSTER: THE MEDIA IS THE MESSAGE (AND THE SOURCE OF POWER). RISK FACTORS OF IMPENDING CHANGE.]

INDUSTRIAL METAMORPHOSIS

In Franz Kafka's novel *The Metamorphosis,* a traveling salesman named Gregor Samsa awakes one morning from an uneasy sleep to find that he has changed into a giant bug. Kafka doesn't say what kind of bug, but the description (brown belly divided into stiff, arched segments, numerous pitifully thin legs flailing around) leaves little doubt that it is a cockroach. Gregor is dismayed and depressed, his family ashamed and confused. What will the neighbors think? What will his boss think? How will he earn a living now? Why did this happen to him?

In the Information Revolution, it will not only be salesmen who find themselves utterly transformed and almost unrecognizable. It will also be bankers, civil servants, entertainers, manufacturers, retailers, distributors, and professional service providers. We will all become new creatures with some new abilities and at least a few unattractive new appendages to go with them. Unattractive, that is, until we learn how to use them. Unlike Gregor, one thing that we know is the cause of our metamorphosis. As cheaper computing and improved data flow throughout the economy take root, relationships within industries change radically. Information is power, and new information will create new sources of competitive leverage. Longtime partners become competitors, and competitors become partners. Consumers will move from the sidelines to become full participants in the processes that go into making and selling products and services.

Changes will occur at an industry, company, and even a personal level. Your career path will be determined by your ability to find, analyze, and apply information, regardless of your job.

What will the process look like to the participants? For some, the changes will unfold over a long period of time, with plenty of chances to adapt and profit from them. For others, transformation will take only a few budget cycles. Along the way, though, everyone will experience at least some sudden breaks in the basic rules of business. Eventually, the economic system created by the Industrial Revolution will take on a new form with few recognizable features, a change as dramatic as the original shifts from hunter-gathering to farming and, in the 19th century, from farming to manufacturing.

A WAR ON THREE FRONTS

Metamorphosis is progressing more quickly in some industries than in others, but in every industry I have studied in the past three years the transformation has already begun. To see the pressure most clearly, consider the *supply chain*, the linked activities that produce, distribute, and sell all goods and services. Since the time of the Univac, information technology has been used as a competitive weapon throughout industries to break down and re-form links in the supply chain to better suit individual companies. In the past five years, however, the speed and frequency of these reconfigurations have increased rapidly, re-forming supply chains in ever-stranger combinations.

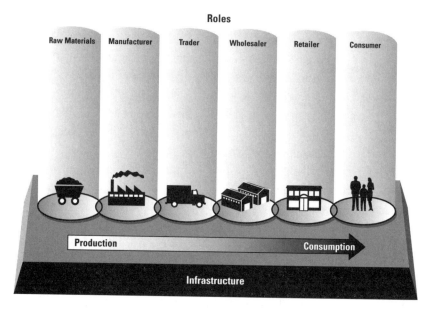

Roles

Raw Materials   Manufacturer   Trader   Wholesaler   Retailer   Consumer

Production   Consumption

Infrastructure

Figure 3.1 The Supply Chain

The process has three distinct stages, but it is important to understand that the stages never happen sequentially—to some degree all three happen at once and at different speeds. Your industry may skip the first stages altogether and head right for the overnight metamorphosis, leaving managers wandering around industry association meetings and trade shows in a daze, like hundreds of Gregor Samsas, wondering where the new limbs came from.

What are the stages? The first is *efficiency,* the stage that will be most familiar to you. In the efficiency stage, information technology is focused on lowering costs by reducing waste in the buying and selling process.

At the *exchange* stage, virtual marketplaces or exchanges (including auctions) expose inefficiencies that are more deeply rooted and harder to see. As exchanges expand, however, their real value appears in the form of information about the market they collect, which can be used to create financial products like hedges, insurance, and derivatives for increasingly specialized kinds of products and services.

In the final stage, the information flow from manufacturing, distributing, and the consumption of goods is standardized from one end of a transaction to the other. The third stage is called *emergence,* because it is here that new industry structures emerge, often with new participants and a dramatic realignment of both power and profits. In the emergence stage, data begins to take on independent uses, a feature we will explore in detail in the next chapter.

All three stages are taking place right now in your industry. In many cases, the same technology is being applied to more than one stage, which is part of the reason large-scale changes are often visible only in the rearview mirror. If the course of your industry's metamorphosis seems sudden or unpredictable to you, it is probably because you focused your attention entirely on the earlier stages, never seeing the big picture.

If so, you are in good company. Most people find it hard to recognize transformation when they are in the middle of it, so it is no surprise that few are able to determine what *kind* of change is going on. The solution is to learn the unique characteristic of each stage and how each is putting pressure on your current supply chain. This is the focus of the rest of this chapter and, in some sense, the rest of this book.

STAGE 1: EFFICIENCY

What drives a company to improve the efficiency of its current activities? The answer, of course, is profits. Profit is the difference between what you

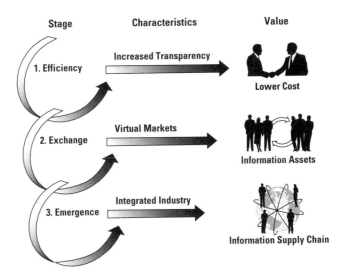

Figure 3.2 The Three Stages of Metamorphosis

collect from selling your goods (products and services) and what they cost you to produce. Profit can be increased in a variety of ways, including charging a higher price, which raises the profit proportionately, or by charging the same price but selling more, which raises the profit by a factor of how many additional units you sell. Unfortunately, in competitive markets, both of these strategies are far more easily said than done.

Independent of competitive pressures, however, you can also improve profits by reducing your production costs. If you lower costs but still charge the same price, you increase profitability proportionately—a 10% reduction in cost would, if price and volume stay constant, flow directly to the bottom line. Communications hardware giant Cisco has for several years cut costs by the equivalent of 7% of its total revenue, generating $1.4 billion in profit. If the same reduction could be achieved by the entire manufacturing sector, $150 billion in improved profitability would appear without raising prices or selling additional goods.

In Cisco's case, most of the savings come from reducing indirect costs. It is not that Cisco is paying its suppliers less money for parts, in other words, but rather that the company has continued to find ways to squeeze inefficiencies from its internal processes. Cisco customers enter and track their own orders with their own computers and their own telephone lines, for example, reducing the cost of customer service. By selling products from its Website rather than through distributors, Cisco minimizes finished goods inventories and receives payment sooner, reducing the need to borrow money. As the company copes in 2001 and 2002 with the first serious sales downturn in its history, the ability to keep inventories low and to eliminate unnecessary activities may prove crucial to its very survival.

In economics, these activities are known as *transaction costs*—general inefficiencies of doing business in any market economy. (Ronald Coase, who won the Nobel Prize in economics for his discovery of these costs, first described them in 1937. I discussed Coase's work in some detail in *Unleashing the Killer Apps.*) In the efficiency stage, information technology puts pressure on the supply chain precisely at the pressure points of transaction costs. So it is worth reviewing the six main types of transaction costs and how information technology is usually applied to reduce them:

Search Costs—Buyers and sellers finding each other within increasingly broad and distributed markets. *Technology connects buyers and sellers across geographies, time, and national borders.*

Information Costs—For buyers, learning about the products and services of sellers and the basis for their cost, profit margins, and quality; for sellers, learning about the legitimacy, financial condition, and need (which may lead to a higher or lower price) of the buyer. *Technology creates standard data structures that can be searched and consolidated over a growing network of computers.*

Bargaining Costs—Buyers and sellers setting the terms of a sale or contract for services, which might include meetings, phone calls, letters, faxes, emails, exchanges of technical data, brochures, meals and entertainment, and the legal costs of contract negotiations. *Much of the exchange of information can now take place virtually, and is standardized in databases for easy reuse in subsequent transactions.*

Decision Costs—For buyers, comparing the terms of the seller to other sellers, and processes such as purchasing approval designed to ensure that purchases meet the policies of the organization; for sellers, evaluating whether to sell to the buyer instead of another buyer or not at all. *Visibility to expanded virtual markets gives both buyers and sellers a truer picture of market conditions from minute to minute.*

Policing Costs—Buyers and sellers taking steps to ensure that the good or service and the terms under which the sale was made, which may have been ambiguous or even unstated, are in fact translated into the behavior of the parties. This might include inspecting the goods and any negotiations having to do with late or inadequate delivery or payment. *Transactions conducted with system-to-system data transfers create a more complete record of the actual performance which can then be captured and queried.*

Enforcement Costs—Buyers and sellers agreeing on remedies for incomplete performance. This could range from mutual agreements for a discount or other penalties to the high cost of litigation. *Electronic records can simplify the process of resolving disputes over what was agreed, what did or did not occur.*

Economists Douglass North and John Wallis have estimated that up to 45% of total economic activity consists of these transaction costs. Eliminating them entirely would translate to a staggering $4.5 trillion in annual savings in the United States alone.

In the efficiency stage, your strategic goal is to find and reduce transaction costs as ruthlessly as possible. This can be a substantial source of savings and, for industries with a complex supply chain, can represent years of profitable activity. It is not surprising, then, to find that most software applications sold today are marketed as tools to reduce these costs. Consider the typical "suites" of applications common to most industries:

- **Financial applications** (accounting systems, credit, and investment management tools) from companies like Oracle reduce the cost of capital for an organization, and minimize its financial risk from paying bills too soon or collecting from customers too slowly or not at all.

- **Manufacturing systems** (enterprise resource planning [ERP], supply chain management, raw materials procurement) from companies such as SAP reduce waste in the production and distribution of goods and minimize the risk of excess or obsolete inventory being produced.

- **Sales and marketing systems** (customer relationship management [CRM], forecasting, and contract management) from companies such as Siebel Systems help sales staff focus on the right customers and the right opportunities, maximize price for any given sale, and reduce future sales costs by providing superior customer service.

- **Administrative systems** (human resources, payroll, and benefit management) from companies such as PeopleSoft reduce the overhead of the business as a whole, which would otherwise be allocated to the cost of goods.

Efficiency and the Supply Chain

The improved profitability that comes from installing packaged software applications, unfortunately, may be short-lived. If your ERP system gives you 10% better profit margins, your competitors will eventually implement these systems as well, leading to renewed price competition. Eventually, the productivity savings will largely flow to the customers, putting producers back in the position they started in, with relatively low margins. As new software is developed, the arms race escalates.

As the ERP example suggests, while efficiency applications are used mostly to cut costs inside individual companies, they can ultimately change the dynamics of an entire industry. Transaction costs embedded in a supply chain often represent somebody else's profit margin. When appliances are more energy efficient, utilities sell less power; when cars require fewer repairs, auto mechanics have less work to do.

To take another example, software startup DiCarta sells products that allow parties negotiating a contract to create a virtual workspace for their documents. The software keeps track of drafts, proposals from the different sides for revisions, and a history of sections that have been accepted by all sides. Using DiCarta's software, the parties can negotiate complex documents without having to print and send them back and forth, eliminating the common problem of losing track of which draft of a particular clause is the most current. DiCarta reduces bargaining costs for the participants, but may eventually put significant price pressure on the lawyers who would otherwise manage the negotiations. A bottom-line savings for the parties, in other words, means reduced revenue for the current provider of the service.

Efficiency applications also promote industry realignment by pushing companies to identify those parts of the supply chain in which they truly excel and focus on them. Few companies today prepare their own payrolls or manage travel arrangements, having outsourced these activities to companies that specialize in them, invariably with the aid of proprietary software (ADP, for example, has its own payroll application; travel agents use one of a small number of professional booking products such as Sabre).

As users evolve from using software to improve efficiency to simply turning over the whole function to someone else, software providers likewise transition from selling products to providing the outsourced services. The original members of the supply chain focus their activities, frequently reducing the number of employees. The outsource providers, meanwhile, improve profit margins by providing the same service to more and more customers.

In the end, competitors who want higher profits on a long-term basis will need to focus on one of two general strategies: become a cost leader, always near the front of the curve at adopting the latest technologies to reduce cost; or become a premium provider, using technology to enhance and distinguish products.

STAGE 2: EXCHANGE

In the exchange stage of metamorphosis, the emphasis shifts from individual companies improving their own efficiency to joint efforts to improve efficiency across one or more links in the supply chain. This stage may begin when companies have achieved sufficient information flow internally to expand their efforts to their most important trading partners, whether customers, suppliers, or both. Outsiders to the supply chain, recognizing large gaps in the current process, may also initiate the exchange stage as a way of skimming savings off the top of an inefficient industry.

The exchange stage is characterized by virtual marketplaces that connect the buying and selling activities of different links in the supply chain, much as the New York Stock Exchange or Chicago Mercantile Exchange do, but with two crucial differences: The virtual exchanges trade new classes of products that have previously been sold only through traditional channels, and, as their name suggests, the virtual exchanges do not have physical trading floors manned by human traders, but are automated through software. Some markets connect only a few links in the chain; some run from raw materials to the sale of finished goods.

The last few years saw a remarkable boom-and-bust of exchanges for just about everything, including bulk chemicals, energy, securities, loans, cars, office supplies, raw materials, appliances, mortgages, and even services like accounting, consulting, and financial advice. In many cases these were "me-too" strategies looking for a market, but you can understand the appeal of the virtual exchange when you consider how quickly businesses and consumers were adopting the Internet and Web technologies, which provide a low-cost platform for building a virtual exchange. The confluence of Moore and Metcalfe created a booming market for exchanges, and a wide range of experiments was launched.

Exchanges like Chemdex, which sold specialty chemicals and other supplies to laboratory chemists, focused on specialized markets where buyers had extensive knowledge of the products they purchased. Others took a wider view, focusing on the sale of indirect materials—office furniture, tools, and packing materials—that were common to many businesses. In some cases the exchanges are transient, such as the specialized auctions run by FreeMarkets, which works with its customers to define requirements for large purchases of raw materials, identifies potential suppliers, and then manages what are called reverse auctions in which the sellers bid their lowest price.

Virtual marketplaces are being built not only by startups but also as private channels for individual sellers, particularly to deal with excess or distressed inventory. And consortia of companies with common needs either as buyers or sellers have banded together with their technology partners to build specialized exchanges, such as Covisint, the purchasing exchange run by the major automobile companies for parts and other components, and Transora, a similar consortium for the packaged goods industry.

Of course the leading exchange operator is also one of the first and one of the few to be profitable. eBay is a completely general exchange open to anyone to be a buyer or a seller, a virtual garage sale that started out making a market for aficionados of Pez candy dispensers but which now hosts auctions for millions of items in every conceivable category, including commercial supplies, services, high-end art, and cars.

Why Exchanges?

In some sense it seems odd to think of exchanges as an evolutionary step forward at all, since open markets and haggling over price are really leftovers of commercial bazaars that go back to the Middle Ages in Europe and earlier in Asia. In geographically diverse, fragmented, or otherwise disorganized markets, in fact, exchanges led to high transaction costs, sometimes too high for transactions to take place. In response to these problems, retailers emerged who took advantage of increasingly standardized, mass-produced goods (another development of the Industrial Revolution) to offer brand-name products at fixed prices. Businesses also entered into long-term contracts with each other, and a series of middlemen emerged to help smooth the process for participants on either end of a sale. No matter what it is you make, do, buy, or sell, your current supply chain was probably forged in the first place to eliminate the costs associated with exchanges.

So why are exchanges making a comeback now? As a pricing mechanism, fixed prices introduce inefficiencies of their own. The fixed price guarantees a certain level of profit to the seller, but may not maximize it. There may be buyers who are willing to pay more for an item, in which case the price tag gives away the excess. There may be other buyers who are willing to pay less than the marked price but still a price that would generate profits. For them, the price tag leads to no purchase at all.

In all cases, market conditions can change, but price tags generally cannot. Coca-Cola tried using technology to create "dynamic pricing" with vending machines that could adjust the price based on outside temperature, charging more for a can of Coke on a hot day. But consumers are so conditioned to the fixed-price approach for consumer goods that the experiment seemed somehow immoral, and Coke stopped publicizing it.

So the medieval bazaar did not so much disappear as it mutated into new forms such as discounting, targeted coupons, and retailing the same goods at different prices as they aged and became less fashionable (or more perishable). Each of these developments reflects fixes to the retail pricing system aimed at getting everyone to pay precisely what they think an item is worth. The return of exchanges, now in a virtual form, is the next step in that evolution. Exchanges, like efficiency applications, are focused on finding and eliminating transaction costs in the current supply chain, but in this second stage the emphasis is on inefficiencies that may be hidden in long-standing relationships between buyers and sellers.

In the energy business, for example, the existing market is grossly inefficient, built on sweetheart deals and old-boy networks, with costs passed on to consumers through the regulated rate-setting process. When Congress passed the 1992 Energy Policy Act, allowing non-utilities to buy and resell electricity for the first time, industry insiders and outsiders alike rushed in to turn the excesses against generators and their distributors.

Energy exchanges were developed by existing commodity trading organizations such the New York Mercantile Exchange, in effect taking the energy business directly to Stage 2. The most successful of these virtual markets, however, has been EnronOn-line which, despite Enron's recent collapse, remains a powerful new force in the electricity business (Enron generated nearly $800 million in pretax profits in 2000 from on-line trading). EnronOn-line connects bulk buyers and sellers of electricity and other products, replacing expensive local sales offices and negotiations in which golf games featured prominently. Enron's own traders were beneficiaries of the improved efficiency of the exchange, improving from 100 trades a day using phone and fax to almost ten times that number using EnronOn-line.

Standardization and commoditization of complex products has benefits beyond efficiency improvements, however. Once an exchange has sufficient trading volume to form a picture of overall market conditions (a state known as "liquidity"), exchange participants can begin to make use of their new information flows to generate new value. Enron, for example, used data mined from EnronOn-line to sell new kinds of financial instruments, including risk insurance for changes in weather conditions. These instruments are a kind of derivative that only exchanges, with their superior visibility into market dynamics, can safely and profitably offer.

As data flow continues to improve and liquidity solidifies into a nearly complete transaction history, the creation of information products and services from exchange data will prove to be the true source of value from the second stage of metamorphosis. In this sense exchanges are an interim step between efficiency and the emergence of a radically altered supply chain. The energy business is already taking steps toward the next stage. Rusty Braziel, CEO of EnronOn-line competitor Altra Energy Services, recently started a new company called Netrana, which aims to build tools and services that will connect buyers and sellers of energy products by linking their own internal systems together. Netrana, says Braziel, will be an exchange with no servers, no Website—and no exchange. If he succeeds, he will have advanced his industry toward Stage 3, emergence.

STAGE 3: EMERGENCE

In the third stage of industrial metamorphosis, the information flow along the supply chain expands beyond immediate trading partners to everyone involved, even to consumers and other ad hoc participants. Extending the data collection over the life of the goods involved squeezes out any remaining inefficiencies in the existing supply chain, but also generates considerable chaos in the process. New information, as we have already seen, leads to new value, and difficult questions of ownership and use quickly surface. The current debate over data privacy wouldn't be happening if there weren't new ways to capture private data. As tools for analyzing and repackaging that data evolve, power will shift at least in part from those who control the movement of physical goods to those who control the information technology that is recording it.

Financial services, entertainment, professional services, and other businesses that primarily deal in information have supply chains that are already heavy on information technology and light on fixed assets, so it is not surprising to find them moving more quickly into emergence than manufacturing and other "brick-and-mortar" businesses. No industry has yet emerged from the third stage, but those that have begun the process point not only to how the change takes place but also to who might be left standing at the end.

The sudden emergence of all-digital music-sharing services in 1999 not only offers a prototype for what the future supply chain might look like for media businesses, it is also an allegory about how unexpected combinations of technologies can unintentionally catalyze radical change long before anyone is ready. The word that came to stand for the sudden unraveling of the music industry, in fact, might be the best word to describe the overall process of emergence-stage transformation: *Napsterization*.

By now almost everyone knows the Napster story. In January of 1999, a college freshman (and soon-to-be dropout) named Shawn Fanning wrote a piece of software that allowed users to easily share recorded music stored on their computer hard drives. He called his program Napster, a nickname he had earned in high school for his perpetually short hair. Using Napster, any computer connected to the Internet could find and make free copies of any piece of music stored on any other connected computer.

As bandwidth to the home—or dorm room—increased, so did the appeal of trading high-fidelity music files. By the end of that school year, over 70% of all college students weare using Napster at least once a month, clogging university networks and panicking the music industry, which sued Napster for copyright infringement 11 months after the service began. Eventually, an injunction was granted that effectively shut Napster down.

Napster itself was a simple tool that harnessed powerful forces, opening a Pandora's box of technologies. As part of the normal process for setting Internet standards, a new compression algorithm known as MP3 had been developed to send high-fidelity sound files over the Internet. Since music CDs could be played on computers as easily as on CD players, music lovers had already learned to transfer songs off CDs and onto their hard drives, converting them into the MP3 format in the process. By the time Napster was launched, a collection that would constitute the world's largest music store—over 375 million files representing a complete history of human sound—had been encoded.

As Napster was spreading, an unintentionally related product launch added further fuel to the fire. In 1998, Diamond Multimedia and others began marketing portable MP3 playback devices that were roughly the size of traditional CD Walkman products. Users could connect MP3 players to their PCs and download MP3 files to the new devices, in effect programming their own music selections. Once loaded, the MP3 player became a portable music library—one with no moving parts, by the way. Following Moore's Law, the amount of available storage on the devices expanded rapidly even as their size and cost held constant. Announced in late 2001, Apple's 6.5-ounce iPod holds the equivalent of 100 CDs of user-programmed music for $400. Within a few years, a same-sized device will store the entire history of human music.

Annihilation of the Supply Chain

In retrospect, it is easy to see why the convergence of technologies—Napster, MP3 compression software, programmable players, and the increasing speed and reach of the Internet itself—signaled almost instant annihilation for the structure of the music industry, a structure that had been largely stable since World War II. The industry had been built on the assumption that anyone who wanted to listen to a particular piece of recorded music would need to buy his or her own copy. Each copy, whether it was an LP, tape, CD, DAT, or even 8-track, was priced to include not only the cost of producing and distributing the copy and a profit margin for each of the participants in the supply chain who handled it, but also a portion that covered the record label's cost of producing the original recording and a royalty for the musicians.

Once Napster was unleashed, it was plausible that one copy could be made available for free to everyone in the world, leaving the record companies and the artists unable to recover their costs and stranding millions of compact disks in their jewel boxes on store shelves gathering dust. (Although, as former Napster CEO Hank Barry points out, recorded music sales actually went up throughout Napster's short life as an unrestricted network.)

The music industry was not caught flat-footed so much as red-handed. Music executives knew perfectly well that their existing supply chain was inefficient, and that eventually digital manufacturing, distribution, and retailing would replace the physical supply chain of prerecorded media. In

1998, for example, the major labels began the Secured Digital Music Initiative (SDMI), a project aimed at building in protections for digital distribution that were similar to those they had achieved by law with DAT. Progress, however, was slow. Implementation of SDMI would have introduced tremendous transaction costs into a digital supply chain, and no one, perhaps not even the labels themselves, was particularly interested in replacing one cumbersome, expensive system with a digital version that left out most of the potential savings.

It is easy to see why the labels, like most industries entering the emergence stage, were in no particular hurry to reconfigure their own supply chain until Napster did it for them. For one thing, built into the price of a CD was a hefty profit margin, one that the industry believed would shrink if it could not control access to recordings as it does today. CDs cost less to produce than LPs, yet sell for four times as much. (Some analysts believe that CD profits finance the riskier businesses that media conglomerates also engage in, such as movies and books.)

One hint of the size of that margin came in the middle of the Napster litigation. In May 2000, the U.S. Federal Trade Commission announced its findings from a two-year investigation of the music industry, and ruled that the labels had illegally restricted their retail partners from discounting the price of CDs, overcharging consumers as much as $500 million between 1996 and 1999. The FTC found that the five major record labels had almost complete control over the retail channel, forcing retailers like Blockbuster and Tower Records to buy and display hundreds of CD titles that sell few copies by threatening to withhold copies of the big hits. No industry wants to change its supply chain when the dominant players are already making excessive profits.

Those profits also translate to control over the supply side of the current industry. Recording artists are more disadvantaged than retailers are in the current music industry because without the ability to make their own CDs and get them into the retail channel, or have their music played on the radio or music video cable channels, they are entirely at the mercy of the labels. Most musicians make no money at all from recordings, and even the successful ones feel exploited. As Hole's lead singer Courtney Love aptly summarized the true nature of the Napster controversy in *The New Yorker*, "If you want to talk about stealing, let's talk about record-company contracts. Stop the pious crap and figure out how we can use the Net to make the music we want."

The Power of the Emerging Supply Chain

We can put to the side the legal problems of Napster use, and assume for the moment that sooner rather than later Napster and similar services such as Gnutella and FreeNet will evolve into legal forms resembling a combination of cable TV and radio, with users paying a monthly fee for unlimited downloads. The fee will cover the cost of everything but the medium itself—specifically, the music label's production costs, the artist's royalty, and a profit margin for the service.

But subscription services will do little to solve the industry's real problem, which has almost nothing to do with protecting copyrights. It is easy to see why if you consider how much an appropriate payment might be. For a pop music CD, production costs are low—perhaps $1 million total. Today, the musician collects a royalty of $1 per CD. So to replace a CD that sells 2 million copies with a service that allows for unlimited downloads of the same music, 2 million users would have to pay $3 each, generating $6 million in revenue—$1 million for production costs, $2 million for the artist, and a generous $3 million to be shared by Napster and the record label. That calculation, of course, assumes that the size of the audience stays the same—if a subscription service attracts more users, the per-user cost goes down. It also assumes that the cost of the download service is not offset by advertising, a conservative assumption given that the MTV network, which plays the music videos at no charge to viewers, is considerably more profitable than any of the labels.

Even so, this hypothetical new supply chain reduces the price to consumers from $13 or so for a CD to $3 for unlimited use of the MP3 files of the same music. The $10 difference is the real reason Napster represents such a dramatic threat to the current supply chain and a true emergence strategy. Ten dollars, or 80% of the price, has just been driven right out of the system. That 80%, of course, comes from the medium itself—the cost of pressing the CD, printing its packaging, and the wholesaling, transporting, and retailing of the physical product. The CD only costs about 20 cents to manufacture, so nearly all of that $10 represents movement through the supply chain, most of it made obsolete by the subscription download service, in which there is virtually no marginal cost to copy, distribute, or sell the product. Participants who today play leading roles in the supply chain—companies who make and press CDs, and music wholesalers and rctailers—drop out altogether. The record labels experience lower profit margins but perhaps higher volume to compensate them, and the musicians, many of whom can't even get recording contracts, suddenly become the power player in the industry, able to connect with their audiences directly and more profitably.

Entertainment businesses, as this scenario demonstrates, are not just their supply chains—not just the set activities that produce and distribute media like CDs, videotapes, and newspapers. To rephrase Marshall McLuhan's famous observation, the medium is *not* the message. At its core, the industry exists to mediate a relationship between artists and their audiences—to deliver entertainment from those who create it to those who consume it. Musical performances are not physical products—they are information. Until the convergence of technologies represented by Napster occurred, however, there was no way to get that information to a large audience without adding the interim step of reducing the performance to a physical medium and distributing that medium as if it were any other consumer product, like a box of cereal or a crate of spare engine parts.

RISK FACTORS

The Napster story is a chilling one, and may leave you wondering just what set of technologies could come together to create a similar threat for your business. Emergence stage activities can develop suddenly even in stable industries, with little activity at the earlier stages. How do you know how far each stage of metamorphosis has progressed in your industry?

One way to predict the pace of change in your industry is to look for three early warning indicators: *deregulation, information,* and *fragmentation.* These three factors are the accelerants in the transformation of industry. If any of these conditions is present in your industry, the chances for sudden and chaotic metamorphosis go up. If two or more are there, the effect is multiplied, like the shock waves of an earthquake.

Deregulation

Regulated industries, by definition, operate largely outside the competitive marketplace. When new competitors appear after a round of deregulation, the old leaders often don't know how to respond. Managers raised in a controlled market cannot instantly adapt to a fiercely competitive environment. Worse, the new competitors can operate outside of the regulated structure, turning protections for the incumbents into obstacles. In response, deregulation often leads to more deregulation. Complex regulatory environments can come down quickly, adding to the chaos. The start-ups attack the supply chain at every point, and incumbents quickly realize that there is little value to the unnatural structure of the industry in its present form—a recipe for rapid innovation and the emergence of a new supply chain.

One easy route for new entrants is to use information technology at all three stages simultaneously. Regulated industries often have little incentive to invest in technology, and may be years behind in installing efficiency products. Improving efficiency is not a priority when profit margins are predetermined, as they have been for decades in public utilities and other quasi-public or public industries, including government itself (if the Department of Defense lowers its procurement costs, who keeps the savings?). Until the Supreme Court stopped them from doing so, bar associations in the United States helped lawyers establish and enforce standard fees, reducing competition but also leaving little reason for lawyers to innovate. Even today, when most law and consulting firms charge clients by the hour, there is a strong disincentive to invest in information technology that yields greater efficiency, since that only serves to lower profits.

Years of inadequate spending on information technology leaves companies in regulated industries without the kind of customer and marketing databases that might otherwise be a chief weapon in a counterattack against new entrants. This has been a painful lesson for deregulating industries, including telecommunications and public utilities. Former monopoly companies find themselves with little to compete with beyond their expensive, aging physical equipment, or what has euphemistically become known as "stranded assets."

Sometimes the regulated market is not a market at all but a geopolitical region. The former Soviet republics ran largely closed economies for decades and countries such as Brazil, Japan, and Germany used high import taxes and inflationary monetary policies to protect developing industries, many of them state owned and operated.

Over the last decade, opportunities to compete in an increasingly global economy have encouraged these countries to dismantle their controlled economies and become world traders. Free trade zones in North America and Europe have opened even more trade to new competition. As in individual industries, the deregulation of national markets quickly reveals the absence of usable technology and the lack of entrepreneurial skill of the current generation of managers.

Information

As we have seen, the emergence of a new, technology-dominated supply chain happens most rapidly in industries where goods never take (or never need to take) a physical form in the first place. In financial services, it is already quaint to think about moving money, stocks, and bonds in armored cars from bank vault to bank vault. Financial instruments are increasingly produced, marketed, exchanged, and cleared virtually. The amount of paper money in the world is trivial compared to the currency that moves exclusively through electronic networks. Trillions of dollars change hands around the world each day through clearing services such as the SWIFT cooperative, which routes over 1 billion communications between financial institutions each year.

Money is not the only information product. Other industries at risk of sudden metamorphosis are those that treat information products as if they were simply physical goods—especially when managers have a difficult time separating the product from the format in which it is sold. Musicians, as we saw, had no choice until recently but to transfer their performances to physical media, and distribute these as one would any other consumable product. In effect, music is information that is transferred to a physical good, and then changed back into information by the stereo equipment of the listener. The high transaction costs of the interim conversion to media defines many entertainment products, allowing production companies, who have the capital necessary to make and distribute physical goods, to dominate the industry and turn artists into contract laborers. With digital technology, the tables are now turning.

Software companies have nearly completed their metamorphosis, though it is not clear who will dominate in the emerging supply chain. Like music, software no longer needs to be transferred to physical media. A majority of consumers now have access to the Internet and sufficient communications bandwidth to receive even large programs. Software manufacturers such as Intuit, McAfee, and Microsoft have created on-line storefronts that take orders, manage program downloads, and provide on-line support.

As a result, the need to copy software products onto floppy discs and CDs is rapidly disappearing, along with the need to package, ship, and sell through retailers who mark up the price mostly for maintaining stores and handling inventory. Egghead, considered a pioneer 10 years ago when it opened retail outlets to sell software, saw its storefronts suddenly transformed into a competitive burden as the on-line distribution channel matured rapidly. In 1998, with little warning, the company fired 80% of its employees, closed all of its stores, and made an unsuccessful bid to enter the crowded field of on-line retailers who had stolen its business.

The shift to electronic delivery of information may have a bigger impact on professional services, including education, law, medicine, and consulting. In the supply chain for these businesses, the principal medium for producing and distributing information is human beings—teachers, doctors, and lawyers. It is the firmly held (some might say religiously held) belief in each of these professions that software will never replace the "human touch," and no doubt systems that can diagnose medical conditions, write a legal brief, or manage a classroom of teenagers are far off at best. Still, there are tremendous inefficiencies in the supply chain professionals use to deliver their expertise today. Dozens of startups have been formed to explore digital alternatives to at least that part of expert work that requires little true expertise, a strategy we will explore in detail.

Fragmentation

Markets in which there are many buyers but no dominant sellers are also prime candidates for metamorphosis. Such markets usually operate at high levels of information inefficiency—buyers have to order from a variety of different suppliers, distributors, and agents, and sellers have to spend resources processing a large number of small orders across large geographies.

Businesses that deal in consumer products such as food and clothing fit this description, as do agricultural products and manufacturing supplies. Because there are no dominant players, such markets are ripe picking for exchanges that allow buyers and sellers to consolidate demand, improve margins, and squeeze out middlemen. Distributors in fragmented markets, however, often enjoy significant leverage over sellers, who could lose their only access to the market if efforts to build an exchange angered their current trading partners. A neutral or consortium exchange often solves this problem.

An exchange for a fragmented market may initially be limited to excess inventory. Exchanges can be made to operate anonymously, so that customers who pay full price do not see that there was a better deal to be had. In the steel industry, there are many small buyers, and producers often overproduce. Metalsite, an on-line exchange for excess steel, handled over 2 million tons of steel in 2000, conducting more than 100,000 auctions and doubling its annual revenue growth. The opportunity is large, since 15% of all manufactured steel is already sold in secondary markets as excess.

Over time, however, exchanges built solely to deal with secondary sales may migrate up the food chain to deal with primary materials, particularly as they develop more complete data on buyers, sellers, supply, demand, and price. ChemConnect and CheMatch, virtual exchanges for chemicals, at first avoided conflict by promising sellers they would only conduct auctions for excess inventory, but both have since graduated to transactions that would traditionally occur through sales offices and distributors. They have been encouraged to do so by buyers who prefer the wider range of sellers and purchase options an exchange provides. If these exchanges can exploit their new role as buyer's advocate, the transformation of the supply chain for some chemicals products will happen quickly.

Fragmentation also exists in markets with many buyers but only a few powerful sellers. Here, buyers (often individuals) have difficulty consolidating demand to get better prices. Power may reside with manufacturers and their complex webs of distributors, agents, and brokers. This is the case in such widely different markets as automobiles, real estate, insurance, and funerals. Cartels in these industries long ago worked out rules of engagement that minimize competition, so the chances of one participant using technology to innovate are slim. Coalitions of consumers, often in the form of nonprofits, are already forming to break the current industry structures in each of these industries, overcoming the resistance of the entrenched participants of today's supply chain.

The danger in markets with fragmentation of buyers is that the customers, who have little to lose, will exploit information technology to help them self-organize. Consumers may form buying clubs and use them to buy directly from manufacturers, sidestepping the expensive network of regional and local sales offices, warehouses, and retail outlets. Costco and Sam's Club consolidate the buying power of a large group of consumers to negotiate the best wholesale prices, and make their money from small markups on high volumes of sales, optimized distribution, and warehouse-style retail locations. The membership fee, also a source of profit, could be thought of as the organizing cost for consumers to help them form "their" firm. (This is also the strategy, to a lesser extent, of Wal-Mart—the parent of Sam's Club—and other discount retailers.)

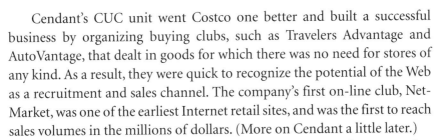

Cendant's CUC unit went Costco one better and built a successful business by organizing buying clubs, such as Travelers Advantage and AutoVantage, that dealt in goods for which there was no need for stores of any kind. As a result, they were quick to recognize the potential of the Web as a recruitment and sales channel. The company's first on-line club, Net-Market, was one of the earliest Internet retail sites, and was the first to reach sales volumes in the millions of dollars. (More on Cendant a little later.)

Consumers are also revolting against the automotive industry, causing considerable chaos for manufacturers and dealers, whose relationships are regulated in detail by state franchise laws. Manufacturers and dealers tacitly agree, for example, not to reveal the true price for new cars, but to provide only a manufacturer's suggested retail price (MSRP), which varies widely from what dealers are actually willing to accept (the "street price"). Dealers then rely on the negotiating skills of car salesmen to sell vehicles somewhere in between the two, hopefully closer to the MSRP.

Haggling, though, is an unpleasant process for consumers, and raises the negotiating transaction cost for everyone. As a result, consumer-oriented information sources like Edmunds and Kelly's Blue Book have developed to demystify the pricing game. The advent of the World Wide Web has greatly improved the customer's access to information, and MSRP has lost most of its usefulness for sellers. J. D. Power & Associates estimates that in 2001 over 62% of car buyers used the Web to get product information before buying, up from 50% the previous year.

Autobytel and other companies go further, allowing customers to submit bids for specific configurations and to have dealers respond with firm offers. In its first two years of operation, Autobytel generated over $26 billion in sales for its network. More important, the company has begun the process of building the emerging new supply chain by organizing a network of dealers from whom they solicit bids on behalf of consumers shopping on-line—a subtle shift in the balance of power away from the dealers. As CEO Mark Lorimar says, "Car dealers now know that sooner or later the last stupid customer is going to walk through the door."

The risk of sudden and catastrophic industry metamorphosis is greatest when the underlying product of the industry in its original form is in fact information. The problem is more acute when the industry has forgotten its roots; that is, when the current participants believe they are making and selling something that turns out to be an interim product that is no longer necessary. (It was never the media consumers wanted, it was always the entertainment.)

Emergence stage activities are already visible—if not quite as dramatically as in music—in many other forms of entertainment, including books, movies, and games. Professional services, such as medicine, law, education, and consulting, are likewise feeling pressure on their once-stable supply chains. In financial services, new supply chains for banks, insurance companies, and securities brokers are close behind. In manufacturing and other asset-intensive businesses, information may represent as much as 50% of the cost of goods, and that 50% is just as vulnerable to Napsterization as any music CD.

Knowing the warning signs for each of the three stages, it is possible both to see the change coming and respond to it with winning strategies. The first step: discovering how better information flow is already transforming your business.

4

THE INFORMATION
SUPPLY CHAIN

Creating New Value from
New Information

The Puritan wanted to work in a calling; we are forced to do so.

—Max Weber, *The Protestant Ethic and
the Spirit of Capitalism*

[FROM A TO Z: NEW VALUE FROM AN INFORMATION SUPPLY CHAIN.
FROM VERTICAL INTEGRATION TO VIRTUAL INTEGRATION. NEW LINKS
AND NEW COMPETITORS. EXPANDING YOUR STRATEGIC FUNCTIONS.
THE PROBLEM OF PRIVACY.]

THE VALUE OF A-TO-Z

In the exchange and emergence stages, information about the supply chain
takes on independent value, repackaged and sold as financial instruments,
marketing databases, and a whole range of new products and services yet to
come. As the new supply chain emerges, in fact, you may find that information about products can be worth more than the products themselves,
especially when, as we saw with prerecorded music, the physical product

simply disappears, replaced by services of which Napster may prove to be an early incarnation.

If you are having difficulty seeing how information in your own supply chain can evolve into valuable products and services, consider a pre-Internet example: *TV Guide*. Launched in 1953, the magazine is an information product in the sense that it describes programs being broadcast on network and cable channels—when they are going to be on, what they are about, perhaps what the critics have said about them. Its function is to consolidate data from several sources and present it in formats that are specific to the days of the week and to the scheduling and channel variations of different parts of the country.

Despite the fact that *TV Guide* is "simply" information about the programs, its value is tremendous. In fact, according to Andy Lippman of the MIT Media Lab, the magazine has consistently made more money than all of the networks—that is, the owners of the programs themselves—combined. What the founders of *TV Guide* recognized was that there is more to television than the supply chain that produces, markets, and distributes programming. There is also a parallel structure, one that manages data about transactions: an *information supply chain (ISC)*.

Like canal builders dredging and then widening, companies build and improve the ISC throughout metamorphosis, introducing new data and improved networks that make it possible for information to flow from one end of the supply chain to the other. The ISC does more than just describe its physical counterpart, however. It is an independent source of value, turning information into products and services that can be sold back to supply chain participants and other interested parties such as advertisers.

The better the ISC, the more opportunities to use it as a generator of new value, just as the founders of *TV Guide* have done for years. Or consider industrial information services, including A. C. Nielsen, Morningstar, and Dun & Bradstreet, who make money from their superior knowledge about the performance of other companies. A good (or bad) word from Moody's or Standard & Poor's, the two companies that rate corporate debt, can have a dramatic impact on your company's ability to borrow money and perhaps your stock price.

ISCs can be built for any supply chain. Even in smokestack industries like chemicals and steel, valuable information is created at every step of every transaction. Today much of it is lost, or captured only on paper, or in systems that cannot communicate across organization borders. For many companies, just being able to get their own information from one department to another is a significant challenge. Sharing it outside the organization, even to trusted trade partners, may be impossible.

Many of today's most ambitious software applications, in fact, are efforts to build one part of the ISC, often undertaken to repair the most broken links. A manufacturer may see its worst problem as sourcing raw materials in the global market, and start a supplier exchange. An insurance company may feel limited by the reach of its network of owner-agent offices, and build a sophisticated Website to sell directly to its customers. In some industries, particularly those coming off long histories of regulation, the supply chain may be so weak that partial repairs like these can yield benefits for years to come. But eventually the easy fixes get done, and the real work begins.

Without the complete ISC, the information these new applications collect will never reach its full potential to generate value. It does little good to improve the process for making a consumer product like soap, only to deliver it to a retailer who has no way to determine how much it needs or how much it has sold. By the same token, Wal-Mart, even with its exceptional information systems, cannot reorder soap at precisely the right time if the manufacturer has a poor production forecasting system or lacks strong links to its suppliers of raw materials. Wal-Mart will know exactly how much soap it needs at which locations, but the manufacturer will be unable to deliver it.

In the long run, real benefits will flow to those who use technology to create new supply chains that tie the entire process together from purchasing raw materials to consumption. Begin by controlling your own information, then expand your visibility in both directions, until you connect every link in the supply chain. It is a strategy that might have the motto, "We make it. We sell it. We deliver it. We service it." It is the connection of business-to-business and business-to-consumer into a single ISC—not B-to-B or B-to-C. Just A-to-Z.

Finding the New Value

Where does the new value come from? In part, the ISC will yield efficiencies that cannot be achieved without complete visibility. The ISC improves every connection in the supply chain—tracking the sourcing and movement of raw materials, pinpointing the location of products in transit, and providing on-demand snapshots of consumer demand broken down into ever-smaller market segments—even markets of just one consumer. A complete ISC, which can move information not just from producers to consumers but also

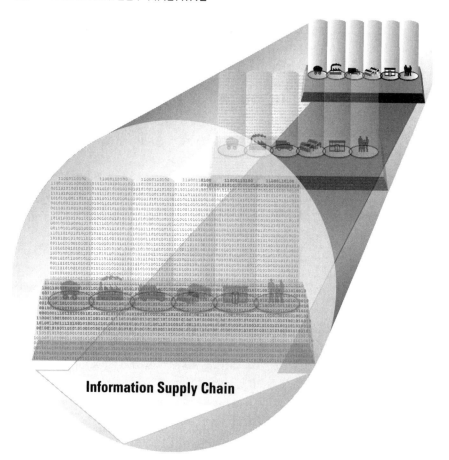

Information Supply Chain

Figure 4.1 The Information Supply Chain

in the opposite direction, does much more than improve productivity, however. Its feedback loop can describe how products have been used and by whom. Knowing how consumers experienced a product or service, in addition to what they bought and when, will be a phenomenal source of value. And it will be new value, not simply an improvement in productivity.

We have already seen that information about a transaction can be more valuable than the transaction itself. *TV Guide* "merely" describes the program offerings of broadcasters, yet 33 million people read the magazine every week. And that is just the beginning. In 2000, the company was sold for $10 billion to Gemstar, owners of cable TV preview channels and the VCR-Plus system for simplified VCR programming. The combined company has leveraged the information collected and organized by *TV Guide* to create an interactive guide and navigator, giving viewers the ability to sort listings by category or individual preferences, issue reminders that signal the TV when programs are about to begin, and perform intelligent searches. The interactive guide is one of the new products and services made possible by the company's control of the ISC.

Think about how your own industry could generate new products and services from a complete circuit of information, and you realize that the process has already begun. Consider these examples:

Customization—*Make exactly what each customer wants, but still mass-produce it.*
Durable goods manufacturers including Electrolux and Whirlpool have been putting software in their products to receive new programming and, not incidentally, build a continuing relationship between manufacturer and consumer. Electrolux leases some of its machines and, via a connection to the Internet, charges customers only for their actual use. Whirlpool is working with Cisco, IBM, Sun, and Nokia to develop new services, such as downloading recipes to stoves and uploading performance data to signal preventive maintenance.

Advertising—*Get the right messages to the right audiences.*
In real estate, home buyers can now search available properties and get virtual tours of homes on-line using sites such as Homestore.com and Microsoft's HomeAdvisor. The information flow is still incomplete, however, and intentionally so. Real estate listing services, owned by the agents, leave out critical information that would allow buyers and sellers to contact each other directly, preserving the agents' sales commission (up to 6% of the total transaction—talk about a transaction cost!). Still, as of 2000, half of all home shoppers start with the Web, and 50 to 75% research mortgage rates on-line.

Production—*Know what to make and when, down to the minute.*
In agriculture, tractors and other farm equipment come equipped with global positioning systems and monitors to check weather, soil conditions, and crop performance. Using these systems, farmers can apply precise mixes of fertilizer at the optimal time. They can also share yield data with seed suppliers, who can adjust their products to maximize yields. Equipment manufacturer John Deere & Co. is developing tools that make use of

GPS-generated data to advise farmers on the complete range of farm activities, including preventive equipment maintenance.

Logistics—*With visibility into product usage, distributors reduce inventory and improve delivery efficiency.*
On-line drugstore PlanetRx experimented with consumer-friendly UPC scanner devices made by Symbol Technologies to simplify the reorder process for its customers. Instead of going to a drugstore or even filling out an order form on-line, customers simply scanned the items they wanted to replenish, connected the device to their computers, and uploaded the order. Customers of Sainsbury's grocery stores in the United Kingdom use similar scanning devices. Since order data begins in digital form, error rates and other costs decrease.

Trading—*Turn complex products into tradable commodities, generating new financial instruments.*
With all exchanges, liquidity requires that the product or service traded be easily compared with offerings from a variety of sellers, in effect treating the good as a commodity. For complex products, such as advertising time for television, sellers argued that exchanges couldn't form, because ad buyers want to match the products they are selling with particulars of a show's demographics. In late 2000, though, Heinz, working with exchange operator FreeMarkets, hosted a reverse auction to buy cable time for one of its products and reduced the two-week process of negotiating by phone and fax to two days of Internet bidding. Over time, local TV and radio ad time will be purchased by exchange, and perhaps network time as well. Beyond reducing transaction costs, commoditization makes it possible to develop new products, including futures, hedges, and other derivative instruments—just as it has in markets for traditional commodities like corn and soybeans.

FROM VERTICAL INTEGRATION TO VIRTUAL INTEGRATION

The origins of the ISC are older even than the examples just given. In some respects, they began with the first wave of industrialization and the growth of large multinational companies in the early 20th century. Strategies that connected every link in the supply chain created some of the most successful companies in history, including Standard Oil, AT&T, and General Motors. Their managers understood that transaction costs between supplier and manufacturer, manufacturer and distributor, and distributor and customer could be high. One way to reduce those costs was to buy up other companies in the supply chain and integrate the functions inside one firm, a strategy known as *vertical integration*. Inside a vertically integrated firm, transaction costs are sharply reduced. Instead of negotiating a contract for components, for example, all you have to do is pick up the phone—the transfer happens, and internal accounting sorts out bookkeeping details.

Visiting the first generation of large corporations in fact led Ronald Coase to his discovery of transaction costs. He wondered why firms left some transactions in the market but brought others inside, and concluded that there must be costs associated with using the market that were not being accounted for; that is, transaction costs. The firm is not a perfect substitute, however. As firms grow both in size and geographic coverage, internal transaction costs also rise. Depending on the company and its industry, Coase believed there should be a perfect size—an equilibrium at which the firm performed only the activities it could carry out more efficiently than the market could. In his famous 1937 article, "The Nature of the Firm," Coase concluded that "a firm will tend to expand until the costs of organizing an extra transaction within the firm become equal to the costs of carrying out the same transaction by means of an exchange on the open market or the costs of organizing in another firm."

The balance, however, changes over time. Since the beginnings of the industrial age, firms have expanded and contracted in cycles that are poorly understood, consolidating now, divesting later. Often, the decisions are influenced for better or worse by regulation. The availability of a tax-free spin-off, for example, may encourage some decentralization. Companies also face the very real prospect of antitrust prosecutions if they achieve too much control over the supply chain, with the definition of "too much" varying depending on the political party in power. Standard Oil, AT&T, and General Motors were all forced to sell off their subsidiaries or divest some key suppliers.

Information technology plays an important part in determining the balance, lowering transaction costs both inside and outside the firm. Some technologies lower the cost of vertical integration. Telephones made possible the kind of coordination necessary to run a global corporation in the first place. The Internet, at least so far, appears to have the opposite effect. It has been lowering transaction costs in the market more rapidly than inside large firms, shifting the balance towards smaller firms and the trend to outsource more and more functions.

The ISC represents the next stage of business evolution: *virtual integration,* in which you lower transaction costs without actually acquiring related companies in the supply chain. As the ISC evolves, you will acquire assets, but the focus will be on your information assets—data that describe the flow of material through the system rather than the material itself. Information assets include customer lists, product inventory and customer demand data, copyrights, trademarks, and expertise about the use and application of products. Using information technology to bring them together across the supply allows you to cut costs even as you build new products and services.

NEW LINKS, NEW PARTICIPANTS

The best way to capture new value from the ISC is to pursue virtual integration within the existing supply chain as it transforms, and use the improved information flow to expand your role into more profitable activities. For example, consider the evolution of specialized logistics providers in industries such as chemicals, automobiles, and aircraft replacement parts. Their origins begin with early inventory control systems, which started with the modest goal of making production planning more efficient by giving companies a better idea of the raw materials they had on hand. Then someone got the idea of hooking together the inventory systems of the suppliers and the manufacturers, so that vendors could manage raw materials for their customers without having to deliver the goods until the last minute.

After a few more improvements, some suppliers developed tools to consolidate demand not only for their customers, but for *everybody.* Soon they were making more money selling inventory management services (or credit management or quality management or logistics management) than they did producing raw materials. They even may have sold off or spun out the production assets that once defined who they were. GE Capital, which began in 1932 as an application to help smooth out the payment process for General Electric customers, can now provide the full range of financial services for any business transaction, and even offers credit cards.

As companies use the developing ISC to offer new products and services, the balance of power in the supply chain shifts, sometimes subtly and sometimes dramatically. Manufacturers who become the principal creditors of their distribution partners, as in the case of farm equipment and seed suppliers, develop powerful tools for evaluating the financial health of customers, encouraging consolidation, acquisitions, and other realignments. They also gain near strangleholds on their customers' operations.

The ISC also encourages new companies to enter the supply chain, and the new entrants frequently extract much of the initial savings generated by new data. Not surprisingly, it is often the technology providers themselves who migrate from arms merchants to combatants in this evolutionary struggle. Technology companies including IBM, SAP, Oracle, and Microsoft have grown rich by offering industry-specific products and services. Once their products become mission-critical for a large segment of an industry, hardware and software providers move into more strategic positions, providing not just gear but also consulting services, joint venture funding for new applications, and outsourced technology support.

Today, a new generation of applications is being deployed to both advance and exploit emerging ISCs. In that process, established technology providers are being joined by startups focused on using information specifically to gain leverage in the supply chain and extract value from the ISC. Ariba and Commerce One, for example, sell powerful applications that can help connect participants in an industry into a virtual marketplace. Both companies store the catalogs of participants, run exchanges, and provide other buyer and seller tools. Not only do these services eliminate waste, they also give their customers virtual access to new buyers and sellers.

Another startup, ECredit, has automated complex algorithms for credit checking, which its customers can tap into as needed, in effect outsourcing the credit function for a variety of transactions. Because the actual credit scoring takes place on ECredit's computers, ECredit's system becomes more accurate the more customers the company signs up and the more scoring it does, reducing risk for everyone while cementing ECredit's place in the supply chain.

Having learned from the success of Microsoft, Oracle, and others, these startups and dozens like them are positioning themselves from the beginning less as software vendors and more as service providers, a new kind of middleman. These new links in the supply chain change the balance of power. Today's middlemen (wholesalers, distributors, and other resellers), who are the most affected, are not surprisingly the most nervous about the introduction of these new links.

Finding Your Place

No matter how the ISC in your industry is built, your role in the supply chain itself will change along the way—perhaps dramatically. As the ISC evolves, roles and responsibilities shift, with producers expanding into transaction financing, or logistics providers taking over order processing between their customers and the customer's customers. In this sense the ISC is the catalyst for the emergence stage of metamorphosis. As the information flow becomes complete, participants in the existing supply chain (along with any new players) use data to improve their leverage and extend their reach, reinventing the original supply chain, perhaps beyond recognition.

To win this game of musical chairs, you must first identify where you are sitting today as well as the other chairs you would like to occupy. Participants in your current supply chain include some combination of suppliers, manufacturers, traders, wholesalers, distributors, agents, transporters, retailers, and consumers. Each participant typically plays only one of the major roles

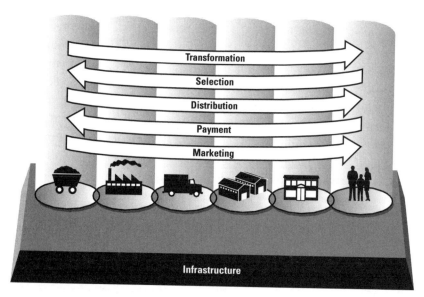

Figure 4.2 The Strategic Functions

involved in producing, distributing, and marketing, and identifies itself in terms of that function ("We're a wholesaler of specialty foods," "We distribute feedstock chemicals to major producers of industrial paints," "We're insurance agents for State Farm," and so on).

Crossing these traditional functions are other activities (we'll call them "strategic functions") that are performed, at least in part, by every company. This is where the real opportunity comes to exploit the ISC. Here's how: The manufacturer may do the bulk of production, but everyone downstream that handles the goods will alter them at least a little, from breaking containers into smaller lots (a trucking company) to configuring and assembling complex component parts (perhaps that is your job on Christmas Eve). A retailer or distributor may provide extensive product support before and after the sale, and the consumer may be responsible for installation and testing, as with most commercial software. Every link in the chain will participate, likewise, in the financing and marketing for each transaction.

Some of these strategic functions move in the same direction as the product flow, that is, from manufacturer to consumer, while others move in the opposite direction, starting with the consumer (payment and selection, for example) and moving back up the supply chain.

The best way to exploit the power of the ISC is to take over one or more of the strategic functions for a bigger part of the supply chain, starting with your immediate partners (customers and suppliers) but ultimately extending out to both ends of the industry. The strategic functions you choose will be those that make the best use of your organization's unique skills and experience. This will take careful analysis and a sober appraisal of where your expertise lies.

The answer you come up with might very well change the way you describe yourself as a company. Today, you might see yourself principally as a manufacturer, with the bulk of your capital committed to production assets. If there are several companies making nearly identical goods, however, it might be that your true calling is in marketing, which you can develop to distinguish your brand and charge premium prices (think of athletic shoes). Once you reposition yourself, you can begin to leverage the ISC to provide marketing and branding as a service to other companies in the supply chain.

The shift to strategic functions is not easy, and requires you to rethink how you make money as well as the allocation of assets on your balance sheet. In traditional roles, profits are a function of markups, commissions, or other crude (and often inaccurate) measures of the value added by the activity. Strategic functions are paid for through service fees, subscriptions, long-term contracts, and a variety of other methods, which necessitate more precise measures of value added. But the effort can pay off; companies that excel at a strategic function often capture more of the profit than they do today, and with less capital at risk.

The change in focus may also lead you to de-emphasize capital assets, or to transfer them to other kinds of investments, perhaps to different equipment and facilities or to fewer buildings but more professional staff. To continue the manufacturing example, you might sell off your poorest-performing product lines, buy the goods of some of your current competitors, and make your money providing advanced customer service.

Consider these examples of companies already expanding to fulfill strategic functions across the supply chain:

- **Financing** Automakers have extended the reach of their financing to cover much of the supply chain, supplementing their production roles with banking activities. (GMAC, the finance arm of General Motors, finances mortgages as well as cars.) In 1998, in anticipation of bank deregulation that came a few years later, new federal banking charters hit an all-time record, including licenses for John Deere, Volkswagen, and Nordstrom's department store. Even without building branches, these companies can offer many of the services once reserved for financial institutions.

- **Payment and Collection** In the United States alone, 29 billion bills are sent out each year, costing companies about 90 cents each plus the postage paid by the payer—pure transaction costs. The push is on to shift customers to on-line bill presentment and payment, which reduces the cost by up to 40%. On-line billing also generates important data for the ISC, making it possible to customize financing options and create new kinds of payments. Targeted advertising attached to on-line bills will generate new revenue and replace wasted bulk mail. Alliances of leading credit card companies working in conjunction with software and network providers such as Microsoft and America Online have been working aggressively to make on-line billing succeed quickly. Paymybills.com, for example, is funded by American Express, Citigroup, and E*Trade, among others.

- **Customer Service** Customers are taking over customer service. After all, they know best what they want and need, and if given the right tools, they even prefer to do their own order entry, diagnose problems, and customize products and services. In the airline industry, which has never been known for high levels of service, mobile computers that are already familiar at rental car return lots are moving into the airport terminals, where delays have increased to the breaking point. Since 1996, Alaska Airlines has offered check-in kiosks, and is now experimenting with smart tags which can be attached to the passenger's key chain and read automatically as the traveler approaches the kiosk. No-frills carriers such as Southwest Airlines have been particularly aggressive in encouraging passengers to serve as their own travel agents, in part by offering lower fares and bonus frequent-flier points to customers who book directly (and pay immediately) through its Website.

The Privacy Problem

Consumers are essential partners in the creation of a complete ISC. Unfortunately, even in the early stages of metamorphosis they have demonstrated considerable resistance, concerned about the loss of privacy that would likely follow from a complete information flow for the products and services they buy. Privacy is a serious problem, the modern equivalent of air pollution during the Industrial Revolution. In the interests of space I describe here only the broad outline of both the problem and its possible solution. It is worth underscoring, however, that without a solution to the privacy problem, there will be no ISC, and therefore no new value from its use.

First, the problem: As consumers ourselves, we can understand fears of data misuse. Companies have been developing information systems for over 25 years, and primitive cross-company initiatives including EDI (Electronic Data Interchange) transferred data long before the Internet became a commercial network. But consumers have been almost uniformly excluded from these developments. It is in this final link, the closing of the loop that makes up an ISC, that the technology of the Information Revolution will play its biggest and most dramatic role. As disposable computing makes it possible to collect more and more consumer data, we can and must find ways to ease privacy concerns.

Consumers have been given few reasons to feel optimistic about these developments. Though the ISC promises improvements in cost, service, quality, and selection, most consumers' only experience with large databases has been with their abuse—in the pathetically low quality of most credit reporting data, or errors appearing on credit card, utility, and other computerized bills. In many countries, lingering fears of governments spying on their citizens are easily fanned into flames. More recently, Internet users (over 100 million in the United States alone) have been distressed to find retailers keeping track of their movements through the World Wide Web and selling these data, leading to a deluge of unwanted advertising and promotional messages.

The privacy problem is made worse by poor public education. Few companies or the trade associations who represent them have explained to consumers in plain English the actual extent of their data collection, nor has anyone helped consumers see the positive benefits that will come with more complete data collection. In the absence of real information the privacy debate has been largely dominated by myth and superstition.

The stakes are high. Already, there are calls for legislation to restrict the capture and use of private data. If done correctly, such regulations can help speed the development of ISCs. If industries resist, or fail to form alliances with their customers, what will more likely pass are restrictive regulations that harm everyone. Earlier data privacy struggles, including the passage in the United States of the Fair Credit Reporting Act, the Truth in Lending Act, and, in the European Union, broad interpretations of the European Convention on Human Rights, have much to teach us, if we will only learn from their example.

The solution begins with better public awareness of the true aims and benefits of the ISC. Beyond that, trade groups and other industry associations must work to establish rules for self-policing that address legitimate consumer concerns about inappropriate uses of transaction data, as well as technologies to allow them to opt out of the ISC at any time and for any reason. These will be the easy fixes. The hard problem will be resolving the link between privacy and propriety; that is, deciding who owns the rights to use consumer information collected during the transaction. This is an aspect of the privacy debate that, so far, no one wants to talk about, but the subject cannot be avoided much longer.

Consumers and the companies they deal with need access to as much relevant information as possible. The more of it that takes a digital form, the lower everyone's transaction costs will be. Once the transaction is complete, however, companies will have to acknowledge (if only because of laws that say they do) that consumers have some rights to the data—at the very least the right to say how the information will be used after their business is complete. Companies who want to use that data in ways that generate new revenue will have to share that income with consumers, either in payment or in kind.

Making individual deals with millions of consumers might sound like an impossible, or at least very expensive, solution. Actually, it is already in place and working in a variety of exchanges, some that you participate in yourself. Consider what happens when you hand over your preferred shopper card to the cashier of a grocery store. The store collects a complete record of your purchase, which can be consolidated with other purchases you have made, correlated with where you live, and analyzed along with the data of other shoppers. This data helps grocers and their suppliers maintain better inventory levels, identify failing products or new product opportunities, and correct bad guesses about promotional prices and coupons.

In exchange for your data, the store provides special discounts available only to its preferred shoppers. Look at the bottom of your last few grocery receipts, and you will probably find that in exchange for your data, the store gave you between 5 and 10% off the total purchase price of your order. That's a strong incentive for consumers to hand over all that data—and all the rights to make use of it—every time they shop.

Grocery stores and their supplier partners understand that to build an ISC they must share with consumers the new value that comes from connecting up the last link in the supply chain. In the case of grocery stores, that data is worth at least 5 to 10% of the stores' gross earnings—that is the amount, in any case, that you have settled for so far. There were no lawyers, no contracts, no negotiations, and, for the most part, no regulations. Despite involving millions of consumers, the solution incurred minimal transaction costs.

This is not to suggest that consumer data will come that easily in your industry. As we understand more about the uses and true value of our information assets, the formula for allocating it among participants in the supply chain will be subject to regular renegotiation. But assigning and divvying up the value of new information being collected as industries proceed through metamorphosis is a crucial step, not only to avoid conflict over privacy and ownership, but to create incentives for cooperation in the construction of ISCs.

No industry has yet emerged from industrial metamorphosis with a complete information supply chain connecting raw materials all the way to the consumer and back again. Still, from the progress made in several businesses, we can say a few things about how you can best prepare for it:

- It costs far less to build an ISC than to build a vertically integrated company. Computing power is cheap and getting cheaper all the time. The company with the most leverage in today's supply chain will not necessarily emerge first from the transformation and, as we saw in the Industrial Revolution, first doesn't always mean best. Minor players with significant information assets, or even new entrants with powerful software, may capture the lion's share of total profits. Share new value with consumers, and you create powerful allies—powerful enough to tip the balance.

- You cannot build an information supply chain if your own link is weak or broken. Your internal information flow must be complete before you can connect with your trading partners and generate new value from the sum of the parts. Proceed with haste to implement core systems including procurement, ERP, and customer relationship management, and build them on an infrastructure that will maximize the potential for data exchange. In 2001, the Internet served as the conduit for close to $1 trillion in orders, most of them between businesses. The same year, companies spent more than $2 billion just to install procurement software.

- Your industry's ISC will not be built solely by a startup company or by an existing participant in the supply chain. Today's participants have the information assets, but startups know better how to deploy them. Every metamorphosis success story involves both kinds of organizations, or what Charles Schwab CEO David Pottruck calls a "clicks-and-mortar" approach.

These are just some of the elements of the strategic response you must design and execute as your industry proceeds through metamorphosis; the details will follow in the remainder of the book. The biggest challenge, however, will be to move fast enough to succeed at all three stages at once,

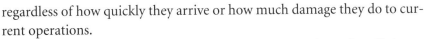

regardless of how quickly they arrive or how much damage they do to current operations.

The only way to do that is to invest simultaneously at the efficiency, exchange, and emergence stages, and to manage your investments together. For that, you will need some new ideas, as well as new ways to implement them: new kinds of investments, new organizational and technical infrastructure, and new partners. In short, a new approach to strategy.

The traditional tools of strategic planning, as we are about to see, won't take you very far in the development of a response to metamorphosis in your industry. But have no fear. While the Information Revolution calls for radical changes in how you plan, most companies already have the skills they need. The hard part will be to find and exploit them—the subject of the next section.

PART II

THE STRATEGY MACHINE

Putting the Pieces Together

5

THE STRATEGY PORTFOLIO

Blueprint for a Strategy Machine

We must all hang together, or assuredly we will all hang separately.

— Benjamin Franklin

[STRATEGY AS A PORTFOLIO. SPREADING THE RISKS: PROJECTS, VENTURES, AND OPTIONS. POPULATING THE PORTFOLIO. FINDING THE BIG IDEA. PROGRESS AT EASTMAN CHEMICAL.]

EASTMAN'S JOURNEY

The Information Revolution is busily transforming your supply chain, a metamorphosis that will happen in three overlapping stages. How will you respond? To win a war on three fronts, you need battle plans for each, and a way to integrate and update your tactics as conditions change. You don't need a strategic plan, you need a series of plans—plans that help you shift from traditional functions to strategic functions, and plans to use the power of disposable computing to build the information supply chain and use it to create new products and services.

Ultimately, those plans will help you build a device as flexible as James

Watt's steam engine, a machine that can be used to make more machines, operate in a wide range of hostile environments, and provide power for whatever projects you undertake—a business engine for the Information Revolution. A strategy machine.

But first things first. Before you build your strategy machine, like any good engineer you need a detailed blueprint. To see how that's done, we need to visit a company that is leading its industry through metamorphosis, cobbling together a working model for the ISC in the process. We travel not to Silicon Valley or Wall Street, but to the foot of the Great Smoky Mountains, in Kingsport, Tennessee—the headquarters of Eastman Chemical Company.

Eastman seems an unlikely candidate to be leading the charge in the Information Revolution. This midsized chemical company, which began life in 1920 making photographic supplies as part of Eastman Kodak, was spun off in 1994, and today produces chemicals, fibers, and plastics for use in paints, pharmaceuticals, food, packaging, and just about any other product you can think of. With annual revenue of about $5 billion, it is roughly one-fifth the size of larger competitors such as Dow Chemical, DuPont, and BASF. Its headquarters, with over 460 acres of manufacturing plants, 15,500 employees, and an average of over 200 railcars per day of raw materials and finished goods coming or going, gives real meaning to the phrase "smokestack industry."

Perhaps because of its relatively small size and short history as a public company, Eastman has shown remarkable courage in defining and pursuing the metamorphosis of the chemicals industry. In particular, CIO Roger Mowen, with the support of CEO Earnie Deavenport and the rest of his executive team, has worked hard to distinguish Eastman from other chemical companies offering similar products, focusing the manufacturing and sales staff on superior customer service through information technology. The company began the process modestly enough by launching its first customer Website, eastman.com, in 1998. The site initially provided product information, but soon added order entry and order tracking.

Eastman was impressed by the response to its Website from old and new customers, and stepped back to develop a more comprehensive plan. Mowen's team reminded themselves of some of the defining features of the $1.7 trillion chemicals market overall. The industry suffers from fragmentation of buyers and sellers, considerable regulatory oversight, and little in the way of information exchange across the supply chain. Because of the high cost and long lead time to build new production facilities, chemical companies also suffer from wild swings in supply and demand. When demand is high, manufacturers begin building new plants to capture more profit. But the plants come on line at roughly the same time and drive prices down. This cycle has created a kind of fatalism in the industry, especially among the largest manufacturers, who believe there is little they can do but lay people off when there is excess capacity, hire them back again when demand catches up, and run their business on razor-thin profits.

Given these risk factors, Mowen and his team concluded that the Internet and other information technologies had the potential to decimate the current industry structure. New technology will make it easier for buyers and suppliers to communicate their requirements, for example, making the supply chain more collaborative but also more competitive. Within a few years, the team concluded, it will no longer be enough for Eastman to offer commodity products at market prices. Instead, the company needs to find new sources of revenue now and exploit the evolving ISC to capture them.

Based on a careful review of its current strengths and weaknesses, Eastman has chosen both customer service and logistics as its strategic functions. The goal is straightforward: Turn Eastman into a customer-driven company, organized around services that enhance the production and sale of chemicals and plastics. To thrive in a future supply chain, Eastman believes it must sell not only chemicals but also *solutions* to its customers' problems. To do that, the company developed strategies for each stage:

- At the *efficiency* stage, accelerate the implementation of important back-office systems, and tie these systems together through an internal network, making data accessible to Eastman employees worldwide.

- At the *exchange* stage, digitize the wealth of technical knowledge Eastman has about products, applications, and services, and use the Internet to make that information available to distributors, suppliers, and customers (including other chemical companies).

- At the *emergence* stage, find ways to innovate with technology more quickly than larger competitors can, becoming a dominant force in a supply chain in which information reduces cyclicality and determines who will be profitable.

THE PORTFOLIO APPROACH TO STRATEGY

As the example of Eastman Chemical demonstrates, strategic planning in the Information Revolution is a very different process from the one with which you are probably familiar—one comprehensive plan, spanning months or even years, often developed by outside consultants and delivered as a total solution. Eastman's decision to develop multiple strategies and to execute them simultaneously is not unique. Many companies understand that the risk of pursuing just one course of action in today's business environment is too high.

I described the limitations of traditional strategic planning in *Unleashing the Killer App,* and there is little to add to that critique other than to underscore it. For those who want to know more, the drawbacks of planning as it has been promoted since the late 1970s (when Michael Porter famously captured the process in his books *Competitive Strategy* and *Competitive Advantage*) have been described in great detail by Henry Mintzberg in his book *The Rise and Fall of Strategic Planning,* the bible for enlightened strategists.

The only thing that has really changed since *Unleashing the Killer App* was published in 1998 is the urgency with which you must move information technology to the center of your planning activities and leave it there. That is not, by the way, what happened during the Internet boom of 1999–2000. The enthusiasm of investors and the business press, along with fears that markets were changing overnight, inspired many existing companies to move "e-business" to the top of their list of things to do. Internet projects were launched in haste and without a clear picture of where companies wanted to go in the brave new world. There was little commitment to any of these initiatives, and at the first signs of internal conflict, unrelated slowdowns in business, or the collapse in value of Internet stock prices, many promising initiatives were quietly terminated, the "strategies" behind them forgotten.

The momentum of industry change continues, however, driven not by the stock markets but by the constant push of faster, cheaper, smaller computing power and the expansion of the global data network. Your industry is experiencing or will soon experience a full range of efficiency, exchange, and emergence threats. New competitors will rise and fall; alliances and partnerships will be made and broken. You may never get a clear view of the new supply chain. While you and your competitors may have gone back to focusing your investments on productivity improvement projects, a few technologies coming together can ignite the later stages with little notice.

The solution is to follow the example of Eastman Chemical and invest in all three stages at the same time, following your instincts about how metamorphosis is proceeding in your industry. That approach may be new to you, but it is hardly novel. The science behind it is well developed. Successful venture capitalists, for example, earn extraordinary profits not by waiting for winners to emerge from the chaos of new markets but by investing in several high-potential companies, placing a range of informed bets on the future.

Investing in several outcomes is also a daily feature in volatile markets such as energy, oil and gas, and agriculture. Managers in these industries measure unknowns such as weather, demand, and the global economy as well as possible, then hedge their bets in case they are wrong. They may offer a foreign customer a fixed-price contract, for example, but invest in currency futures to protect the company if the economic balance between countries shifts unexpectedly. Their goal is not to guess right every time—indeed, many of the bets will pay off only if others do not. Rather, their hope is to balance as many outcomes as possible.

The techniques used to place these bets are based on the economics of options, first described in the 1970s by Myron Scholes, Robert Merton, and Fischer Black, and known as the Black-Scholes model. Following Black-Scholes, financial managers avoid big investments in an uncertain future by purchasing an *option,* a fee that protects your right to make the actual investment at a later date. Instead of buying stock or commodities, in other words, they purchase an option to buy them at some point in the future at a predetermined price—a price their research tells them is likely to be lower than the market price.

When the exercise date arrives and the manager's prediction turns out to be correct, she exercises the option and gets the stock at a discount. If she was wrong, she will let the option expire, forfeiting the option fee (but *not* the amount by which her estimate was off). The collection of options a manager holds at any one time is called a portfolio, and it is the *overall* performance of the portfolio that determines whether or not the investments are profitable.

The theory behind options is complex, but the application to your strategy is simple: The more uncertain the future, the more you need to place low-cost bets, or options, on a variety of possible outcomes. Instead of the linear approach of traditional strategy, you must develop strategies for all three stages now, and stand ready, willing, and able to execute them simultaneously. You must create, in other words, a *strategy portfolio*.

The drivers of the Information Revolution—Moore's Law, Metcalfe's Law, and the economic power of transaction costs—are the guideposts for developing your portfolio, but they do not point in only one direction. In developing your strategy portfolio, you must learn to invest at least a little in many different outcomes, some of them contradictory. As part of the process of managing your portfolio, you will also learn to start some projects quickly even as you scale down your efforts elsewhere. By monitoring the changing landscape inside and outside your business, you will recognize when it is time to make incremental change and when it is time for a leap of faith.

Once you place the initial bets, the real strategy process begins: monitoring the health of your investments and doing what you can to make each of them successful. When it becomes clear that an investment at any stage is not going to pay off, you must learn, as with any option, to terminate it quickly and definitively, rather than letting it linger and waste valuable resources. Remember that it is the overall performance of your strategy portfolio that matters, not the return on investment of each individual initiative you undertake.

Developing a strategy portfolio, by the way, is not the same as diversifying your business by buying or investing in unrelated companies and activities. The portfolio is always built around your approach to getting the most use from your current assets. Unlike simple conglomerate building, the strategy portfolio extends into the future. And it begins with small investments, few of which ever lead to outright acquisition or mergers with companies you invest in.

SPREADING THE RISKS

Uncertainty, as options theory teaches, does not mean inaction. Even though there is more risk associated with the later stages of metamorphosis, it is still possible to make investments today using the tools of portfolio management. Not all investments are the same, however. Each stage has a different kind of investment, with its own unique characteristics (see Figure 5.1). At the efficiency stage, for instance, investments take the familiar form of projects, developed and managed just as you do today with other information technology projects.

For the exchange and emergence stages, manage risks by making small investments in different initiatives and attaching options to each investment. The option lets you capture most of the potential value if the venture succeeds. At the exchange stage, for example, consortia and joint ventures are excellent ways to manage risk. At the emergence stage, you invest as a venture capitalist does, taking small stakes in several entrepreneurial ventures, some inside and some outside your company.

	STAGE		
	EFFICIENCY	EXCHANGE	EMERGENCE
Investment Type	Project	Venture	Option
Risk	Low	Medium	High
Duration	6–12 months	12–24 months	2–5 years
Initial Investment	High	Medium	Low
How Financed	Capital Budget	Discretionary Funds	Venture Capital
Technologies Used	Mature	Old and new/ Integration	Experimental
Review Frequency	Weekly	Monthly	Semi-annually
Investment Ratio	3	2	1

Figure 5.1: The Strategy Portfolio

Let's take a more detailed look at each of the investment types.

Efficiency: The Project

Projects are the most familiar technology investment for most companies, and require little introduction. The goal of projects is to improve productivity, which may be accomplished by forging tighter links between departments or with customers and suppliers. To win approval for new projects, managers prepare a cost-benefit analysis that shows the expected cost savings or additional revenue the system will create. Projects are budgeted for 6 to 12 months at a time and are expected to pay for themselves within 18 to 24 months of completion.

Projects often cost millions of dollars, especially for large-scale systems like ERP. Consequently, once they begin, they are the focus of intensive, full-time management review, with weekly progress reports and monthly reviews by a project steering committee of sponsoring executives.

Efficiency projects use mature technology, often packaged software and databases that have been in use in other organizations for at least a few years. Project teams work closely with the hardware, software, and communications vendors, and with trade partners (buyers and suppliers) for projects that cross organizational borders. Projects are usually executed internally, with some contractor support.

Exchange: The Venture

Investments at the exchange stage represent efforts to expand a company's access to trading partners—perhaps to a global audience—using a virtual marketplace. Because the risks associated with exchanges make them difficult to cost-justify as projects, the most appropriate method to develop them is with an experiment limited in both time and budget—not a project but a venture.

A venture is an experiment with a new way of doing business, often done in conjunction with other organizations testing similar ideas. As a sponsoring organization, you do not fully commit yourself to the venture. You may invest only a small amount of money and loan out a few of your employees. Once the exchange is operating, you may sell only some of your goods through it, perhaps excess or distressed inventory, or limit your participation to markets or channels where a competitor so dominates that you have little to lose if the exchange initially results in lower prices or profits.

Exchange ventures are subject to frequent changes in scope, partners, and technology, so an annual or even semi-annual budget is inappropriate for financing them. Instead, fund them out of research and development accounts or special innovation funds (remember, the initial investment is a modest one). Your company may not be in charge of the venture, but may instead serve as a key investor, outside advisor, and a source of goods necessary to give the exchange liquidity. Rather than providing day-to-day oversight, your management of the venture is limited to monthly progress reviews and steering committee meetings, especially once the exchange begins operating. Your commitment (along with that of your co-investors) may fund the venture for 12 to 24 months. At that point you decide whether to invest again—that is, whether or not to exercise an option to continue.

One important risk of exchange ventures is that they are dependent on new and immature software products, often from startup companies who may have no prior track record. In a rapidly developing application market such as auction management, you may not even know who the leading vendors are. Companies who are the most successful at identifying good venture partners maintain advanced technology groups (ATG) as part of the information technology (IT) department. The ATG is staffed by senior IT professionals, who follow developments in new software architecture, applications, hardware, and services. They cultivate relationships with companies building promising new products and services, and serve as liaisons to the rest of their companies.

Your relationships with other participants in an exchange are significantly different from those you have with contractors and vendors for your projects. Since everyone is an investor, including the companies supplying the technology, the connection is a deeper one—more a partnership than a customer and vendor. In many cases the software or hardware provider will run the venture on a day-to-day basis. If the exchange succeeds, you may take over its operation and future development, and treat it like a project.

Emergence: The Option

Even when the emergence stage arrives quickly, you are unlikely to know much, if anything, about how the industry will be affected. The only way to develop a better understanding is through basic research, most of which will not lead to anything of direct or immediate value. Few companies today make regular investments in the emergence stage, with the exception of companies whose businesses are by their nature dependent on finding dramatic new breakthroughs. Information technology companies fit that description, as do companies involved in biotechnology, pharmaceuticals, chemicals, and education. University professors spend much of their time on exploratory research.

Because these companies have developed techniques to manage investments in an uncertain future, it is important to understand how they operate. Their basic research, for example, is never limited to one investment or to large commitments of money. Instead, they place several small bets on a variety of technologies that have the potential to change the world. Every investment in the emergence stage is an option, and most will not be exercised.

One technique for managing options is to operate a corporate venture capital fund. For example, wireless communications giant Nokia created Nokia Venture Partners in 1998 to find and manage options. In order to keep the Finnish company at the forefront of new developments in its core business, Nokia Venture Partners is located not at the company's headquarters but in the heart of Silicon Valley, with offices in other world technology capitals. A team of 18 investors (many former venture capital or investment banking professionals) manages a portfolio focused on the development of mobile Internet applications and infrastructure. Nokia provided the funds for the first set of investments, but for the second portfolio the venture group solicited funds from other companies as well.

Nothing so involved is required to create an option. Sometimes all you have to do is launch an experiment. At a time when shopping mall operators forbid their tenants from telling customers they also had Websites, Simon Properties, one of the largest retail landlords, decided to test the future instead. In 1999, Simon formed a subsidiary called Clixnmortar, whose charter was to create small pilot applications that used technology to bridge the gap between shopping malls and on-line retailing.

One of the experiments was called FastFrog, in which teenage shoppers were given a lime green bar code reader as they entered the mall. The readers were used to scan all of the items the teens wanted but couldn't afford to buy at stores like Abercrombie & Fitch. Once they returned the scanners, their wish lists were uploaded to a personal Website, which could be emailed to parents and other adults. The items could then be purchased either from the Website of the merchant (if it had one) or sent from the mall.

FastFrog generated more ideas for Simon to test, and began the process of building a new kind of relationship between the company and its retail tenants at the malls. Though Clixnmortar went on hiatus in 2001, the investment was never large, and can easily be restarted.

Finding Your Golden Ratio

How many of each type of investment should you have? How big should your portfolio be? Obviously there is no general rule about how much money you should invest in a strategy portfolio, or what percent of your total budget to assign to it. Many companies start by committing a fixed percentage of gross sales (perhaps 5% or less). Others combine their current information technology and product research budgets together, treating them as a single fund from which to make all portfolio investments.

Within the fund, you allocate money based on risk. Spend more on projects than on ventures, in other words, and more on ventures than on options. To maintain a healthy portfolio, however, you will need to make investments at all three stages. One client recommends an investment proportion of 3 efficiency dollars for every 2 exchange dollars and 1 emergence dollar, or 3:2:1, which has a certain mathematical elegance. The ancient Greeks called such proportions Golden Ratios, because they occurred frequently in nature. Applying that formula to a $1 million budget would mean $500,000 for projects, $333,000 for ventures, and $166,000 for options.

Whatever allocation you decide on, stick to it. The temptation is always there to cut off funding for the riskiest investments—the options—whenever market conditions change for the worse. But remember that options are your hedge against an uncertain future, and the one guarantee you have regarding that future is that the business environment will mutate many times along the way. Don't forget that the goal of the strategy portfolio is to develop new products or services that can put you on firmer ground. If you abandon your strategy at each downturn, you will continue to live at the whim of the market, responding to every change—good and bad—as a crisis.

Waiting for business to improve before restarting your long-term investments, moreover, means waiting until you are too busy serving customers to concentrate on the portfolio. The best time to invest, as we saw in reviewing the Industrial Revolution, is when the economy is slow or depressed.

If budget cuts are unavoidable, don't fall into the lazy manager's trap of simply reducing every investment by an equal percentage. Instead, take the time to review the entire portfolio again. You are likely to find that some investments can simply be canceled, leaving you enough money not only to balance the books but perhaps to accelerate development for some of the remaining initiatives.

POPULATING THE PORTFOLIO

We have been talking so far about the strategy portfolio in theoretical terms. Let's shift gears and consider how you might actually go about populating an initial set of investments.

As Eastman Chemical did, you start as you would in a traditional strategy effort—by evaluating the current state of the supply chain and the forces affecting its transformation. From this analysis, generate a set of hypotheses about how the industry could change and when, along with as many interim steps as seem plausible. The number of different strategies you start with will depend in part on the risk factors at work in your industry, an honest appraisal of your current assets, and the current state of the ISC. Try to have at least two hypotheses.

For example, in a manufacturing industry in which many competitors make products identical to yours, information technology could make it easier for buyers to compare prices, putting downward pressure on profits for the producers. If so, your goal might be to de-emphasize manufacturing and move toward one of the strategic functions described earlier, such as financing. Or you might buy factories from less efficient competitors, and succeed by selling more goods at a lower price. If you excel in customer service, you could try translating your customer relationships into bulk purchases on their behalf, and make money by collecting market data you turn into new products and services.

At this point, you should be able to describe your strategies on a portfolio map, in a format similar to Figure 5.2. Notice that for each strategy and each stage, there is a space to identify how you might test the hypothesis. You will not test all of them, and the way you test will depend on your level of uncertainty—the more uncertain you are, the more you should test with a venture or an option rather than by launching a project. The key again is to

SAMPLE STRATEGY PORTFOLIO
SCENARIO 1—CONSOLIDATION AND PRICE TRANSPARENCY

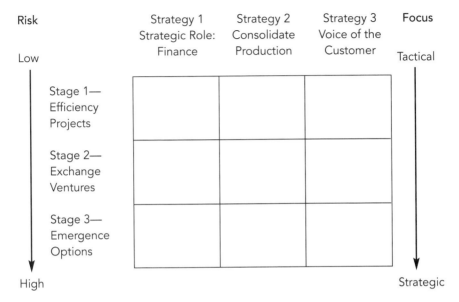

Figure 5.2: Sample Portfolio Map

create a balanced portfolio and to work diligently to keep it balanced—beginning new initiatives, shutting down others, and developing new or modified goals continuously. To become the provider of transaction financing, for example, you may have to invest in companies offering virtual credit scoring or simplified payment processing.

For each hypothesis, you can narrow your investment decisions more by choosing a general strategy to pursue at each of the three stages. The general strategy will be based on your strengths and weaknesses, as well as on your relationships with other participants in the supply chain.

This sounds complicated, but it is not. Remember from Chapter 1 that there were five winning strategies in the Industrial Revolution, approaches that can be applied to any technological revolution. They are reviewed briefly and shown added as another layer on the portfolio map, which is simplified to just one strategy.

1. *Innovate*—Rather than invent technologies, invent ways to adapt the technologies of others to problems in your supply chain. Like

Thomas Edison and GM's Alfred Sloan, you need patience as well as a fanatic commitment to your strategy.

2. *Supply*—If disruption is likely to affect your customers more than you, go into the business of supplying arms to the combatants. You may be a supplier of raw materials, like U.S. Steel during the 19th century or Intel today, or the builder and operator of key infrastructure—a railroad, a communications network, or application software. In either case, succeed by understanding your customers' business better than they understand it themselves.

3. *Regulate*—Governments and other organizations that identify and solve common problems for an entire supply chain often become key players in the new order, able to use their leverage to generate new value for themselves or their sponsors. This is the job of administrative agencies and trade associations, but over time they may become complacent and forget their mission. If so, revitalize or replace them.

4. *Promote*—In many cases open standards can generate more overall wealth than can privately owned systems. Make modest investments in the short-term benefits of a proprietary system, but for the long term create or join open standard groups, and use your influence to shape the standard in your own best interest. The Auto-ID Center for intelligent tags, mentioned earlier, was started by Procter & Gamble after the company realized an open standard could be deployed more quickly and generate value faster than a private standard.

5. *Finance*—Even if your company is not in the banking business, your best strategy may be to invest rather than invent. Investing does not always require cash. You can invest intellectual assets—brand, expertise, and relationships. At the emergence stage, few companies manage options without outside participation, and in most cases you will be a minority investor. On the other hand, if the opportunity to take control at the right price presents itself, be prepared to move quickly.

Going back to our example, you may decide to pursue an innovation strategy at the efficiency stage. This would make sense if your company has a good track record of installing systems quickly, usually before competitors do. Check that box if you believe you could offer financing services to your trading partners by upgrading your current systems and keeping them at the

SAMPLE STRATEGY PORTFOLIO

SCENARIO 1

STRATEGIC ROLE: FINANCE

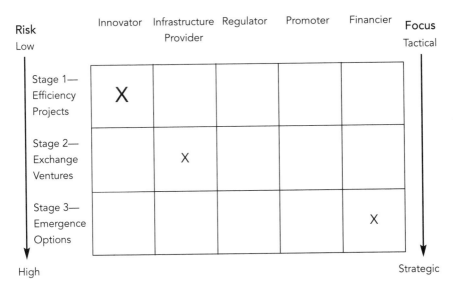

Figure 5.3: Sample Portfolio Map, Version Two

forefront of new developments in related technologies—in essence betting that you can stay ahead of others who have access to the same technology.

WHAT'S THE BIG IDEA?

Once you have a map of your strategy portfolio, how do you develop or locate the projects, ventures, and options to invest in? For emergence options, we have already noted several sources, including research consortia, advanced technology groups, and individual initiatives of inspired managers and executives.

The best source for investments at the efficiency and exchange stages, however, are the options themselves. Managing the options naturally filters out bad or unprofitable ideas, leaving the rest to become investments for the other stages. As options mature, in other words, their risk decreases, and they become ventures and then projects. In effect, the options form a kind of investment funnel, wide at the top and narrow at the bottom. That is one reason to have as many emergence stage investments as possible. The more small bets you place, the better your chances of having something valuable left to implement.

Whatever sources you use, you will want to start with a long list of interesting ideas. Right now you may have little more than a blank sheet of paper. If out-of-the-box thinking feels uncomfortable, getting anything down may seem a daunting prospect. Don't get intimidated! Over the last several years, I have worked with and watched dozens of companies develop their first strategy portfolios. One thing that continues to amaze me is how easy and fun the idea part can be. Under the right circumstances, even managers in the most staid companies can tick off a dozen plausible investment ideas in an hour or two. And once you've gone through an idea-generation exercise once, it becomes easier to feed the idea pipeline on an ongoing basis.

The best way to get started is simply to get started. The best ideas are generated in meetings (whether face-to-face or virtual) of groups representing each of the parts of your organization. To begin, remind participants of the forces driving the Information Revolution and give as many relevant examples as possible of how competitors and others are already tapping those forces to disrupt today's business for you or your trade partners. If you have trouble finding hair-raising illustrations from your own world, look for them in other industries ("What's happening there will happen to us the minute the regulatory environment changes," "What's happening in entertainment will happen here, but more slowly because our products are only partly information-based," etc.).

One technique that works particularly well is "The Worst Nightmare," the technique GE's Jack Welch used to start his managers thinking creatively. Tell each team that they have just left their current jobs to work for a startup that will compete directly with their old employer. Once you remove the practical constraints of budgets, antiquated information systems, and human resource problems, it takes remarkably little time for teams to come up with ways to destroy businesses and whole industries that have been around for decades. They rarely need any help connecting the dots between the exercise and reality: "If we could do that to ourselves, somebody else is probably already working on it. And why do we have to leave the company to do something like that, anyway? Our company has a brand, it has strong relationships with customers and suppliers, and it has industry expertise. It has information it isn't leveraging."

Sometimes great ideas come from field trips to information technology meccas such as Silicon Valley or Cambridge (Massachusetts *and* England). After an eye-opening visit to California in 1999, the CEO of Procter & Gamble's beauty unit was inspired to start Reflect.com, a cosmetics Website that offers customized products based on customer-input data. Convinced that this option needed to go on the fast track, P&G set up Reflect as a separate company, funded in part by Institutional Venture Partners (IVP), a venture capital firm. P&G provides the expertise for product personalization, brand management, and marketing, while IVP gives startup advice, help with human resources, and access to additional capital. Most stand-alone cosmetics Websites have folded, but Reflect continues to generate new business and raise more money to continue its development.

If you still need help finding the big ideas or separating the good from the bad, here are a few tips to get the juices flowing:

1. **Focus on the customers' problem, not your current offerings.** "Web enabling" your current business might help cut costs, but it is a strategy with little long-term value. Forget about your current offerings and put yourself in the customers' shoes. What problems are they are trying to solve when they buy from you? You probably provide only a piece of the solution, and your big idea could be a combination of products and services that takes care of everything. This means offering your products along with whatever other products and services will eliminate the buyer's pain. Focusing on the customers' problem is the difference between a 34-cent first-class letter and a $12 FedEx letter.

   My consulting colleague Peer Munck got his big idea while working on a project for Alliant Foodservices, a large restaurant supply company. Munck was initially interested in developing an on-line ordering system for restaurant owners, which would simplify food purchasing and help Alliant optimize its deliveries. But in the course of early interviews with potential users, Munck discovered almost by accident that the owners had bigger problems than broccoli. During a visit to one of Alliant's customers, the lunchtime staff failed to show up, and Munck's team wound up putting on aprons and pitching in.

   The experience convinced Munck that on-line replenishment wasn't enough. To solve the real problem for Alliant's customers, food and supplies ordering had to be bundled with other tools sorely lacking in the restaurant business, including labor scheduling, advertising, and accounting. Munck convinced his client to fund development of

The Sauce, a startup company providing full-service assistance to restaurant owners, including a suite of software applications on wireless computers, business advice, and help using the Internet for promotions and on-line reservations. Their motto: "86 the headaches."

2. **Go for the passion play.** The most successful Internet businesses to date are ones that focus on sex, sports, money, and shopping. That is no surprise. There are only so many hours in a day, and people spend their free time on things they actually care about. And that's okay, even if you don't sell anything on that list. In most cases your interaction with customers is closely connected to something that's near and dear to their hearts, even when your customers are other businesses.

   This is one lesson that the vast majority of on-line banks still haven't learned. Bank customers are people first and account-holders second, but you wouldn't know it from looking at the Websites of companies like Wells Fargo, Citibank, or the now-defunct on-line bank Wingspan.com. They're all about banking—paying bills on-line, checking account status on-line, and applying for loans on-line.

   There's a much more exciting way to think about banking. Banks, after all, are intimately involved in the issues people have dealing with their personal finances. They are also experts in solving money-related problems. Nobody particularly wants to open an IRA account, but they do want to retire. No one wants to apply for a mortgage, but they do want to own a home and send their kids to college. Customers don't get excited about learning to pay bills on-line, but they can appreciate what a few extra minutes a day with their families can mean. Approach the design from the customer's point of view, and the big ideas present themselves.

3. **Find the related communities.** One of the reasons Web-based communities like America Online and eBay have proven to be powerful generators of value is that they provide increasing returns the more people they sign up. If you can find, organize, and arm a group of like-minded people, they'll become the most potent sales, marketing, product service, and product development departments you'll ever have. Regardless of who your customers are, there is a community very close to the products and services you provide. One experiment would be to give that community a useful place to gather and interact,

and then derive revenue directly or indirectly (retailing, advertising, referrals, and so on) from the energy they create.

I once described this approach at a luncheon, and the man sitting next to me challenged me to find his community. His catalog company, The Company Store, sells high-quality bed linens and comforters. With a table full of strangers working on the problem, it took only a few minutes to come up with a big idea. Few people care to talk about their sheets and pillowcases, it's true, but everyone is concerned with sleeping, especially when they have trouble doing it. Some estimates say as many as 40 million Americans suffer from sleep-related problems.

Rather than just replacing the catalog with a Website, we suggested he create an on-line community for sleeping disorders sponsored by the bedding company—with the company catalog sitting right behind the community. The site could offer the latest research on sleep and sleeping problems, and chat rooms that let sufferers offer each other advice and sympathy. The site, we said, could even offer hosted on-line Q&A from leading researchers—presented, of course, at 3 A.M.

A Case Study: Eastman Chemical Company

To see the complete process of developing a strategy portfolio, let's return to Tennessee and Eastman Chemical. When we left them at the beginning of the chapter, CIO Roger Mowen's team had identified strategies for all three stages of metamorphosis, and was preparing to create and populate an initial portfolio. Before he could do that, however, he needed to create an organization capable of managing the different kinds of investments the company was preparing to make.

Fred Buehler, who led the original development of eastman.com, took over the efficiency stage, and quickly consolidated all of Eastman's external and internal Internet projects. But for ventures and options, Mowen and Buehler knew they were unlikely to find good investments or learn how to manage them from Eastman's headquarters. So they decided to open an office in Silicon Valley. They sent Mark Klopp, an energetic young director with a background in sales, and gave him what sounded like a simple mission—build Eastman Ventures, a corporate venture capital arm. *From scratch.*

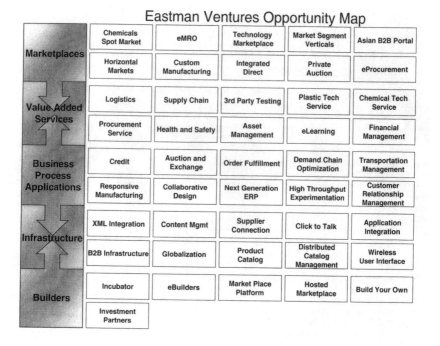

Figure 5.4: An Early Portfolio Map—Eastman Ventures (used with permission)

Klopp began by developing a portfolio map (an early version is shown in Figure 5.4). His group identified several ways Eastman could use technology to change the overall structure of the chemicals industry, including the development of virtual marketplaces, automating strategic functions such as credit and logistics, and adding customer service enhancements to keep eastman.com at the forefront of on-line destinations for buyers. Once these categories were established, Eastman Ventures set about evaluating potential providers and partners. As they completed their research, each element in the map was assigned to one of the three stages, indicating which hypotheses would be tested by projects, ventures, or options.

Buehler and Klopp then set out to fill in the boxes with investments. Between May 1999 and May 2000, for example, eastman.com completed nine major upgrades, improving the on-line catalog and enhancing order entry, adding a private auction feature to sell excess inventory, translating the site into multiple languages, and extending on-line sales to all Eastman's customers worldwide. In California, Klopp and his team made venture investments in 10 companies the first year, including WebMethods, a company that develops software to help buyers and sellers connect their systems, which became Eastman's key technology for opening an integrated, direct channel with major customers and suppliers. By late 2001, Eastman Ventures had a portfolio of 20 companies, covering nearly every category on the opportunity map.

At the exchange stage, Eastman entered into its first joint venture in 2000 with G-Log, a transportation management startup. Together, the two companies launched Cendian, which provides logistics and delivery services for the chemicals industry over the Internet. (Eastman exercised an option to acquire the company outright later that year.) Eastman is using Cendian to leverage its expertise in shipping chemicals, offering it as a service to small and mid-sized chemical companies for whom transportation is an expensive and frustrating part of doing business. Cendian has already taken over transportation management for Eastman itself, as well as several other chemicals companies—the first step in Eastman's goal of generating new revenue through professional services.

Eastman has also enjoyed positive results from other portfolio initiatives. At the efficiency stage, Eastman now receives more than 10% of its sales revenue on-line, and purchases 20% of its raw materials over the Internet. Out of 22 venture investments at the emergence stage, three companies have completed initial public offerings, generating substantial returns for Eastman Ventures. In its first two years of existence, in fact, Eastman Ventures has delivered a rate of return higher than the company's average for traditional investments. Indeed, the venture group, despite its youth, is delivering returns in the top quartile of all venture capital funds.

The most important benefit, however, has been Eastman's ability to integrate its options, ventures, and projects, using the strategy portfolio to pursue its long-term vision. Senior management works hard to ensure that the company maximizes its investments by encouraging managers to use the technology of its startups whenever possible, and Eastman Ventures gets many of its investment ideas by talking to managers running today's business. Over 80% of the companies Klopp invested in have other dealings with Eastman. On eastman.com, for example, order flow management, private auctions, requests for quotes, and contract management are all powered by technology from companies in which Eastman holds equity interests. Often, Eastman is their first chemicals industry customer.

Portfolio management ultimately led Eastman's board of directors to conclude in early 2001 that the company was really two businesses that were moving in very different directions. One part of the business (specialty chemicals) was beginning to leverage its expertise in customer service by developing digitally delivered services, while the other (plastics) increasingly generated profits from manufacturing economies of scale. In 2001, Eastman announced its plan to split into two companies, reflecting the need for each to pursue its own destiny. This unexpected consequence of developing a strategy portfolio, itself a sign of the breakdown and re-creation of the industry's supply chain, allows both companies to focus on their separate visions of the emerging chemicals supply chain.

There is one more feature of Eastman's experience worth mentioning. From its earliest investments in the exchange and emergence stages, Eastman has discovered strengths it never knew it had. When Mark Klopp first arrived in California, he was concerned that a mid-sized chemical company would stand a poor chance of being allowed to invest in promising new technology companies, especially when the competition came from long-established venture capitalists who had considerable experience in helping their portfolio companies.

What he found was precisely the opposite. What startup companies need almost as much as money is customers. Eastman discovered that its brand, customer base, supply chain relationships, and expertise in chemicals design, manufacturing, and distribution are a kind of currency, one that is often worth more than cold hard cash. These intangible assets had tremendous value to Eastman's new partners, value that never showed up on a balance sheet, value that Wall Street analysts didn't seem to recognize. Almost as if it was invisible.

6

INVISIBLE CAPITAL

Turning Products into Services

There is only one thing in the world worse than being talked about,
and that is not being talked about.

—Oscar Wilde, *The Picture of Dorian Gray*

[DISCOVERING THE HIDDEN BALANCE SHEET. INFORMATION ASSETS
AND THE DANGERS OF IGNORING THEM. FUEL FOR THE STRATEGY
MACHINE: TRANSACTION COST LEVERS, INFORMATION FLOAT, AND
INFORMATION GOODS. THE POWER OF THE VALUE CURVE.]

THE HIDDEN BALANCE SHEET

In 1896, Charles Dow created the Dow Jones Industrial Average (DJIA), a
weighted index of 30 key stocks traded on the New York Stock Exchange.
The Average, along with supporting market details, was reported every day
in his newspaper, the *Wall Street Journal*. The DJIA is a simple, shorthand
way to determine the progress or decline of the broader market for stocks,
and over time it has become iconic, a daily fixation (or worse) for millions.
Today, the *Journal* has almost 2,000,000 readers, making it one of the most-
read papers in the world. In 1997, Dow Jones began licensing the index to
companies who use it to create new financial instruments, including

futures, options, and other derivatives. The index has become, in effect, a product.

As the experience of Eastman Chemical suggests, one of the happy side effects of developing a strategy portfolio is discovering the true, often hidden value of your company's stockpile of information—your private stash of Dow Joneses. Even companies that do not deal directly with consumers, or whose principal activity is manufacturing, depend on information for profitability, including information that often exists only in the heads of employees. Digitize these assets, and you can use them to gain both leverage and value in the information supply chain developing in your industry. Your company is sitting on a gold mine of unearthed capital, a treasure trove of information assets you've barely begun to exploit. The good news is that these assets are renewable. The bad news is that, for now, they are also invisible.

If the portfolio is the blueprint for a strategy machine, *invisible capital* is the fuel that keeps it going. Its most useful form, as we have already seen, is the information asset, but before we can understand how to develop and apply information assets successfully, we need to understand how they work and why they are so undervalued.

Accountants refer to all the valuable information in your business— your invisible capital—as "intangibles," because, as the name suggests, they never take a physical form as factories and inventory do. The intangibles include intellectual property such as copyrights, patents, and trademarks. Your brand and logos are also intangible. Expertise in product design or use, customer service, training, customer retention, supply chain management, information technology, customer loyalty—these are all intangibles. Even a company's CEO can have intangible value. Think of General Electric under Jack Welch, Herb Kelleher's Southwest Airlines, and Bill Gates and Microsoft.

It's easy to think of famous examples of information assets. Take Coca-Cola. Its two most valuable assets are its logo and its secret formula, not the few bottling plants it actually owns. Coke has invested millions of dollars over the last 100 years to associate its brand with all sorts of positive emotions, and now derives revenue from the logo itself in the form of clothing and toys. Harvey Entertainment Company, which used to publish comic books and cartoons about a stable of characters that includes Richie Rich and Casper the Friendly Ghost, hasn't produced any new content for 10 years. All of its revenue comes from renting out its creations for film and merchandising deals.

Taken together, information assets drive large parts of the economy and did so long before the Information Revolution. Whole industries, including law, education, and consulting, are based entirely on intangibles. Organizations that deliver financial services, entertainment, medicine— even governments and religions—own buildings and equipment, but their real value is in diagnostic skills, market intelligence, and the ability to change your life, if only for a few hours. The services sector alone accounted for 80% of the United States GDP in 1999, roughly $9.5 trillion.

Service providers are the most dependent on information assets, but manufacturers are hardly excused from this discussion. Just to get a sense of how much you rely on information assets for your own profits, think of the main elements of the price you charge for your goods. How much of that amount represents information? Don't forget to include order processing and other administration, inventory costs for expired raw materials, and sales and marketing expenses. Perhaps you charge a premium to help customers determine what products and quantities they need, or have less obsolete inventory than competitors do because your market intelligence is good. If so, these too are part of the information cost. No matter what business you are in, at least 50% of the price you charge represents information.

Fall into the GAAP

What are information assets such as the DJIA, the formula for Coca-Cola, or Casper the Friendly Ghost worth? Given all the independent revenue these properties generate, the response is a surprising one. According to their companies' financial statements, the answer is: nothing.

Information assets, at least as far as the balance sheet is concerned, are not only intangible—they are worthless. As entertainment giant Time Warner summed it up in their 1999 annual report, generally accepted accounting principles (GAAP) "do not recognize the value of such assets." All public companies must follow GAAP. This is one reason most professional services companies such as law and consulting firms, which under GAAP have almost no assets, have chosen to remain private companies, and why most (though not all) universities and religious organizations operate as not-for-profits. It may even have something to do with why America Online acquired Time Warner and not the other way around.

Accountants argue that they cannot value these "intangibles" because there is no accepted method for calculating their worth—principally because accountants haven't developed any. Saying they aren't recognized because there's no way to value them is tautological, and in a sense an indictment of the profession. Over the last few years, leading academics, including NYU's Baruch Lev, have started to develop ways to measure intangible assets, but there is still a great deal of groundwork that needs to be done. Meanwhile, the importance of information as a measure of value increases with Moore's Law and Metcalfe's Law. The misalignment between accounting value and real value has become acute. Reading a balance sheet (which often fails to show even the *visible* capital accurately) has become an exercise in futility.

Every company has valuable information, of course, but the companies that suffer most from the problem of invisible capital are those that create and own large stocks of intellectual property and expertise. Entertainment companies are prime examples, as is any organization that makes its money through services rather than products. You will look in vain to find values for lucrative properties like Mickey Mouse, Bugs Bunny, or Batman, or the brainpower of thousands of consultants working at IBM, KPMG, or Accenture. From an accounting standpoint the real worth of these companies appears, like magic, only when the company is sold.

When Disney bought the ABC television network in 1996, for example, ABC's balance sheet showed a net worth of $5 billion. Disney paid $19 billion. Why? GAAP notwithstanding, some clever investment bankers working on the deal managed to put a price on ABC's information assets, including the long-term potential of existing programs like *Dateline* and *Politically Incorrect,* the network's relationships with affiliates and viewers, and its stockpile of old programs. The bankers were also able to come up with a value for ABC's programming expertise—the set of skills that led it to import the game show *Who Wants to Be a Millionaire?,* ABC's most successful new show in years.

In this case, not only were ABC's information assets invisible, they represented the bulk of its value. Together, ABC's information assets were worth an additional $14 billion, nearly three times the total value of the company according to GAAP. The shareholders of both companies agreed.

Oddly enough, so did the accountants. Look at Disney's balance sheet now, and you will find buried in Footnote 11 an "intangible asset" of $14 billion, representing Disney's "cost in excess of ABC's net assets acquired."

Once Disney paid that amount to ABC shareholders, GAAP allows it to appear on the books where it behaves like any other asset. (If you are looking on your own balance sheet, sometimes the information value of acquired companies appears as "goodwill" or "going concern.") Information assets are not recognized, in other words, *until someone decides to pay for them*. So there is a method for coming up with their true value after all—it is the amount a buyer is willing to pay.

Information Rules

GAAP ignores information assets not out of spite but because valuing information is hard to do. You cannot determine the price of a logo or a customer relationship with the same tools you use to depreciate a piece of equipment. That does not mean that there are *no* rules for information assets. Economists have done very little to work them out, however, so few managers understand what they are or how they work. At some point in your career you probably signed an employment agreement promising to protect your company's intellectual property, but in all likelihood you can't describe the difference between copyrights, trademarks, and trade secrets. Even CEOs of large companies regularly get it wrong when they talk casually about "owning an idea" or "trademarking a word" (you cannot do either).

What we do know is that information has very different economic properties than its tangible cousins. Capital assets lose value as they are used, equipment becomes obsolete, and raw materials are depleted. Information assets behave precisely the opposite way. Brands and reputations become more valuable the more they are exercised, in theory generating revenue forever. Like the black holes of outer space, information assets obey their own physics. Thinking about information rules tends to cause vertigo for everyone.

For many industries, there has been little incentive to flesh out the physics of information or even to integrate what is already understood into daily business operation. But information assets are the principal source of new value in the emerging economy and, as such, the fuel for your strategy machine. For a complete study—everything you need to know about information economics but were afraid to ask—Carl Shapiro and Hal Varian's 1999 book *Information Rules* does the trick nicely. Meanwhile, here's a primer of the most important properties of invisible capital:

1. **Information does not get used up.** Unlike raw materials, fossil fuel, and factories, information does not degrade or diminish when it is used in the production of goods. As the DJIA became shorthand for the status of the capital markets, more and more people referred to it, not only in the *Wall Street Journal,* but also on TV, radio, and the Internet. At the end of the trading day, however, Dow Jones still has its property. Physical assets are sometimes referred to as "scarce goods." Information is a renewable resource.

2. **Everyone can use information at the same time.** If I am using my factory to produce steel, or my warehouse to store books, or my fields to grow corn, no one can use these assets until I am finished. Information assets, on the other hand, can be used simultaneously by an unlimited number of people, all for completely different uses, if need be. Within your company, the finance department may use the customer list to review credit policies while sales and marketing analyzes it for ad campaigns and promotions. Every one of your customers can review your catalog at the same time, and if it is on-line, you don't even need to print copies.

3. **Using information makes it more valuable.** Under the law of supply and demand, the greater the supply of a good the lower the price you can charge for it. With information it is precisely the opposite. The more places my brand appears, the higher the value customers attach to all my goods. Use makes the brand more, not less, valuable. The increase in value accelerates, in fact, as the information spreads, creating what economists call "network effects."

   It is not supply and demand but Metcalfe's Law that operates here: The value of information increases geometrically as new users absorb it. Since no one owns the protocols that make up the Internet, they have spread easily, resulting in the explosive growth of the 1990s. The standards are now more valuable than they were when only a few people used them, and the value is increasing faster all the time.

4. **The more easily information flows, the more quickly its value increases.** Restricting the flow of information may protect current profits, but in the end it is a losing strategy. The legal attacks on Napster and other music-sharing services echo a similar fight that occurred when videotape recorders reached mass-market prices. Disney in particular feared

VCRs would destroy the market for first-run movies and interfere with a strategy of keeping its library out of sight so that every re-release was a major event (in effect treating their information assets as a scarce good). Despite the fact that VCRs, like MP3 players today, were being used to make unauthorized copies of broadcasts, the U.S. Supreme Court refused to ban them. This turned out to be a good thing for the studios, which now make far more profit from videotape rentals and sales than from theater releases.

5. **Value can be destroyed through misuse.** As any brand manager will tell you, the value of information can be reduced and even wiped out by misuse. If you license your company's name (and reputation) to an inferior product, or a product that does not have or make a clear connection to your brand, you risk confusing consumers about what your logo stands for. Marriott offers lodgings under nearly a dozen different brand names (e.g., Courtyard, Fairfield Inn, Renaissance)—each with its own amenities and price range—in an effort to maximize occupancy rates at the highest possible price per room. In reality, consumers have difficulty distinguishing the different types of hotels, and confused customers may actually value the Marriott name less overall.

FUEL FOR THOUGHT

Few executives—and even fewer stock market analysts—obey information rules, leading companies to mistreat their information assets, putting their long-term value at risk. In many cases they sell them on the cheap or let them waste away. Harvey Entertainment, as mentioned earlier, has done nothing to continue developing its cast of characters as it focused on licensing deals. The company's failure to produce new Casper and Richie Rich comics pitched at the next generation means the potential audience for movies and licensed products is smaller all the time. By mid-2001, in fact, Harvey was nearly bankrupt.

Throughout the supply chain, undervaluing information assets slows the development of the ISC. As metamorphosis advances in your business, however, both the opportunities to use your invisible capital and the risks of losing it multiply. You need to encourage the development of these assets at each stage in your strategy portfolio, starting now. As with any feature of the portfolio approach, investments should be weighed most heavily on information assets that will propel efficiency projects, but if you do not make parallel investments at the exchange and emergence stages, your chance of capturing value from the emerging ISC is zero.

The urgency may be difficult to see. In most industries, very little data actually makes it from one end of the supply chain to the other, and almost no information travels upstream from the consumer. Much of the most valuable data is not in a digital form at all. Information is trapped in incompatible systems that cannot be shared between companies—sometimes not even between departments.

Progress at digitizing information has been slow, but the pace is picking up. Over the last 10 years, in particular, software companies and systems integrators have worked hard to develop technologies for capturing, storing, and applying information assets. Data warehouses, for example, pull information together from different systems, while business intelligence and data analysis tools simplify the process of extracting, reporting, and making sense of the information. Knowledge management applications such as Lotus Notes capture more complex information (documents, presentations, and other forms), helping colleagues share their "best practices."

Many of these applications need only a few more turns of Moore's Law and Metcalfe's Law before they become irresistible. No doubt your company has invested in some of these applications; perhaps you have already spent millions of dollars without seeing the promised productivity improvements and new revenue, or at least not on the timetable you expected. Even if the products available today are not quite ready for prime time, you cannot simply wait until they are. Indeed, their implementation should be a key focus of your strategy portfolio.

If you are still not convinced of the power and value of information assets, consider the brief history of the World Wide Web. The Web, after all, was designed to link information in any form (including text, graphics, sound, and video) across computers. In only a few years, this information database has exploded in size, and there are now several excellent tools to search, index, cross-reference, and even rank the value of its contents, making it easier to sort the wheat from the chaff. Without intending to, the Web has become the de facto standard for knowledge management systems.

In professional service industries, including medicine and law, the existence of the Web as a source of information, even in its primitive form, is already wreaking havoc. Patients now have access to medical research and a global network of fellow sufferers, giving them the tools to make more informed decisions about their own care. Doctors feel overwhelmed and unsure how to answer questions from patients who may know more than they do. Lawyers and accountants find that basic software for simple legal problems like wills, divorce, bankruptcy, and tax preparation are freely or inexpensively available, leaving them with more complex but perhaps less profitable problems to solve.

In financial services, the failure to recognize and exploit information assets threatens not only revenue but the very existence of large banks and full-service brokerage firms. The "full service," which is recognized in trading commissions of $100 or more per trade, includes the broker's cost of gathering relevant information. More and more of that information, however, is available for nominal fees or for free directly from its sources, including company Websites, news agencies such as the Associated Press and Reuters, and the evaluation services Hoover's and Dun and Bradstreet. On-line brokers package these digital assets and offer them to customers on a self-service basis for vastly lower prices ($30 per trade for Schwab, as low as $5 for others). Morningstar, which began life rating the performance of mutual funds, now offers advisory services and portfolio analysis products directly to investors.

In the brokerage business, the Web has clearly shifted the balance of power to the customer, putting even the most respected firms on the defensive and their commissions at risk. A few years ago, I sat in the boardroom of a large Swiss bank with senior executives of its brokerage business and asked them why their customers continued to pay its fees. I was surprised to hear the answer: the bank believed it was the efficiency of its back-office trading system which allowed them to clear trades at an attractive price. That was their asset, or so they believed. "What would be your internal cost to trade 100 shares of stock in your own company?" I asked the president.

"One hundred dollars," he said proudly. With my laptop, I went on-line in his company's own boardroom and completed a trade with discount broker Charles Schwab for 100 shares of the bank itself. My cost, including Schwab's margin: $29.95. That's when the conversation really began. It wasn't the back office after all, but information that customers valued, and not just information they could find for themselves. We have expertise, the executives said, in developing portfolios, serving customers, and reading beyond the data.

Because that expertise didn't appear on the balance sheet—didn't generate revenue the way the back office did—the bank had a hard time seeing it as an asset until its value was seriously threatened. Three years after that meeting, the company—Union Bank of Switzerland—had merged out of existence. In its latest incarnation as UBS PaineWebber, the bank lives on only as a brand. PaineWebber now provides the "back office."

If you want to avoid such an ignoble fate, make it your top priority to find your company's information assets and apply them to every investment in the portfolio. How do you do that? As with the portfolio map, the best way is to look for opportunities at each stage of metamorphosis. We have already seen in the case of Eastman Chemical how information assets like brand and market intelligence can be a source of capital for your investments, more valuable to venture partners than your cash. What you will also discover is that information assets (new ones and improved old ones) are one output of a successful investment, able to serve as independent generators of revenue. Like the DJIA and the Coca-Cola logos, they may take the form of new products.

STAGE	INFORMATION ASSET	SOURCE	EXAMPLES
Efficiency	Transaction Cost Levers	Brand, Expertise, Customer Loyalty	Cendant, UPS
Exchange	Information Float	Transaction Data, Virtual Services	PayPal, Nielsen
Emergence	Information Products and Services	Information Supply Chain	Boeing

Figure 6.1: Information Assets by Stage

1. *Efficiency: Transaction Cost Levers*

The best way to capitalize on information assets at the efficiency stage is by making better use of information you already have. That is the goal, in some sense, of every information technology project—to improve the flow of information within your company, making employees more productive and reducing transaction costs. Once you have a base of integrated systems, you can start to find new uses for the expanding set of data you capture in digital form.

Henry Silverman, CEO of Cendant, perfected a unique form of value investing built around the simple idea of exploiting the hidden value of transaction systems and databases. Throughout the 1990s, Silverman bought up distressed companies including Ramada Inn, Howard Johnson hotels, Avis Rent A Car, Coldwell Banker, and Century 21. Though the companies were in businesses as different as hotels, rental cars, and residential real estate, they had one thing in common: a recognized consumer brand. More important for Silverman, they also had information assets that supported the brand, including reservation systems, listing services, and extensive customer data.

Those were the assets Silverman really wanted. So first he sold off the physical assets (hotels, cars, and offices), often to the employees. Then he licensed the information assets, franchising them back to the owners. The manager of an Avis location or a Coldwell Banker office owned his or her business, but rented the brand from Cendant and paid a fee for using its systems. An ill-fated merger in the late 1990s with buying club giant CUC sidelined Cendant for a few years, but in 2001 Silverman came back with a vengeance, buying the Apollo travel reservation system for nearly $3 billion. Apollo processes 100 billion transactions a year.

United Parcel Service (UPS) also understands the potential to turn internal efficiency into a new service that can be sold to its customers. As home-based shopping took off, first with catalogs and later with television, UPS learned to optimize its systems for high-volume delivery of small packages. When Internet shopping began its rapid growth, UPS was ready. Today it is the preferred shipper for Internet commerce.

FedEx not only has missed its opportunity, its chairman Fred Smith argues that the failure of startups Kozmo and Webvan prove the folly of ever trying to make money in home delivery. In today's retail environment, after all, every item has to be picked, packed, and delivered, but that cost is borne by consumers (their time, their vehicles, their routes). How could a carrier take over these costs and make a profit?

In fact, those substantial transaction costs could be reduced by applying expertise in logistics—precisely where FedEx has information assets to spare. But again it is UPS that has taken the lead. In addition to over $1 billion a year spent on information technology, UPS has been refitting its fleet of trucks to handle smaller items and more frequent stops. Using money raised from a 1999 public offering, UPS Logistics has so far acquired seven companies specializing in supply chain management for the service parts industry alone, signaling further investments in the company's information assets.

2. Exchange: Information Float

At the exchange stage, companies must look beyond improved efficiency to find the value in the new information generated by virtual trading activity. Over the last few years, many companies built on-line marketplaces in the mistaken belief that they could get rich collecting transaction fees from buyers or sellers or both. Since the cost of operating an exchange is largely fixed, more transactions at least in theory mean lower operating expenses for each and, therefore, higher profits. The more trading volume through the exchange, the faster profits rise.

The problem? Given the relatively low cost of duplicating the technology, buyers and sellers can and do threaten to build their own exchanges, a threat they use to force exchange operators to lower per trade fees. As a result, most new exchanges fail to become or stay profitable. Fee pressure is a problem not only for virtual exchanges. Physical trading floors, including the stock markets and mercantile exchanges, faced similar issues early in their development—the reason most today are run as member-owned cooperatives. (Several on-line exchanges are member owned, including Covisint, the auto parts market built by the major car makers.)

Physical exchanges have developed an alternative source of revenue: short-term investments on the money they collect from buyers, sometimes referred to as *float*. Float is the main source of revenue as well for insurance brokers and other escrow services, who hold funds for as long as 30 days before turning them over to sellers, investing in the interim in low-risk instruments such as overnight bank transfers and government debt. Internet payment services including PayPal also operate on float. PayPal processes credit card payments for on-line retailers (including eBay auctioneers) whose business is too small for most merchant banks. By operating virtually and holding the seller's money for three to four days, PayPal can charge less for its service than a typical credit card processor but still make money.

These services hint at the source of actual value for virtual exchanges:

information float. Information float is the ability of a market operator to use the information it collects about each transaction to form a clearer picture of overall market conditions such as price, volume, and risk. That knowledge can be translated into products and services, including credit, insurance, and specialized hedge instruments to protect market participants. Once an exchange reaches liquidity, information float generates profits not from the control of funds so much as the control of transaction data. The more transactions an exchange processes, the more profitably it can underwrite them.

To achieve information float, however, exchanges must work to group transactions by standard characteristics, just as physical exchanges have done in making markets for different categories of securities, currencies, and metals and other commodities. Market operators must also collect data on every trade they process, including buyer and seller history, price ranges, volatility, and other indicators of changing conditions. The ability of virtual markets to collect and consolidate this data for millions of related trades reflects the real potential for exchanges, not service fees.

Virtual exchanges, including eBay, are only beginning to collect enough data to consider how they will make money from information float, but the concept is not new. Nielsen Media Research simply keeps track of who is viewing a TV program or Website, but their products are essential to advertisers and broadcasters. The Zagat's guide, likewise, collects customer reviews of over 20,000 restaurants and publishes them in books and electronic formats. These are products and services derived from the very happening of a transaction and the careful collection of the associated data.

3. Emergence: Information Goods

As a repository for information about all the transactions in your supply chain, the ISC is itself an information asset, one that is shared among the participants (though often put to better use by some than others). We have already seen examples of companies using the ISC, even when it is incomplete, to create new products and services. Web-based offerings from ECredit, DiCarta, and Eastman's Cendian subsidiary, for example, all collect information about particular aspects of their customers' transactions (credit, contract negotiation, and logistics) and use it as a feedback loop to improve the quality of their own products and services.

The more complete and better integrated your own databases are the more they capture a complete picture of your company—your transactions, your expertise, and your market intelligence—making it possible to offer customers new information products and services, and deliver them virtually. As your revenue shifts to emergence stage activities, your business transforms as well, changing the structure of your organization (the information technology department becomes a profit center, not a support function, for example), your allocation of assets (more employees, less equipment—or the other way around), and perhaps even what industry you are in.

If that sounds like science fiction, consider U.S. aerospace powerhouse Boeing. The company announced in 2001 that it was leaving its headquarters in Seattle and relocating to Chicago as part of an effort to transform itself from a product company to a service company. The shift is not as dramatic as it might sound. As Boeing lost market share in commercial airplane production to Airbus and others, the company has steadily de-emphasized manufacturing, making fewer than half the parts that go into its newest model aircraft, the 777. Instead, Boeing focused its efforts on automating and digitizing its expertise in a variety of related fields, including maintenance, design, modifications, equipment financing, and crew training, all of which it now offers as services to its airline and government customers. The headquarters move was in some sense symbolic—from the giant factory where Boeing makes planes to the city with some of the largest customers for its services business.

In addition to moving from products to services, Boeing is also changing its emphasis from physical to information assets. Boeing, along with Microsoft and Cisco, was given a contract to build and operate a product design network for the U.S. military. The new network will be based on the system Boeing used to create the 777 jumbo jet, in which Boeing and all its suppliers collaborated in a virtual environment. Boeing is providing industry expertise to the project, and will operate the network as an information service, open to all defense contractors. At least for this project, Boeing is a software design company, not an aircraft manufacturer.

THE VALUE CURVE

You may have noticed that the more we talk about information products and services, the more difficult it is to distinguish between the two. Is an on-line catalog of products from several vendors, such as those developed by software startup CommerceOne, a product? When CommerceOne collects orders and feeds them directly into the information systems of the vendors, is that a service? Does the answer depend on whether you are a buyer or a seller in the transaction?

These are interesting questions of philosophy we need not dwell on. As companies in the same supply chain uncover and digitize information assets, the ISC develops in increasingly complete form. In fact, the potential to use it to create new goods (products *and* services) is what drives industries into the emergence stage and a radically reconfigured supply chain. Those new applications are invariably software of some kind, and in software the distinction between product and service means little. Most software already has elements of both—the product you buy may run on your computer, but essential services such as upgrades, product support, and training have moved to the Web. Products become services, and services become products.

How do companies decide when to offer a product and when to offer a service? A simple economic tool called the value curve gives the answer (see Figure 6.2). The value curve shows the relationship between the available quantity of a good and the price sensitivity of its customers. At one end, unique goods are those that cannot be easily obtained from another seller or substituted with a similar item. Buyers of unique goods are more concerned with the quality of the item than its price (the economic term is *elasticity*). No one shops around to get the best price deal for a painting by Picasso.

At the other end of the curve are commodity goods, where no effort is made to distinguish one supplier's products from another's. Here customers are principally interested in getting the lowest price, with all other features of the product considered irrelevant. Every soybean that meets a certain defined grade is identical to the rest, which is why commodities traders can deal in enormous volumes and future prices.

Unique goods command premium prices and high profit margins, but only for a few items, while commodity goods are sold close to cost but in large volumes. Dealing with either item, of course, can make for a profitable business.

Information exhibits many of the same properties as other goods under the value curve. Unique information, like unique goods, commands a premium price, but has few buyers. Information that is shared by many,

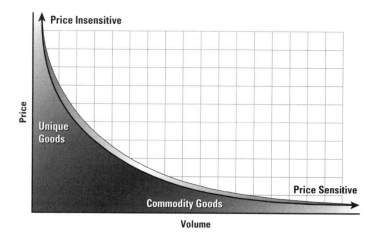

Figure 6.2: The Value Curve

what we might think of as common knowledge, can be sold profitably only in bulk. The one doctor who can diagnose a rare disease can charge her patients whatever she likes, as can the one lawyer who can save you from going to jail. For common knowledge, customers select their providers based on cost—and may not even be willing to pay at all, or at least not directly. Many people go to Home Depot to get advice on repairs and renovations, information the store gives away to encourage sales of tools and materials.

What is different about information assets is the ease with which they migrate up and down the value curve. Intuit's tax preparation software, TurboTax, started life as a product, which automated the preparation of only the most basic tax forms. As Intuit's user base grew, the company added missing functionality and put in more of the expertise that had once been thought the sole domain of tax preparation professionals, including a library of video clips in which tax experts explain esoteric concepts in lay terms.

Today, TurboTax has over 22 million users, and the product can handle all but the most complicated personal returns. Tax professionals, who charge $500 or more to help each customer prepare a return, find they are competing with software that may do a better job for less than $50. The "service" of tax preparation has become a "product."

TurboTax also shows how digital information can move in the other direction. Frequent changes to tax law translate to annual software updates, and Intuit has used its open channel to millions of customers to leverage a suite of related services, including additional software for state returns and financial planning, product support, and a subscription-based version of its products in which a Website provides answers to unique tax and financial questions. TurboTax on the Web, a product converted back to a service, has over 1 million subscribers. Intuit's understanding of the inherent malleability of products and services has allowed it to take on strategic functions in a variety of supply chains, including credit card approval, insurance, and on-line bill payment services.

For Intuit, as for any company operating near the emergence stage, products *are* services, and all capital, ultimately, is invisible capital. To understand why, close your eyes and imagine for a moment that all of your information systems are integrated, that you have built the perfect data warehouse and have a set of business intelligence and knowledge management tools that have uncovered all your information assets.

In such an environment, you can separate your information along the value curve, and begin to apply it to the most appropriate investments in your strategy portfolio. Product design skills would live on the unique end of the curve, to be used, as at Boeing, to reinvent the company as a service provider. Information about the status of an order is commodity knowledge, which is useful, as at eastman.com, to reduce transaction costs.

The value curve will also help you reassign information assets that are misplaced, translating common knowledge into low-cost products and unique knowledge into premium services. Figure out the 20% of questions that represent 80% of your telephone inquiries, for example, and make the answers available in an easy-to-use interface customers access directly from the Web, telephone, or any other device, as FedEx famously did by offering customers on-line access to its tracking database.

Now, open your eyes. How far are you from being able to turn products into services and services into products as new opportunities and new technologies present themselves? If you've discovered all your invisible capital and applied information assets to all three stages of the strategy portfolio, you're most of the way there.

There is one more thing you need, and that is the discipline to constantly reinvent who you are and what you do—to keep putting new ideas into the portfolio and develop them into products and services regardless of the stress they may put on your current technology investments and the structure of your business. That discipline—the merger of strategy and operations—means reinventing your business not once every decade or every few years, but every day.

If you're ready, put the pieces together, crank up the engine, and turn on the strategy machine.

7

PERPETUAL MOTION

Starting Up the Invisible Capital Engine

The idea becomes the machine that makes the art.

—Sol LeWitt

[THE PERPETUAL MOTION MACHINE. SOLVING THE INPUT-OUTPUT
ERRORS. TECHNICAL ARCHITECTURE BY STAGE: INTEGRATION, LIQUID-
ITY, AND DECONSTRUCTION. ORGANIZATION ARCHITECTURE BY STAGE:
ALIGNMENT, INCUBATION, AND CORPORATE VENTURE CAPITAL.]

THE PERPETUAL MOTION MACHINE

One of the great lost causes of science has been the pursuit of a machine
that can operate without an external source of energy: a perpetual motion
machine. Its benefits are obvious, and everyone from Leonardo da Vinci to
your freshman year college roommate has tried to figure out how to build
one. The 14th-century Italian philosopher Marcantonio Zimara, for
example, dreamed up a perpetual windmill powered by its own bellows.
The machine begins with a fan being turned by air from a bellows. The fan
in turn drives a belt that turns a crank, and the crank moves the bellows,
which keeps the fan going.

Give the bellows one good start, and the machine operates itself, right?

Of course the answer is no. Over time, the bellows pushes out less air, the fan moves with less force, and eventually—in this case, probably very quickly—the bellows doesn't move at all.

A perpetual motion machine, unfortunately, is impossible for many reasons, not the least of which is, as Isaac Newton observed, "the seekers after perpetual motion are trying to get something from nothing." A machine simply cannot make more energy than is put into it. Even a device that needed to do nothing more than operate itself would fail. The problem is the inefficiency of the machine. At every stage of operation, from bellows to crank to fan, energy disappears from the system, in the form of heat or noise or wind or any number of other ways. Physicists call that inefficiency friction. Economists call it a transaction cost. Without a continuing energy source the machine will slow down and eventually stop. Perpetual motion, we now know, is impossible.

Or is it? What if your business operated a machine that did not follow the laws of physics? What if instead of fighting friction, the machine ran in a universe where every action had not an equal and opposite reaction but a *greater* reaction, producing more energy than it used? Could you change your focus from producing individual goods or services to operating the machine itself, leaving the machine to create the value?

Information does not follow the same rules as physical goods. It does not get used up. Everyone, inside and outside your company, can use it simultaneously. Information becomes more valuable the more it is used, and if nurtured, generates new value over time, becoming more useful as a source of new products and services. Your supply of invisible capital does not obey the laws of thermodynamics. In the Information Revolution, strategy is a machine powered by information assets. Strategy is perpetual.

We come at last to the strategy machine. Any organization can develop the first set of investments for its strategy portfolio, unearth its most obvious information assets, and watch for the early warning signs of an emerging ISC. But what then? Innovation is a difficult process under the best of circumstances, and in many companies it is nearly impossible. Companies such as Microsoft and Charles Schwab, which have not only reinvented themselves but done so with the same leaders, are the rare exceptions.

As metamorphosis transforms your supply chain, the only way to retain your competitive advantage is to reinvent your business. Not once, not even once a year, but *every day*. The portfolio must be renewed and replenished, filled at the top with options you can develop into ventures and projects. Finding your invisible capital is not enough—you must develop the ability to transform it into new information products and services, moving up and down the value curve.

Strategy is not an event. It is a process. Like James Watt's steam engine, your strategy needs to function in a wide range of hostile environments and provide power for whatever projects you undertake. To reinvent your business every day you need a machine with information as its input and its output—an invisible capital engine, an information breeder reactor, your strategy machine. The portfolio is the blueprint, and invisible capital is the renewable fuel. Put them together, and you have a perpetual motion machine.

Here's how it works. Your initial investments act as the first turn of the crank. As you manage your investments, new information products and services are found and developed along the value curve. The new goods generate more ideas, and these go into the next round of investment decisions as potential options, ventures, and projects. Linking together your strategy

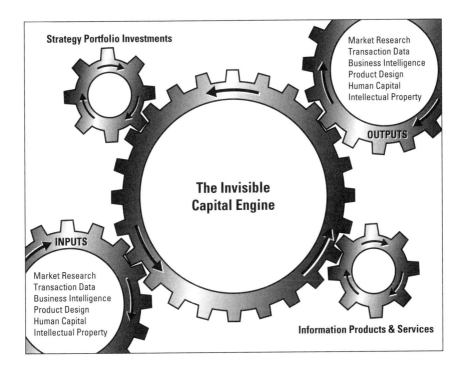

Figure 7.1: The Strategy Machine

machine with those of your trading and investment partners creates the information supply chain. Over time, strategy and operations converge.

Perhaps the most remarkable feature of the strategy machine is that its inputs and outputs are the same. Market intelligence, transaction data, design expertise, brands, and other information assets are first used to formulate investment ideas. As the investments generate information products and services, new data flows back into the system. As more invisible capital goes into the engine, more valuable assets come out. Information is the input; better information is the output.

Figure 7.2 shows the strategy machine of an engineering consulting firm. Here the company's most valuable information asset is the expertise of its professional staff, nurtured through extensive training and the hands-on experience of working with clients. Today, expertise is used in a variety of products and services across the value curve. At the high end, the firm conducts customized engagements for clients to solve specific problems, often with on-site project teams. To reach a broader audience with less specific information, the staff writes articles, speeches, and books. The firm has also repackaged some of its research and experience with clients into self-service databases sold on a subscription basis, offered in conjunction with bulletin boards where clients can post simple questions which are answered by younger engineers and other subscribers.

To build its strategy machine, the most important change for the engineering firm was a change in priorities. The development of the initial strategy portfolio maps made clear that all revenue was generated from a single collection of invisible information assets, which included speeches, engagements, books, and research reports. Now, rather than measuring each product and service as a separate source of revenue, the company measures only the development of new information assets and the return on its strategy portfolio. Revenue takes care of itself.

More elaborate changes were made to the firm's technology and organization architectures. Information assets stored in incompatible information systems or left in the heads of the engineers could not be used as input to the strategy portfolio. The systems needed to be able to capture the knowledge of the firm's engineers, and the engineers needed a reason to contribute their expertise to the engine. This required a new set of databases and knowledge management applications and new desktop and mobile computers for the engineers. Engineers are now evaluated not on their billings but on their contributions to the firm's knowledge base.

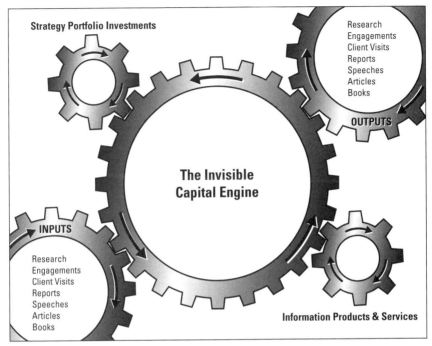

Figure 7.2: Strategy Machine for a Professional Services Firm

INPUT-OUTPUT ERRORS

The hypothetical engineering firm I just described actually exists, although I have changed some facts about the development of its strategy machine to simplify the example. Let's put one of those facts back in: the firm's difficult and ongoing struggle to locate and organize its information assets in reusable forms, which has limited its ability to create new information goods. Until the firm captures more knowledge, the strategy machine will not operate at peak efficiency, any more than a computer can when it has faulty input and output processors.

In part, the firm is unable to solve its I/O problems because the ISC for its industry is incomplete. The ISC, like the power, water, and transportation systems of the Industrial Revolution, can only function if everyone agrees to use the same standards. For decades, railroad operators refused to settle on a single gauge for track width, which added tremendous cost when freight had to be transferred between railroad lines. (In the United States, agreement on a single gauge was delayed nearly into the 20th century.) AT&T achieved a monopoly on long distance only because it was the one company that could provide connections between hundreds of local exchanges.

Similarly, the engineers rely heavily on data from outside sources—statistical databases, building codes, government agencies—and there are few standards for most of that data. These issues will be resolved, as they were in the Industrial Revolution, through the eventual emergence of common formats and protocols, both technological and organizational, across the supply chain. That is the truly revolutionary feature of the Internet and the process by which it adopts new data exchange methods. For the first time in the history of computing, an open, nonproprietary approach to standardization has been spreading more quickly than closed solutions. Metcalfe's Law to the rescue.

For the engineers, and for you, standardization will make the strategy machine possible, but it will also require dramatic changes both to data and knowledge management. Think of the ISC as the transportation system for your industry as it emerges from metamorphosis. Like the railroad, power, and telephone networks, the ISC will improve efficiency and make new kinds of business possible, but only if you follow the rules of the road. Your own data must conform to the standards, and your information systems must be able to send and receive information across the ISC without anything getting lost in translation.

This is not, it should be emphasized, a problem that can be delegated to your Chief Information Officer (CIO). The strategy machine is as important a piece of operating technology as any of the equipment or other assets you use today to produce your goods and services. Its design must be the responsibility of the entire executive team—including but not limited to your CIO.

Depending on your industry, it will take some time for the most important standards for storing and exchanging information to emerge. In the meantime, there are a few basic design principles to bear in mind. This is not a technology book, but every executive should understand these principles, at least in as much detail as they are described in the next few pages.

Build on Open Standards

Even if you do not work for a high-technology company, the data and knowledge management systems you create should be as flexible as possible. Throughout metamorphosis your systems and data will be required to communicate with new systems and devices that cannot be described today. Trading partners will want to interact with you in different ways depending on the device or interface they are using at any given time.

The best way to ensure (although not guarantee) your ability to participate fully in future data exchanges is to build your systems on Internet standards, including the important commercial standards—XML for form data and MP3 for audio, for example—that have been added to it. In a market of competing standards, choosing the winner is difficult. The best technology does not always become the most widely adopted, perhaps because of cost or simply poor marketing. Most video engineers will tell you that Sony's Beta standard is superior in quality to VHS, but VHS nonetheless became the dominant standard in the United States. In choosing standards, follow the portfolio approach and hedge your bets.

It is also important to recognize open and closed standards regardless of what they are called. Many hardware and software vendors, anxious to retain their current market position, will offer their protocol to the market as a standard, but often with strings attached. Sun, for instance, tried to make its Java technology a standard while maintaining it as a proprietary product, a mistake that held back the spread of Java as a programming language by at least a few years.

Dick Costolo, vice president of wireless software company 724 Solutions, distinguishes between true standards that are developed, tested, and willingly adopted by users, and standards developed by consortia of technology companies "that are forced on users as an expression of the members' market power." In the former category he places XML, a robust data exchange language that is replacing traditional Electronic Data Interchange (EDI). In the latter category he places Bluetooth, a wireless protocol invented by Ericsson, which is being aggressively marketed by a powerful group of vendors that includes Intel, Toshiba, Nokia, IBM, and Motorola (a lower-cost standard, with the unfortunate name 802.11b, is spreading more rapidly). Bluetooth, he says, is overly complicated, expensive, and bulky—designed to sell the equipment of the consortium more than to solve the problems of users. "A foisted standard is no standard at all," as Costolo puts it.

Separate Data, Application, and User Interface

In their rush to respond to the first generation of Internet startups, most companies quickly built simple "brochureware" Websites, and then added features such as order processing over time. Little thought was given in the first instance to transaction processing, creating enormous headaches as companies tried after the fact to integrate data coming to and going from the Website with data from older systems. Data definitions were often hard-coded into the layout of the site. When new devices—Blackberry, pagers, cell phones, and PDAs—came along as alternatives to the Web, most companies found it difficult to reformat data to send to them.

In designing new systems and databases do not start by assuming that today's environment will remain for long. Expect to interact with special-ized new devices that will send and receive small units of information. Assume as well that new technologies for interaction, including live video and instant messaging, will become part of the standard environment users expect. And imagine that nearly all the functions only your employ-ees have access to will eventually migrate out to your trading partners as well.

If these expectations had been part of your business strategy a few years ago, what decisions would you have made differently? For one thing, you would not have started by building a Website. You would have begun instead with the information design, and committed to keeping data, application logic, and user interfaces separate so that each could adapt to new and improved technologies as they became available. Starting now, store your data in abstract forms, perhaps using object-oriented databases. Application logic should also be written in small, component-sized pieces, separated from other logic and from the data by high-level software known as Application Programming Interfaces (APIs).

Nobody knows how future applications of Internet technology will actually be used. Inventors are surprised by unintended uses that evolve (sometimes quickly) from their creations. They start out believing that new devices are merely improvements over existing ones—just as cars were thought to be "horseless carriages" and television was first described as "radio with pictures." With experimentation and serendipity, new appli-cations emerge. The less you hard-code old metaphors—the Web, the Windows interface—the easier it will be to respond to new opportunities.

Establish and Enforce a Basic "Building Code"

As with any structure, your information assets will be easier to develop if their design includes enforceable rules that ensure compliance with the overall strategy. These rules constitute the building code that employees, trading partners, and technology vendors must follow. Overly restrictive rules, of course, will make it just as difficult to build a working strategy machine as having no rules at all, so it is important to find the right balance between what is necessary and what is merely desirable. Here are some suggestions, based on rules adopted by several organizations that are building strategy machines:

• New applications must follow the rule of true separation between data, logic, and user interface. This rule applies not only to custom development but also to packaged software purchased from vendors.

• Choose one database management system (e.g., Oracle, MS SQL Server, DB2). Do not develop or buy any applications unless they support it. All applications must support data import and export capabilities using Internet protocols and languages such as XML.

• Start with an ambitious design for your data warehouse, but fill it in carefully. Make sure the data can be easily shared inside and outside your organization's borders. Consistent rules about data elements (e.g., "What is a customer?") are crucial.

• For applications that are not central to your business, choose one major packaged solution and insist all business units install it. Companies as large and diverse as GE have standardized on Oracle's financial applications. Do not customize non-core applications.

• For applications that are core to your business, on the other hand, do not buy software packages. Build them yourself, embedding as much of your invisible capital as possible.

• Define the components for an organization-wide desktop computing environment that specifies hardware, operating system, and key application selections, including office tools and email. Do not allow individual departments, business units, or geographic areas to vary from the standard environment.

• For any application that may be used by customers and suppliers— which means, by the way, *every* application—construct a layer of software between these new front ends and existing databases. Doing so will keep the "plumbing" between systems manageable, particularly when components are upgraded or replaced.

- Provide financial incentives to departments and employees to share their data and keep it accurate. Sharing it widely helps to identify where errors exist and who is best suited to correct them, including suppliers and customers.

Adopting these rules for information asset management does not mean building the ultimate system from the beginning. If anything, err on the side of detail in the design but keep the initial implementations simple. Remember The Sauce, the startup that wanted to solve the big problems plaguing restaurant owners? The company's plan was to start modestly, offering a food ordering application that would run on hand-held computers such as the PalmPilot. Rather than leave gaps in the design to add more features later, however, the design team struggled to build a first version that handled everything. This led to delays, budget overruns and, in the end, a first version that was too complicated for its users.

In this case, trying to build a system that worked for an ISC that didn't yet exist proved fatal. The Sauce ran out of money before it could get its strategy machine going, and shut down in 2001.

Problems with the inputs and outputs of a strategy machine are not unique to startups or to professional services firms, however. They are everyone's challenge. Technology for capturing, storing, and manipulating complex information is still in its infancy, but few companies make the best use of the tools that are available, and almost none are organized to quickly adopt better tools when they mature.

Many companies, moreover, have policies against sharing valuable knowledge with trading partners, no matter what the application might be. Internally, employees are rarely rewarded for behavior that develops invisible capital—indeed, the saying "knowledge is power" describes the pecking order in many companies. Those who have it are more likely to hoard it than to feed it into the portfolio.

You cannot solve any of these problems overnight, but you can begin to rethink and rebuild your technology and your organization now to better support a strategy machine. Below, I describe the process of developing the machine's *technical architecture* and *organization architecture*. These are the most important parts of its design: the rules, policies, and systems that will help realign your company.

TECHNICAL ARCHITECTURE

As the name suggests, a technical architecture represents the high-level design of your strategy machine. Before you can begin construction, you must first determine the requirements for your machine, draw up plans to satisfy them, and then test those plans in a variety of ways. Will the engineering design support the intended uses? Will the materials work together? Can the design adapt to changing conditions and demands, and be expanded, remodeled, or retooled when necessary without having to start over?

As you refine your strategy portfolio, the investments will reaffirm the wisdom of some architectural decisions and challenge others. Retrofits, redesigns, and additions to the strategy machine will be regular events, and need not be traumatic. It is, however, important to understand the general demands on the architecture that will be made by investments at each stage of metamorphosis.

STAGE	INVESTMENT	DATA ASSET	KEY REQUIREMENT
Efficiency	Projects	Transaction Cost Levers	Pull data together from existing internal systems to improve cost and productivity
Exchange	Ventures	Information Float	Pull data from key links in the supply chain to improve the performance of the market
Emergence	Options	Information Products and Services	Pull data from the information supply chain to create new products and services

Figure 7.3: Technical Architecture Requirements by Stage

Efficiency: Integration Architecture

At the efficiency stage, your technical architecture must encourage easy, accurate, and flexible exchanges of data between applications. To test your design, ask yourself whether data can flow smoothly between:

- existing applications, even those built and managed by individual departments (e.g., finance, manufacturing, and marketing);

- older systems and newer Web-based applications, or applications aimed at other Internet devices, including PDAs and cell phones; and

- your organization and those of your closest trading partners, including key suppliers and leading customers.

Successful efficiency projects hinge on your ability to mine useful information out of existing ERP, CRM, and supply chain databases. This represents your best opportunity to demonstrate superior customer service, optimize vendor relations, and increase manufacturing efficiency. On the other hand, if your architecture cannot expedite the exchange of data and integration of applications, then the worst features of your current systems will soon be exposed to the world.

For many companies, valuable information assets are probably already in reusable digital form, locked away in the data warehouse. You may have spent years building up vast stores of valuable data about customers, inventory, suppliers, and manufacturing performance, but now find that few executives can make use of it. Information assets are frequently hidden inside older applications and databases that were never designed to integrate with each other, let alone with the systems of customers and suppliers.

According to David Kellogg, VP of marketing for leading business intelligence and analytics tools provider Business Objects, part of the problem is cultural. Both information technology and non-technology professionals treat the contents of application databases like delicate flowers that will wither the moment they are exposed to sunlight. "Companies have some strange ideas about information and customers," notes Kellogg. "They ask, 'Should we expose our data to customers? What if the data isn't perfect?' They may as well ask 'Should we expose our products to customers? What if the products aren't perfect?'" The real fear isn't about data quality—it is about losing control.

The ability to determine the value of information assets buried in the data warehouse is improving, driven in part by companies such as Business Objects and Informatica, which provide software and services that help companies extract and process data from disparate sources. The original focus of their products was internal, making it possible for companies to join databases together and answer basic questions such as "Who are our largest customers?" Recently, however, both companies have enhanced their products to cross company boundaries and to support Internet data exchange standards.

Homegrown integration efforts can also yield impressive results, and demonstrate the importance of a flexible technical architecture. Consider two examples in very different industries: Eastman Chemical, whom we have already met, and Silicon Valley Bank, the dominant provider of financial services to high-tech startup companies. Both launched their first Websites without worrying about how old data could get to the new systems or back the other way. In essence, this was a calculated risk. Both companies believed the most important goal was to get on-line, and planned from the outset to retrofit their sites to connect them back to the data warehouse once the software was already working.

Eastman.com started off simply. The first release gave customers only those functions that were the most common source of support calls, including order tracking and printing "certificates of analysis," which are legal documents required to ship chemicals. To offer these tools, however, Eastman had to build elaborate connections to several different systems, including SAP and the Oracle data warehouse. In the interest of time, they wrote logic into the Website software that extracted the data directly out of the different databases.

The tools were a hit with customers. Seeing what appeared to be a simple way to get data from Eastman, they soon asked for real-time access to inventory, pricing, and order status data. The largest customers and suppliers offered to connect their systems directly to Eastman's, bypassing the Web altogether.

Eastman was gratified to have the opportunity to use technology to strengthen its ties with trading partners, of course, but design decisions made during the first projects were beginning to haunt the eastman.com team. Had they continued building direct connections between old and new systems, satisfying the new requirements would lead to a maze of software, which would slow the performance of the Website and constrain future enhancements to the transaction systems.

Eastman's information technology leadership team took a deep breath and reconsidered its approach to integration. They jettisoned the ad hoc connections and replaced them with a comprehensive plan to supply data to all the new applications. One helpful step was to accelerate Eastman's conversion to SAP's latest version, R3, which offered better tools for data import and export. Using a product called Yantra, Eastman then built a new layer of software that sends and receives data to and from different application databases. All requests for data go through this layer. The redesign was an expensive decision, but paid for itself by making it possible to continue to change and improve the back end without undoing the customer interface.

For direct connections to major suppliers and customers, Eastman exercised an option. One of Eastman Ventures' first investments was in a company called WebMethods, which makes XML integration software. Working with WebMethods, eastman.com selected XML as its standard for sending and receiving information to and from non-Eastman systems. WebMethods is now the centerpiece of the "integrated direct" program, and Eastman has become the first chemical company to use it to build links between their own systems and those of their trading partners. Web-Methods, like the internal integration software, insulates each side of the exchange from technical changes made by the other.

For Silicon Valley Bank, it was relatively easy to Web-enable some basic transactions, including transfers and stop payments. "But after that," says CIO Erwin Martinez, "it became an unnatural act. What we have are basically batch systems, and they can't be made to operate in real-time." Batch systems expect transactions to come at the end of the day, when database synchronizations can be handled off-line. In addition, many of those systems needed to be replaced because of rapid expansion in the bank's business. To continue moving its transactions on-line, the bank needed a new approach.

Martinez's solution was to rethink his overall technical architecture. He developed a new plan to replace many core systems and introduced a set of guidelines to make it easier to add or remove different vendors in the future. One of Silicon Valley Bank's "rules of the road," for example, is that all new applications must use Oracle as their database-management product.

Martinez sees the long-term solution, however, in a technology that, like data warehousing, has become increasingly important to efficiency stage projects: object-oriented programming and databases. Object-based applications abstract logic and data into smaller packages that represent basic business activities, offering at least the potential for easier modification and reuse of common elements. Selling the object-based rewrite of core applications isn't easy, but Martinez has made progress with the rest of the executive team. "My customers—internal and external—are no longer in the mood to compromise."

Exchange: Liquidity Architecture

At the exchange stage, your technical architecture will be challenged by the need to increase the trading activity in whatever kind of virtual markets you participate. As we have seen, the real value of an exchange comes from greater visibility in the market as a whole; encouraging as many transactions as quickly as possible, then, is the key to success. With critical mass comes liquidity, and liquidity is what creates information float and the ability to profit from it. Like the old joke has it, you may lose money on every transaction, but you'll make it up on volume.

Features that will help you achieve liquidity quickly include:

- Capturing all transaction data and making it available to the participants;

- Offering buyer and seller rating systems; and

- Making it possible for exchange participants to share relevant information with each other.

Several companies have been working to build general-purpose software that satisfies these requirements for a wide range of industries. At the exchange stage it may be possible to buy a technical architecture solution from one or two partners. FairMarket, for example, is a Web-based service provider that connects merchants to markets. On the merchant side, Fair-Market provides tools to vendors, including Dell and TicketMaster, to manage auctions for distressed merchandise. On the customer side, FairMarket replicates the merchants' listings on high-volume Websites, including Excite and Boston.com. The result is that auction listings placed by vendors through FairMarket appear simultaneously on numerous sites, increasing the pool of potential buyers. FairMarket provides not only liquidity but other services for both sellers and buyers, including listing composition, bid management, and payment processing.

FairMarket focuses exclusively on providing technical architecture for consumer auctions, and has used its specialized expertise to make their service more compelling for sellers. The company recently released its

"Performance-Based Markdown Engine," for instance, which helps merchants evaluate current consumer demand and optimize pricing for clearance merchandise.

As exchanges improve, they begin to resemble miniature, virtual versions of the market itself, a prototype for a fully functioning ISC. The next advance in exchange architecture will be software to tie together as many exchanges as possible using an approach similar to FairMarket's. Another company, Trade Dynamics, has designed an open exchange that makes possible simple connections across exchanges. In addition to standards, they offer common management services, including content searches, user profiles, bid histories, and post-transaction services such as escrow, payment, data mining, market analysis, logistics, order tracking, and dispute resolution.

As these examples suggest, market makers must embrace open standards passionately if they want to achieve liquidity, even if this means abandoning proprietary networks that may be working perfectly well today. Visa, for example, one of the leading providers of credit card processing services, recently launched Visa Direct Exchange, an open standard for sharing transaction data between merchants and Visa member banks. Visa Direct Exchange replaces a proprietary network Visa had spent millions developing over the course of many years.

The new system lowers the cost and improves the speed of data exchange, a crucial feature if credit cards are to remain a dominant form of payment in a world of higher transaction volumes with smaller dollar amounts, the world, that is, of electronic commerce. More important, the Visa Direct Exchange architecture captures more data and is thus better suited than the old system to mining valuable marketing information from transaction data, a key source of future revenue for Visa and its partners.

Emergence: Deconstructed Architecture

The most difficult challenge for your technical architecture is to anticipate uses that are almost entirely unknown today—the focus of emergence stage options. But it is important to try. As new devices begin sending data, the technical architecture's flexibility will be severely tested. Already, companies that invested millions of dollars in systems built for the World Wide Web are finding it difficult if not impossible to refit their applications and data for the next generation of interfaces, including cell phones,

PDAs, and game consoles. And these are just the beginning of a wave of new interfaces that will develop in the Information Revolution.

Extensions to today's interfaces also pose maddening design problems. Adding instant messaging and live audio and video will push the limits of abstraction and componentization. Then there is taste and smell: Trisenx in Savannah, Georgia, has already developed equipment that dispenses edible wafers "printed" with flavor cartridges, allowing users to sample food as they see it on a Website. Another startup, DigiScents, has a product called iSmell that plugs into a personal computer and produces hundreds of unique aromas. Applications for taste and smell may be far off (or may not be), but the more abstract your technical architecture, the better positioned you will be to exploit these technologies when they are ready.

Planning for the unknown, of course, takes time and builds complexity into the architecture. Remember, however, that the strategy portfolio is designed to allocate costs appropriate to the level of risk at each stage. Your technical architecture can take emergence stage requirements into consideration without much expense. It may be enough simply to be on the watch for next-generation applications and features.

Given the uncertain requirements of the emerging information supply chain, your best bet is an architecture that keeps data, applications, and user interfaces separate. You will have already done much of the necessary work to achieve this "deconstructed" state for the previous stages, but your resolve will be tested by several new technologies. The most important of these are described here, and provide a dry run for your technical architecture. How would you handle them?

- **New devices and interfaces for communicating with customers, suppliers, and other trading partners.** The era of the browser, in which the world's information is linked together through Websites, navigated with search engines, and collected and reorganized through portals, is coming to an end. Even if your customers, suppliers, and other stakeholders are thrilled to interact with you today exclusively through the Web, it won't be long before they'll demand new services and new interfaces that operate through PDAs, cell phones, pagers, and other computing devices, as well as new interaction tools such as instant messaging. A few more cycles of Moore's Law, and your applications will need to communicate directly with non-computing devices—cars, refrigerators, clothing, and packages.

- **Information requirements that vary depending on the device or application being used.** As we enter the next generation of information exchange, efforts to force complex user interfaces on simpler devices will not work. Just as a car is not a "horseless carriage," a car is also not a "browser with wheels." New devices and applications bring with them new metaphors for interaction. You cannot shove a Web page onto the display of a cell phone, and even if you could, that much data would not make sense from the user's point of view. Users adopt roles that are appropriate to each device or interface, each of which has different requirements for information, timeliness, interactivity, and speed. The user who wants a full history of a company's financial performance in the office, where she has a high-speed connection and a large monitor, wants just headlines sent to her cell phone.

- **Automatic exchanges of information through "agent" software will scale up rapidly.** Products from wireless software companies like 724 Solutions are in the forefront of emergence architectures, designed around information and how it might be used rather than the layout of today's Websites. The company's technology allows users to identify information that is important to them, what changes they want to be informed of, and how and where they want to be told. This is the first step toward an architecture in which browsing isn't done by individuals at all, but by software agents that are delegated to watch a variety of conditions and report through a variety of media. From here, the natural extension is to authorize the agents with actions beyond notification, such as buying or selling.

  Morningstar, which provides evaluation services for mutual fund customers, uses these tools to allow its users to signal how and when they want to be notified of changes to their portfolio. At the end of the day, software agents can send the customer an email with the closing prices of all the funds she owns. If a fund in her portfolio goes up or down by 5% during the trading day, however, the agent can be taught to page her instead. Each notification, no matter how small, gives Morningstar another opportunity to interact in some important way.

ORGANIZATION ARCHITECTURE

Even as you reorganize your technology, technology will reorganize you. Your strategy machine cannot operate, let alone perform at peak efficiency, unless and until you change the very structure of your organization. At best, your company today operates well only at the efficiency stage, but as we have already seen you cannot treat ventures or options like projects. Budget processes, for example, only approve investments with quick (but modest) returns, rejecting investments with longer-term potential and higher risks. Where today's investments may largely be treated as independent initiatives, moreover, the strategy portfolio will only achieve your vision if the investments are coordinated—managed, in other words, as a true portfolio.

There is a simple solution to problems like these: match your organization to the structure of the portfolio. As Figure 7.4 suggests, each stage of metamorphosis requires its own organization—project teams for projects, an incubator for ventures, and corporate venture capital for options. This may sound like a lot of new overhead, but it doesn't have to be. Many companies already have pockets of expertise in executing joint ventures and in making venture investments. For them, the hard part will be to align that expertise around a single vision, common management, and one set of portfolio tools.

In my experience, unfortunately, that alignment is often the hard part, harder even than building new organizations. Cultural and political obstacles,

STAGE	INVESTMENT	ORGANIZATION TYPE	KEY REQUIREMENT
Efficiency	Projects	Project Team	Alignment and integration of technology and strategy functions
Exchange	Ventures	Incubator	Strategic joint ventures with key technology and industry partners
Emergence	Options	Corporate Venture Capital	Visibility into emerging technology developments and relevant investment criteria

Figure 7.4: Organization Architecture Requirements by Stage

which are discussed in detail in the following chapters, require more resources and more creative thinking to overcome than learning how to form joint ventures or choose venture investments. As with any business transformation, reorganization around a strategy machine will only succeed if it is led by senior management. Not that leadership alone is sufficient for success, of course. It is simply a necessity.

Efficiency: Align and Integrate Technology and Strategy

If your company knows how to run projects, you already have the tools you need to implement your efficiency stage investments quickly and with minimal risk. Skills like project management, team leadership, budgeting, scheduling, design, and testing must be continually improved with regular training and formal evaluations.

Before you start up the invisible capital engine, however, it is essential to widen communications channels between team members and between teams. In many companies, deep political divisions separate the information technology organization from the business units and the corporate strategy organization. Historically, the CIO is not included in the strategy process.

These barriers cause friction that can sidetrack or stall successful implementations. As older systems mature and new capabilities are added, it becomes possible to convert more complex invisible capital such as customer relationship skills and product design into digital forms, bringing information technology squarely into a strategic role. The days of focusing information technology in the back office are over. That means, by the way, that you need a CIO who can and does function as a member of the executive team.

Better alignment across departments can be achieved in a variety of ways. Using the same information technologies to improve internal communications that you use for external communications is the most obvious and effective. The more information about company strategy and the portfolio investments that goes into a common database, the more people can work on improving it. Company intranets with internal Websites are regularly used today for handling benefits and insurance. The same technology can be applied to give employees working on all stages of metamorphosis news about the strategy machine. Discussion groups, distribution lists, and collaborative workspaces can also help to unearth and cultivate information assets.

Managers in the efficiency organization must work closely with their counterparts in the exchange and emergence groups. The strategy portfolio is a funnel, with options winnowing down to ventures, and successful ventures evolving into implementation projects. The better informed the efficiency organization is, the better the chances are that ventures and options will not be victims of the "not invented here" syndrome. Eastman Chemical's decision to include the efficiency organization in the venture capital process, for example, has led to investments in the most promising technologies, and opened the door to leverage Eastman's real-world experience in shaping product development at many of the companies in which they invest.

Eastman did not begin its strategy machine with such good alignment, by the way. Internet applications were initially developed by the customer service organization, leading to both technical and cultural friction with the information technology group. CEO Earnie Deavenport solved the problem by making Roger Mowen—who already headed the customer organization—the company's CIO. Under a common director, relations quickly improved. E-Business Director Fred Buehler found one interesting way to bridge the gap between strategy and technology: "At joint team meetings, the business experts have to give the technical presentations and vice versa. That gives both sides a working knowledge of the challenges faced by the other." As well as an ample dose of humility.

Exchange: Build an Incubator

Although project organizations are common in most companies, few have the skills to launch successful ventures. By definition, ventures are more speculative and cannot be budgeted and managed with the same precision. To hedge the higher risk, ventures are almost always done as joint investments with key partners, including developers of the technologies being tested. As a result, the exchange organization must have strong partnering skills and the ability to create new business entities quickly, some of them with separate legal status. Not all ventures succeed, so it is also important to be able to dismantle the new organizations as quickly as they were put together. Because ventures live close to the emerging industry structure, they are often seen as threatening to managers in the existing business and need some degree of insulation from day-to-day decision-making.

For all of these reasons, the organization that designs, launches, and nurtures your ventures must be staffed by experts in new business creation who can act as coaches. The venture organization must provide common development services, including human resources, finance, marketing, office infrastructure, and systems development, both to achieve economies of scale and to get the ventures launched quickly and without distractions. In short, what ventures need is a corporate incubator, an organization whose "products" are new businesses.

I hesitate even to use the word *incubator*. It is associated today—and correctly so—with some of the worst excesses of the first generation of Internet startups. Young entrepreneurs got the dangerous idea that they could shorten the time to a public offering of stock by launching multiple companies at the same time, and created incubators to attract less experienced entrepreneurs to help them build new companies with dispatch. Companies such as Idealab, Cambridge Incubator, eCompanies, Softbank Ventures, 12 Entrepreneuring, Internet Capital Group, Divine Interventures, and others began promising their investors that they could bring new ventures from infancy to self-sufficiency in as little as 100 days. They raised considerable venture funding to build elaborately designed spaces where ventures were co-located, surrounded by a core of experienced professionals and shared services. Every one of them closed their incubators or shut down completely when the stock market changed course and investors disappeared.

The idea of incubation is not a bad one, but these were nurseries of dubious quality. I visited several incubators, and found all of them lacking in the requisite features of a successful business. Many were run not by executives with a track record of building businesses, but by ex-consultants who had never run one, or by Internet entrepreneurs or project leaders who had sold their first companies or left corporate jobs before proving that their efforts had succeeded. Though most incubators claimed to have elaborate proprietary methodologies for launching companies, none did. Support services were fragile, and the incubator staff often had less experience solving difficult business problems than their hatchlings did. Even under the best of conditions, no viable business can be created in less than 100 days—any more than nine women can be organized to deliver a baby in one month.

Happily, the Internet incubators are gone, and with their departure we can begin the process of rehabilitating the term. In fact, the concept of venture incubation, aside from the abuses of the late 1990s, has a long and successful history. Twenty years ago, universities built incubators to commercialize the discoveries and inventions of their research faculties. These were shared facilities near campus where professors could work part-time with entrepreneurs to bridge the gap between applied research and product launch. Cisco Systems, to pick a multibillion-dollar success story, began life in 1984 in a Stanford University incubator.

Developing or working with a properly staffed incubator, as Eastman has done with Eastman Ventures, is the best way to manage the ventures in your portfolio. For many companies, the problem is not a lack of invisible capital, but of an organization in which that capital can be turned into ideas, along with an environment in which to test them. Your company's managers are focused—appropriately—on operating a business, not reinventing it. Incubators help germinate the ideas and sift through those that deserve the modest investment of a venture.

Developing your ventures inside an incubator has important financial benefits as well. If your company is publicly traded, one strong disincentive to launching new ventures is that the losses of those businesses must be deducted from your quarterly earnings. If, however, your ventures are partially owned by others, you can avoid that problem and still reap the financial gains if the venture is successful.

Here's how. Reporting requirements for subsidiaries do not apply to ventures if your company does not control their operation (accounting rules defines "control" a few different ways—check with your CFO for the safe harbors). Public companies can develop their new ventures in incubators or joint ventures in which they own a minority share, with options to buy back some or all of the venture from their business partners at a prearranged price. Not only does this keep the venture's losses off your books, it also minimizes investment risk. As a minority owner, more of the venture's operating costs will be borne by others, perhaps by companies that have cash but not the invisible capital you bring to the venture.

Emergence: Develop Corporate Venture Capital

To manage emergence stage investments, the best organization architecture is one that has been proven over decades of development in another business altogether—venture capital. Since the 1970s, U.S. leadership in funding and nurturing very early stage companies, not only in information technology but also in biotechnology, materials science, chemistry, and power generation, has become one of its greatest assets in the global marketplace.

This leadership comes as a result of significant investments made by the private and public sectors in research universities, as well as corporate and individual tax incentives that encourage long-term investing with lower tax rates. A unique network of venture capitalists, investment bankers, underwriters, and corporate lawyers brings the pieces together and guides entrepreneurs who may have no capital other than their ideas.

At the emergence stage, you must re-create that environment in miniature. This could include tapping into the existing organization architecture of Silicon Valley and other technical centers throughout the world, as Eastman did by opening its office in California. Unlike institutional investors, however, the capital you invest will consist not only of cash but also your information assets—your invisible capital.

How do you do it? Whole books can—and have—been written on the subject of corporate venture capital, and those who have little experience are encouraged to seek them out. For the rest, a few brief comments here:

Leadership—The corporate venture organization must have strong backing from senior management to succeed. Many of the ideas and concepts the venture group brings to the organization will seem strange; the process itself will be unfamiliar. The venture group may be seen as a virus by the corporate culture, and must be protected by the company's leadership, especially in the beginning. The venture group must work diligently, at the same time, to communicate its activities and deliver benefits to the company as quickly as it can. Rotating venture capital staff back to the business, and business managers into the venture group, can go far toward building bridges to the other strategy organizations.

Relevant Investment Criteria—From 1998 to 2000, many companies with no prior experience in corporate venture capital jumped into the game, only to be badly burned. In 2001, for example, Ford Motor Company wrote off almost $200 million in failed information technology investments. Many of the novice corporate venture capitalists were simply being greedy, throwing money at Internet startups that had nothing to do with their industry, let alone with a carefully designed strategy for responding to the three stages of metamorphosis. Corporate venture capital is not a casino game—to succeed, your investments must be chosen not only for the soundness of the ideas behind them, but also for their relevance to the rest of your portfolio.

Organization—The venture group should start small, and grow organically as its portfolio expands. There are no rules of thumb on the size or budget to run the venture group itself. Some companies do everything with two people; large technology firms may have as many as 100. The mix of needed skills includes business development, mergers and acquisitions, and marketing, as well as experience in venture investing.

Finding Opportunities—The portfolio maps serve as the investment agenda, but in the fast-paced world of startups, the venture organization must be opportunistic. Venture investing still works largely on personal connections and referrals; getting into the "deal flow" requires physical presence. Attending training and meetings of groups such as the National Venture Capital Association and the Venture Capital Institute can help, but it is more important to simply meet with other venture capitalists and communicate the value your company can bring with its cash. Once your venture group is part of the network, maintaining a good reputation is essential. Returning calls and responding quickly to proposals is a good start; sticking with the companies you invest in and maintaining a consistent set of priorities is even better.

Evaluating Opportunities—Venture investing opportunities cannot be evaluated as if they were project proposals, but that does not mean decisions to invest are made solely on instinct. Senior management must commit to a fund, then leave investment decisions largely to professionals. Successful corporate venture capitalists develop procedures for screening opportunities and investigating carefully ("due diligence") those that pass the initial screens. The ability to evaluate companies is a skill that can be learned, and borrowing best practices from established venture capitalists is a perfectly good way to get started.

Managing the Portfolio—Regular reviews of the portfolio by the venture team can identify quickly those investments that require more attention, or ones where new opportunities have developed for other parts of your company. The venture team should always be on the lookout for executives who can serve as internal champions to introduce and adopt technologies from the venture investments. The venture team should review the portfolio with senior management sitting as a steering committee, every six to nine months. Revisit the portfolio maps and market conditions at least once a year, and develop ballpark estimates of how many new investments will be made and how much money will be required.

In *Unleashing the Killer App*, I wrote about British Petroleum's (BP) regular efforts to reinvent its business by describing two of the company's long list of innovative projects. One was an experiment that put video kiosks in gas station convenience stores, giving customers the ability to order a wide range of goods, including food and clothing. The other was BP's implementation of a common operating environment (COE), a technical architecture that replaced some 30,000 desktop computers and a jumble of incompatible software products with a single set of integrated applications. The COE helped BP coordinate its worldwide exploring, refining, and retailing businesses.

Since then, the company has successfully completed the acquisitions of Amoco and Arco, two former competitors, as well as Castrol, which produces lubricants, and the European chemical operations of Mobil—all told, about $120 billion worth of new assets. It has also completed a major corporate reorganization that broke the traditional oil industry model of central control into smaller, autonomous organizations. BP now has over 140 separate business units and a dozen senior executives who run the company under the strategic direction of CEO John Browne. In a way, BP has transformed its superior management skills into a service it now performs for other oil companies—its former competitors.

BP's technical and organizational innovations are closely related. The decentralized command and control structure fosters innovation by reducing the overhead of extra management. At the same time, the COE keeps the businesses connected for common activities such as financial reporting and sharing of operational data. The COE played an instrumental role in the successful completion of BP's acquisitions. By choosing one set of applications built on Internet protocols, BP essentially bought an option to extend its systems and data not only to customers and suppliers but also to some of its largest competitors. That option has paid off handsomely.

The company has now tied the two efforts together. In 2000, BP announced a $200 million project to redesign 29,000 retail locations, which includes the extension of the COE all the way to the gas pumps.

Following up on the kiosk experiment, BP is now working to move on-line shopping, as well as Internet services for weather and traffic information, to the pumps themselves. These new devices will connect through the stations to BP's expanding network, eventually sending data all the way up the supply chain—critical steps in the creation of a valuable ISC.

Of the many valuable lessons from BP's example, the most important is that combining a good technical architecture with an equally agile organization structure can multiply the value of both. The BP story also demonstrates the absolute necessity of a passionate and committed executive team. Many of BP's technical and organizational decisions were not only expensive, but ran counter to long-standing company and industry traditions. It took the strong will of John Browne and his team to formulate a winning strategy and maintain the courage to see it through to what is now the brink of a metamorphosis success story.

Passion, commitment, and a strong will (along with a strong stomach) are all forms of invisible capital, and you will need plenty of each to build and operate a strategy machine. Even after you put it together and turn it on, keeping the machine running is no easy task. The strategy machine requires regular maintenance, precision tuning, and occasional overhauls. And as we are about to see, there are many people inside and outside your organization who, regardless of how much value the machine creates, would like very much to shut it down.

PART III

THE EXECUTIONER'S SONG

Reinventing Your Business Every Day

8

THE SOCIOLOGY
OF STRATEGY

Confronting Grief, Overcoming Inertia

Sanity clause? Everybody knows there ain't no sanity clause.

—Chico Marx, *A Night at the Opera*

[THE FIVE STAGES OF GRIEF. OVERCOMING INERTIA. PARADIGM SHIFT
HAPPENS. OUTBREAKS OF SECOND SYSTEM SYNDROME. THE LITIGA-
TOR'S DILEMMA.]

ON CORPORATE DEATH AND DYING

This chapter opens with a short digression—a personal story of strategy
execution and its discontents. Many years ago I was a project manager at
a large software company. One of my last assignments was to develop a
technical architecture that would unify all the company's products, which
included financial, manufacturing, and distribution applications as well
as software engineering tools. Though each product had its own architecture, they all had a common origin. The company maintained separate
development and support organizations, but all of them followed an
identical and precise methodology, right down to the specific headings in

documentation. It was relatively easy to find a single design that would not require significant changes to any of the products. The engineering problem was no problem at all.

I met with the product managers every week, and every week they came up with new reasons why it was impossible to bring their software together. The meetings always began by reviewing the objections raised in the previous meeting, followed by my team's findings that none had merit. Although my group was composed of representatives from each of the support organizations, their own managers doubted every one of our conclusions. At the end of the meetings, the managers would deliver a new set of objections, and promised that if these could be addressed, they would support moving forward.

The company was fortunate to have on its advisory board Alan Kay, one of the greatest software architects in history. Kay had served as chief scientist at Xerox's famed Palo Alto Research Center, where he first developed many of today's most important breakthroughs, including the graphical user interface and visual programming. Our CEO, who was concerned by the slow progress of my project, asked Kay to sit in on one of the weekly meetings. As usual, the agenda was filled with objections to the common architecture. The meeting ran long, and Kay got up to leave before the end. "Wait a minute, Alan," said the CEO. "You haven't told us what you think of the project."

Kay stood in the doorway for a moment without saying anything. "I think," he said at last, "that sociology is a very interesting subject."

Years later, I finally understood what he meant.

This last section explores the obstacles—the business sociology—that will try to upend your strategy machine. More important, we will also see how to reverse these obstacles, jujitsu style, and turn them into catalysts that will make the engine even more powerful. The focus here is on the black art of strategy execution, which makes finding big ideas to populate your portfolio seem easy by comparison. We will look at case histories of several companies who got as far as their first set of investments only to run into roadblocks, some of which were overcome and others which proved insurmountable. Barriers to innovation, as we will see, come in all sizes, one for every organization.

In particular, this chapter focuses on how to avoid a few general problems of execution, particularly those that plague the first months of the process, after the portfolio has been designed and the technical and organization architectures have been put in place. Often, it is only then—after the invisible capital engine is given its first supply of fuel and starts to rev up—that caution flags appear: the first expressions of management doubt, the first intrusion of company politics, the first indication that something is holding the machine back, slowing it down, and creating drag.

Familiar management tools are of little help, by the way, because the resistance to moving forward, as in my personal story, is not a rational problem that can be solved by logic and analysis. Focus groups, workshops, and research reports won't do the trick. You are facing a problem of psychology or rather two problems of psychology—one that affects the company as a whole and another that drives the individuals who work there. Solving these problems will require that you unearth and confront the hidden sources of resistance in the corporate psyche. The best place to start is with a most unpleasant field of study: *thanatology,* the science of death.

Why talk about death? The promise of a strategy machine is the transformation of your industry, your company, and the careers of everyone involved. For many, that process is a kind of corporate death, and the first steps toward change provide concrete evidence that it is happening to you. Whether you acknowledge it or not, grief naturally follows. So, for your own sake and the sake of your colleagues, you need to understand the dynamics of grief and how you can accelerate them. Until you accept the inevitable—the metamorphosis—your progress will be minimal at best, and unprofitable in any case.

We start with the most famous book on grief of any kind. In 1969, University of Chicago psychiatrist Elisabeth Kübler-Ross published *On Death and Dying,* a psychological study of patients coming to terms with terminal illness. Through extensive interviews, Kübler-Ross discovered that patients experienced a common set of emotional responses as they approached their demise. The five stages of grief she identified will be familiar to you even if you have never read the book, as they are now a part of popular culture, referred to in daily life by people who may not have any idea of their original context:

1. **Denial**—An irrational refusal to accept the reality of approaching death ("It must be a mistake.")

2. **Anger**—Resentment, often displaced to family members, doctors, and God ("Why is this happening to me?")

3. **Bargaining**—Secret deals to accept one's fate only if certain short-term goals can be reached ("If I can dance at my child's wedding, I'll be satisfied.")

4. **Depression**—Preparatory grief for the imminent loss of everything ("What will happen to my loved ones?")

5. **Acceptance**—A period of calm and a quiet coming to terms ("I led a good life.")

Without intending to, Kübler-Ross wrote what is probably the most important book on management science of the last 50 years. *On Death and Dying* applies as much to industrial metamorphosis as it does to human mortality, a fact I have been reminded of many times over the last few years.

When *Unleashing the Killer App* was published in 1998, it was clear beyond any doubt that a new generation of information technology had matured, but it was still common to find executives, particularly in traditional companies, who were deeply in denial. Most Fortune 500 executives have moved on, but some did not, and went to their graves—at least from a career standpoint—unaware that new forces were reshaping their industries. For a poignant example, consider A. G. Edwards & Sons, the 100-plus-year-old brokerage firm. Its CEO, Benjamin Edwards III, great-grandson of the firm's founder, went out of his way to announce in May 1998 that the firm would *not* be offering on-line trading. His rationale? To protect customers from themselves: "To the extent we can get your eyes off the short term and onto the long term," he told the *Wall Street Journal*, "we can protect you from human nature. Everyone gets very emotional with their money."

Almost a year later to the day, Edwards announced he had changed his mind. The company would offer on-line trading after all, a service he hoped would be ready within a year. Although he still didn't think on-line trading was good for clients, he was "pressed by the competition to provide it." Indeed he was, but even as Merrill Lynch from above and Charles Schwab from below were dismantling his supply chain, Edwards still denied what was happening. "We're not pursuing a commodity-type business where all we offer is execution," he told the *Journal*. He also said he wasn't sure why his company's stock was selling at a lower valuation than

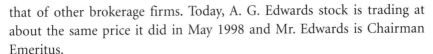

that of other brokerage firms. Today, A. G. Edwards stock is trading at about the same price it did in May 1998 and Mr. Edwards is Chairman Emeritus.

As the old supply chain breaks down and the ISC emerges, professionals understandably fear for their careers, their companies, and their industries. Working through their doubts, they exhibit behavior characteristic of all five stages of grief. Consider these examples from my consulting work of the last few years:

Denial: During one killer apps project, the president of a large equipment leasing company insisted that even though competitors were already doing business over the Web, he saw no need to meet that challenge. Why not? Because "our customers don't have computers and won't anytime soon." Our project team checked—over 65% of his customers already had computers.

Anger: During the dot-com boom of 1998–2000, as startup companies were quickly going public and at least temporarily making their investors and managers wealthy, the mood changed to the second stage: "We've been busting our hump for five years to improve margins, and now some dot-com with no profits at all has a higher market cap than we do." Dwelling on the injustice of public markets didn't make the reality disappear any more than it did for Kübler-Ross's patients.

Bargaining: For many, 1999 was the year of bargaining, as in "We have to focus on Y2K this year, but if we get through that, then we'll figure out our Internet strategy." Analysts and reporters encouraged this form of avoidance, just as family members often do for the terminally ill.

Depression: As Y2K passed without incident, the promise evaporated and depression set in, just as Kübler-Ross predicts. Despair was often expressed in human resource terms: "Even if we had a killer app idea, we could never build it. The startups are stealing all our people with stock options and work environments we just can't offer."

Acceptance: Following the stock market decline and recession that began in mid-2000, many executives have slipped back to an earlier stage. For those who have reached acceptance, however, it usually appears in one of two forms. Either you stand ready to acknowledge the end of the old supply chain and everything that goes with it—ready, that is, to start building something new—or you prepare for early retirement, convinced that you just don't have the energy to make another shift in thinking.

OVERCOMING INERTIA

There is, of course, one important way in which corporate death differs from terminal illness and it is the difference between a happy and a sad ending. As part of industrial metamorphosis, every organization will die. If you develop a strategy portfolio, however, your chances for reincarnation are excellent. There is even a strong likelihood of being reborn as something better.

In the early days of operating your strategy machine, however, you may still find yourself face-to-face with that powerful force of physics that is the bane of all perpetual motion—inertia, the resistance of a body that is at rest to being set in motion. The complexity of existing relationships with customers, suppliers, and regulators, as well as information technology systems that hard-code that structure, create tremendous organization drag. The bigger you are, the more resistance you will feel.

If you wait long enough the same forces driving the Information Revolution will give you the push you need, like it or not. As we have already seen, many industries are already being pulled from their orbits, often against their will, by the power of disposable computing and the explosive growth of data networks. But rather than wait for the ground beneath your feet to move, why not walk away under your own power?

Corporate inertia takes as many forms as there are people working at companies, but there are three common variations: the paradigm shift, the second system syndrome, and the innovator's dilemma. The rest of this chapter explains not only what they are and why they exist, but also how to overcome them.

Paradigm Shift Happens

Industrial metamorphosis begins with a paradox. Today, as with the Industrial Revolution, it is the existing companies, financiers, and regulators who eventually capture most of the new value created by new technologies—most startups, even those that break new ground, fail. Yet established companies historically put up the most resistance to changes that will, in the end, make most of them better off.

Why? The answer comes not from management science but from the work of a historian, the late Thomas S. Kuhn. In 1962, Kuhn published *The Structure of Scientific Revolutions,* a remarkable study of the sociology of science. Kuhn analyzed breakthroughs in several fields to find out how scientists internalized big changes. What happened, he asked, when Albert Einstein discovered relativity, or when Antoine Lavoisier discovered oxygen? How did they get their colleagues to abandon old theories that formed the foundation of their discipline and embrace a revolutionary change—what Kuhn called a paradigm shift? (Yes, Kuhn is the source of that abused and often misused phrase.)

The answers are surprising. For one thing, Kuhn found that new paradigms took much longer to achieve general acceptance than could be explained by the need to verify the accuracy of breakthrough discoveries. Even after the old theories were clearly disproved, scientists were slow to embrace the new science. Many scientists were so comfortable with their beliefs ("the sun revolves around the earth" or "fire is the release of phlogiston into air") that they could not reorient their thinking.

In the worst cases, he found, scientific revolutions take as long as 20 years, the length of time it took for the current generation of scientists to retire. The closer the revolution is to a central principle and the longer that principle has been around, Kuhn concluded, the harder it is for the field to absorb the new reality, no matter how powerful the evidence is that supports it.

Kuhn explained this resistance by pointing out that scientists are not trained to invent and discover, but rather to refine and extend what is already known. For most practitioners, a career in what he called "normal science" is devoted not to exploring but to working out new details of the existing paradigm. Indeed, many of the biggest breakthroughs he studied came about by accident and were first ignored or discarded. Scientists, he said, are not innovators but "expert puzzle-solvers." If you spend your career working out precise details of a science as you first learned it, it is no surprise that you resist its overthrow—particularly if you have established a reputation as a champion problem-solver.

That description may sound familiar to you. Managers, like scientists, are rewarded for their ability to solve the day-to-day and quarter-over-quarter problems of their businesses, not for thinking of ways to replace the framework of the industry. The best managers get promoted to senior exec-utives, which means most strategic decisions are made not by visionaries but by the best problem-solvers, experts in "business as usual." Today's leaders have been trained and groomed by predecessors who went through their careers practicing business as usual. In industries with long histories of regulatory control, dominant companies may not have experienced any changes to normal business for several generations of managers.

Scientists and managers aren't lazy. They just aren't likely to exhibit visionary thinking. Your job is to run today's business as efficiently as pos-sible. Ferdinand de Lesseps, recall, learned the hard way that shipping companies would not at first use the obviously beneficial canal he built in Suez. Likewise, a few years of noise about how executives "don't get it" is hardly enough to overcome the invisible grip of inertia in the boardrooms of the world's largest organizations (governments included) when it comes to the Internet. Managers need time to adjust—their systems, their processes, and their attitudes.

Leaders who do see change coming may be unable to develop a responsive strategy, or at least not quickly enough to turn their insight into advantage. After a new discovery has shattered the old ways, execu-tives, like the scientists in Kuhn's study, may waste the last years of their careers trying to put the pieces of the old paradigm back together. Instead of solving the new puzzles, they come up with increasingly strained rea-sons to avoid them. They lack the context—or the tools—to do anything else.

Resistance to new paradigms is a potent force in privately held compa-nies, but it is far worse in public companies, where stock market analysts encourage inertia by administering painful reminders to managers who do not stay utterly focused on the current quarter. Discount broker Charles Schwab, for example, tried at first to treat on-line trading as a new channel for new customers. Analysts who covered Schwab's own stock approved. But when the old customers found they were paying higher commissions than the on-line customers, even when they too used the new channel, CEO David Pottruck was forced to abandon the double standard. The company made an abrupt about-face, quickly merged on-line and traditional operations and offered everyone the same price. Overnight, $150 million in projected revenues disappeared.

Stock analysts revolted, and Schwab's share price plummeted, losing more than half its value. As the total investment pool managed by Schwab added billions of dollars, however, Pottruck's strategy proved itself. One anxious year later, Schwab's stock soared to dizzying heights. After increasing over tenfold from its price before the two-tier strategy was abandoned, it now trades at about three times that amount, still a healthy increase.

Following Kuhn, you might generalize Schwab's experience as a mathematical formula: *A company's inertia is the sum of the resistance of all of its stock market analysts.*

Inertia can be overcome, but moving deeply entrenched organizations may take the combined power of outside forces like globalization and deregulation, along with breakthroughs in information technology, all acting together. The energy business supplies a cautionary example of what can happen when all three converge at one time. Until recently, the supply chain that begins with exploration and mining and ends at consumer meters was operated as a quasi-governmental monopoly in which prices, profits, and barriers to competition were strictly controlled by legislation and regulation.

The regulation protected against the potential waste of redundant production and distribution facilities, but at the same time eliminated competitors and stifled innovation. Like professional service providers who bill by the hour, public utilities with fixed rates of return on capital investments had no incentive to develop information or other systems that would improve their productivity.

The industry is now experiencing the first tastes of competitive business in its history. Provider monopolies are being ordered to separate themselves into different companies for generation, distribution, and retailing. At the same time, regulated pricing and guaranteed profit margins are being phased out in favor of an open market.

The interim steps toward open energy markets have been awkward, and in the case of California, have been accompanied by near-catastrophic results. In the long term, however, it doesn't matter. Inertia has been overcome. The old supply chain is simply gone, and the legislators who dismantled it know that going back to the old structure would require even more political capital than what has already been spent.

Talk about a paradigm shift. Before deregulation began in the early 1990s, the utility industry had not changed significantly since the New Deal. There have been plenty of revolutions in the basic science of energy itself (nuclear, solar, turbines), but no change to the relationships that defined the industry—who performed what functions and who kept what part of the total profits. Suddenly everything was up for grabs. All the old rules were suspended. It was as if the law of gravity had been repealed.

With deregulation came a second shock to the system, as startups such as Altra Energy Services and distributors that included the once-mighty Enron rushed in with new information technology to begin attacking gross inefficiencies in the supply chain. Because the industry's technical architecture was so weak, the energy business skipped efficiency applications and went straight to the exchange stage. Energy products turn out to be perfect for a virtual exchange, because products are standardized and delivery takes place simply by reallocating supply already traveling through pipelines and transmission grids. At the wholesale level, the virtual marketplaces achieved liquidity in record time, capturing over half the total market for high-volume commodities such as natural gas and electricity.

Few industries have had their basic assumptions ripped away so violently, but there are warning signs of similar transformation in nearly every other industry. In many cases, deregulation has been a factor. In every case, though, information technology is both the root cause of the chaos and the foundation for the emerging order.

Developing a strategy portfolio is your best tool to overcome resistance to paradigm shift. By making modest investments in emergence stage options, for example, you acknowledge that visionary thinking is best left to those who are in the business of creating chaos. You can and should outsource innovation. Even leading technology company Cisco Systems recognizes that focusing on existing customers may blind them to major technological shifts. Their strategy has been to invest and ultimately acquire new companies that can develop next-generation products for them.

As the options filter down to ventures and projects, your company also has time to internalize radical changes. When the new supply chain takes its first steps out of the primordial slime, you'll already be standing by, ready to help it up.

Outbreaks of Second System Syndrome

A second form of inertia that threatens your strategy machine is the second system syndrome, a condition first diagnosed by Frederick P. Brooks, Jr., in his classic 1975 book *The Mythical Man-Month*. Brooks managed the development of the OS/360 operating system, which powered IBM's most-ambitious mainframe computer at the time. But Brooks' insights on long, complex projects involving entire companies have value far beyond the world of software engineering. Brooks' warnings about the habits of technical architects, for example, apply equally well to those charged with maintaining a strategy machine. "An architect's first work is apt to be spare and clean," Brooks wrote. "He knows he doesn't know what he's doing, so he does it carefully and with great restraint."

Brooks found that once the first system was done, however, the architect suddenly becomes overconfident, believing that the problems he encountered during his first project represented every possible obstacle. Having dispatched them, he could proceed to build his masterpiece. There is still a great deal the architect doesn't know, however, and his second system is invariably overengineered and full of unnecessary "frills and embellishments"—a mess, in short. The second system, Brooks wrote, "is the most dangerous system a man ever designs."

Second system syndrome spread rapidly during the first generation of Internet ventures, and the strain was particularly virulent. The overheated market for venture investing that drove the NASDAQ from 2000 to 5000 in less than a year and a half served as irresistible proof to many entrepreneurs, both startup as well as those inside mature companies, that their first systems had been complete successes. Partly out of greed and partly out of hubris, the founders of these ventures were, not surprisingly, eager to get started on the next big thing.

Just as Brooks warns, these second systems were often opulent palaces that were so overdesigned as to be uninhabitable. In the worst forms, entrepreneurs such as Garage.com's Guy Kawasaki, Idealab's Bill Gross, and Divine Interventures' Andrew Filipowski announced that rather than starting a second venture they would instead open incubators, boot camps, and virtual Silicon Valley garages. There they could teach the next generation of entrepreneurs everything they knew about launching new economy companies. Meanwhile, most of the first ventures languished, their strategy machines sputtered out, and the companies came to an abrupt and often permanent halt.

Jay Walker presents a classic case of the syndrome in its worst form, and is worth studying in some detail. Walker's first venture, Priceline.com, represented a genuine breakthrough in fixing one of the most intractable problems in the airline industry: pricing. Seats on airplane flights are a perishable good—if they aren't sold, the plane still flies, and the airline absorbs nearly all of the cost. Airlines want to sell every seat, but at the highest price possible. Holding out too long risks an empty seat, but selling at too low a price may mean forgoing profits. Every day airlines play this game thousands of times, using complicated mathematical models called yield management systems.

Walker believed he could sell excess inventory to bargain shoppers early enough to ensure no seat went empty, and do so without drawing away business travelers who would otherwise pay full price. In Priceline's exchange, customers "bid" the price they are willing to pay for the trip, but cannot choose the specific airline or flight time. Those features keep away all but bargain-hunters, exactly as Priceline wants.

Walker secured early investment from Delta Airlines, which gave Priceline enough inventory to be liquid and attract the target customers. The system seemed to be working. But instead of refining his nascent system, Priceline's wildly successful IPO emboldened Walker to extend his idea to other commodities—first in other parts of the travel industry (hotel rooms, rental cars) and soon to just about everything. Before long, he offered the "name your own price" service for home mortgages, long-distance telephone service, even gasoline. These products, however, are not as perishable as airplane seats and thus not as good a fit for the Priceline system. Most of the new exchanges failed to attract buyers or sellers, and Walker was forced to write off hundreds of millions of dollars.

Rather than rehabilitate the company he started, Walker quit its board of directors in December 2000 and returned to Walker Digital, his intellectual property holding company. Walker Digital, which describes itself as a company whose products are "business solutions," is Walker's think-tank for coming up with Priceline-like ideas. Walker's new idea was to have Walker Digital simply sell its ideas, and leave to others the concerns of turning them into successful businesses. Unfortunately, so far the company has only had one idea—Priceline.

Twenty-five years earlier, Frederick Brooks wrote that a good architect has to finish three or four successful systems before he can begin to "identify those parts of his experience that are particular and not generalizable." Without that experience he still doesn't know what part of his success is solid engineering and what part is dumb luck. That is what makes the second system so dangerous.

The key words here are *successful* and, even more important, *finish*.

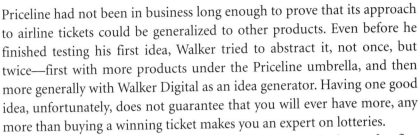

Priceline had not been in business long enough to prove that its approach to airline tickets could be generalized to other products. Even before he finished testing his first idea, Walker tried to abstract it, not once, but twice—first with more products under the Priceline umbrella, and then more generally with Walker Digital as an idea generator. Having one good idea, unfortunately, does not guarantee that you will ever have more, any more than buying a winning ticket makes you an expert on lotteries.

Second system syndrome ultimately led investors to bail out of unfinished companies, but it was those same investors whose enthusiasm helped spread the disease. How? Their stock-buying frenzy misled entrepreneurs into believing their first ventures had succeeded. A successful public offering certainly looks like a victory, after all. The winners believed they had uncovered a new formula for building companies: articulate a good idea, build the shell for a business around it, and get going on the next one. The markets encouraged them to generalize their experiences before the party was over, but also before they proved their first ideas were any good.

The willingness of public investors to buy into early-stage ventures had other unfortunate side effects. It panicked otherwise rational business people into believing that new products could be developed in the blink of an eye. Because information products and services, which do not require new factories and equipment, can be built and marketed quickly, it is true that their development cycle or "time to market" is shorter, a phenomenon referred to as "Internet time." But it began to look, for a time, as if "time to market" hadn't just compressed. It had disappeared.

The epidemic of second system syndrome that ran from 1999 through 2000 confused many entrepreneurs about what was driving Internet time. It was not, as they believed, the increased speed with which startup companies and internal ventures could first be offered to public investors. It was and remains a function of Moore's Law and Metcalfe's Law, and has accelerated only slightly from the beginning of the Internet age. After the pendulum of the public markets swung from a high-risk back to a conservative disposition, the worst excesses of second system syndrome became painfully obvious.

If second system syndrome afflicts you or your company, the cure is simple: portfolio management. For each investment, make certain that you do not remove it from your radar screen until one of three things happens: you sell your interest, the investment becomes a freestanding and profitable operation, or, if the idea didn't pan out, it is terminated—a noble failure. No more declaring victory and walking away after the first positive press coverage, after the initial partners are signed up, or after the IPO ends its first day of trading.

Finishing the first venture does not mean pursuing only one idea at a time. As you manage the investments in your portfolio, you will take out many options, launch multiple ventures, and complete several projects simultaneously. The point is simply not to assume that everything you do will end up as a full-fledged business. Give each investment only the foundation and framework it needs and you not only minimize your investment exposure, but at the same time you give each idea its best chance to blossom.

The requirements for long-term business success haven't changed, Internet time notwithstanding. The characteristics of companies that deliver value to customers, employees, and shareholders from one generation of managers to the next were firmly established in the Industrial Revolution. No matter what stage your investments are in, the basics remain: high-quality, well-engineered products and services; adequate cash and reasonable accounting controls; a healthy organization populated by talented individuals; and sales and marketing activities that are coordinated with the rest of the company. Burn those requirements into the engine of your strategy machine, and you can overcome any symptoms of second system syndrome that might appear.

Innovate or Litigate

The third common problem of corporate inertia that may appear in the early days of operating your strategy machine is the difficulty of introducing new technologies into existing products and services—what Harvard Business School's Clayton Christensen calls "the innovator's dilemma." In his book, Christensen argues that established companies face an intractable problem when their principal products are threatened by new technologies that offer superior performance at a far cheaper cost, or what he calls disruptive technologies. Since the strategy portfolio's goal, in part, is to find such technologies, you will very likely face this problem from the outset.

Here's the dilemma in a nutshell: as disruptive technologies transform the supply chain, they generate a paradigm shift. In one example, Christensen describes how hydraulics made their way into steam shovels, back-hoes, and other digging products, eventually replacing cable-operated shovels and the manufacturers who built them. Hydraulic technology uses pressurized air to lift and move the arm of the shovel, but at first worked only with smaller equipment. At the time, digging equipment was used primarily on large projects like mining or sewer construction. Cable-based manufacturers experimented with the new hydraulics, but found it could not meet the needs of their customers, so they rejected it.

New suppliers such as J. I. Case, John Deere, and Ford instead created a new market, using hydraulics to produce small, low-cost diggers for con-tractors riding the wave of the post–World War II housing boom. Since hydraulic machines didn't compete with the cable-operated diggers, they initially posed no threat to the old manufacturers. As hydraulic diggers improved, however, they worked their way up the food chain until they were both better and cheaper than cable machines. Within 25 years all the leading cable-based companies had left the market for digging equipment entirely. A revolution won without a single shot being fired.

Paradigm shifts are particularly difficult to see coming, as this exam-ple suggests, when today's customers encourage you to ignore them. Your customers may not need the smaller backhoe, additional data storage capacity, or telecommunications bandwidth that disruptive technologies make possible. So why make the difficult adjustment to new designs, new manufacturing, and new products now, especially when doing so would undercut the market for products you plan to keep selling for several years?

The answer is that if you do not, companies without your customers and your investment in the current generation of technology will. They will find the profitable applications with different customers, develop expertise with the new technology as it is perfected, and establish the scale needed to creep into your markets. You will be forced into smaller and smaller niches, and be left, like Kuhn's scientists, working out the last details of a paradigm that has already shifted. Commercial banks, for example, have lost most of their consumer business to brokerage firms, insurance companies, and other financial services specialists. They lost customers, then deposits, and finally products, convinced each time that what was disappearing was an unprofitable part of the business anyway.

How do you overcome the innovator's dilemma? Christensen's solu-tion presents a hard choice. If a truly disruptive technology threatens your core business, he believes that corporate antibodies will kill any effort to transform the business. Instead, he recommends creating a new company to work with the new technology or acquiring a startup. Either way, the new entity's charter is to compete with the parent and ultimately replace it in the emerging supply chain.

There are at least two other ways to respond to disruptive technology, though neither may strike you at first as a "strategic" response. One is to lobby lawmakers to restrict the ways in which new technology can be used, protecting current markets with regulation. Failing that, the second avenue is to use the courts to slow or even stop the migration of new entrants up the supply chain—litigate rather than innovate, in other words. Both options are of limited use, and may only work for a short time, but if applied judiciously can buy you and your supply chain partners time to proceed through metamorphosis at a more manageable speed. Entertainment industries have used both regulation and litigation, for example, in their battle to delay the emergence of digital distribution—closing "loopholes" in intellectual property laws on the one hand and closing Napster by court order on the other.

In addition to entertainment, professional service industries such as medicine and law are past masters of these alternative solutions to the innovator's dilemma. Regulating and litigating have worked with remarkable success, for instance, in the market for legal services. It may surprise you to learn that in 19th-century America, there were few restrictions on who could appear in court, counsel clients, or draft contracts, wills, and other legal documents. Anyone could act as a lawyer.

Between 1850 and 1950, bar associations pushed for laws that shut nonlawyers out of all these services. To protect profit margins, the bar restricted its own membership to those who had taken first two and later three years of law school, and who had passed the bar's examination. Lawyers were prohibited by law (much of it administered by the bar) from advertising, practicing law in other states, and often from charging any less than fees set by the bar.

Since 1960, many of these restraints have been dismantled, the victims of more consumer-friendly legislators and courts. But the remaining regulatory controls are still powerful weapons with which to combat the disruptive technologies of the Information Revolution. The bar associations of several states have successfully sued to restrict the activities of companies using electronic channels to deliver legal information. Software companies offering commodity tax and estate-planning products will eventually eat into protected markets at the unique end of the value curve, but their progress will continue to be impeded by law.

Regulation and litigation can also exacerbate the innovator's dilemma. In many industries, established companies may see a threat and have the skills to respond but cannot do so because they are constrained by regulation. As we saw in the case of energy and other public utilities, the inability of generators to recover the costs even of efficiency stage applications created disincentives that were all but impossible to overcome. The more highly controlled the industry, the more difficult it is to innovate.

Industries that have used law to suppress innovation on the one hand and those that cannot themselves innovate for the same reason are the extremes, but these examples suggest the range of outside influences that can shape or even determine how your strategy portfolio can be implemented.

Developing the tools to overcome inertia in all its forms is a kind of conditioning, preparing you for the main event. You won't have to wait long for that. From the moment you switch on your strategy machine—no matter how carefully you prepare your portfolio, no matter how many information assets you unearth, and no matter how well your technical and organization architecture have been designed—you are guaranteed to run into more specific forms of inertia. Eight of them, to be specific.

The internal and external obstacles described in the next two chapters have killed more good ideas and destroyed more strategy machines in the last few years than any other cause. Some, including conflicts in your marketing messages and problems integrating the strategy machine with your employment policies and information systems, will appear as internal obstacles. Others, such as clashes with channel partners and regulators over portfolio investments that threaten the status quo of the supply chain, take the form of external threats.

Don't be fooled—all eight originate from the same wellspring of resistance—the one buried deep inside you, the one that resists any change with the same ingenuity and persistence exhibited by Dr. Kübler-Ross' patients. I know, because I have experienced that resistance myself, as have executives at every company mentioned in this book.

The internal and external obstacles will prove to be your greatest challenge in transforming your company and keeping the strategy machine humming. Overcoming them, however, begins neither with company nor industry, but with you. Inertia, in all its forms, is quite literally a drag. To achieve escape velocity, you will need to apply as much as you can of the force that is its opposite: leadership.

9

INTERNAL CATALYSTS

Overcoming the Inside Obstacles

A man is known by the company he organizes.

— Ambrose Bierce

[OBSTACLES TO CATALYSTS. THE ORGANIZATION BAN. CULTURE SHOCK.
SELLING THE BIG IDEA. OF HUMAN CAPITAL. INTEGRATING FOR PROFIT.]

OBSTACLES TO CATALYSTS

Two days after the 1970 Apollo 13 mission launched Jim Lovell, Fred Haze, and Jack Swigert into space, things began to go seriously wrong with the rocket's electrical system. The ship was 200,000 nautical miles from Earth and heading—quickly—in the wrong direction. Lovell, the mission commander, found he had insufficient fuel to turn his spacecraft around. His solution: continue heading toward the Moon, enter an orbit around it, and, as he came around the back, fire his rockets, using the Moon's gravity as a slingshot.

You can do the same. Obstacles may exert a gravitational pull on your strategy, but that gravity can be used to your advantage. Turn the problem around, and it undergoes a metamorphosis of its own, from an obstacle gumming up the works of your strategy machine to its opposite—a *catalyst of change,* hurtling you toward your destination with added momentum.

The real sources of execution failure for strategy portfolios—for any strategy—are ethereal, invisible to the naked eye. Managers may sense hesitation in the voices of senior executives and scale back their ambitions, or find their projects quietly stabbed in the back by company politics that have more to do with personalities than with business objectives. Perhaps the paperwork, meetings, and delay associated with funding and staffing new projects, even small ones, dissuade you from starting them in the first place. Or, if you do manage to get started, vague unease expressed by a key supplier or customer may sink the effort, if not your career.

Steering the strategy machine past potential obstacles, many of which appear at the very beginning of your journey, is a task that requires a steady hand, a keen eye, and an intuitive ability to sense the invisible. There are a few general techniques you can use to avoid them. You can also learn from examples of companies whose engines stalled but were restarted, as well as those who ignored the warning signs of trouble only to have their machines seize, the moving parts fusing together.

There are eight obstacles—five internal, three external—that most frequently upset a strategy machine in its first 12 to 18 months of operation. If you can get past these it is largely smooth sailing from then on. This chapter explores the internal ones—organization, culture, marketing, human capital, and technology integration. Chapter 10 deals with those that are outside your organizational borders—channel conflict, law, and financing. Any one of them, or more likely any combination of them, can attack you from the moment you first populate your portfolio. You must begin now to develop skills to identify and defuse them.

These internal obstacles test the ability of your company to invest in a future that directly challenges who you are and what you do today:

1. **Organization**—Rules and controls necessary to keep your business operating smoothly that act to constrain or suffocate innovative ideas.

   Can you organize such projects, even if it means taking them outside the company?

2. **Culture**—Embedded understandings of the current power structure and operating philosophy of your company that limit how you generate new ideas and how you implement them.

   Can you manage transformation without losing your identity?

3. **Marketing**—Assumptions about the meaning and value of your brand that are challenged as you develop new information products and services.

   Can you develop new marketing techniques appropriate to new channels without destroying existing brand value?

4. **Human Capital**—Explicit and implicit limits on your ability to innovate that result from inflexible methods for hiring, training, and retaining talent.

   Can you find, hire, and retain entrepreneurial talent, even in a seller's market?

5. **Technology Integration**—Holes in the technology architecture left by previous strategies and operating decisions hard-wired into your hardware, software, and communications infrastructure.

   Can you integrate new software and standards with your existing systems, turning your data warehouse from an albatross into an asset?

Forces outside your company, including suppliers, customers, investors, and regulators, generate the external obstacles:

6. **Channel Conflict**—Resistance from existing sales organizations to new ways of marketing and selling products and to deeper, information-rich interactions with customers further down the supply chain.

   Can you proceed with emergence stage initiatives that may realign your loyalties without alienating channel partners you still need today?

7. **Law and Regulation**—Real or threatened legal action from regulators or other participants in the supply chain who believe the strategies you pursue violate the agreed rules of engagement in your industry or the local jurisdictions in which you operate.

   Can you make the regulatory system work to your advantage?

8. **Financing**—Objections from shareholders, institutional investors,

and stock market analysts to portfolio investments whose long-term value they either do not or will not recognize.

Can you find ways to finance your strategy portfolio without incurring the wrath of Wall Street?

THE FOUR STEPS

Before exploring the individual obstacles, I want to describe the four basic steps that will help you convert each of them into catalysts of change. The four—identify, immunize, internalize, and invert—make up a kind of pre-ignition sequence for your strategy machine. They are the prerequisites to successful execution. Read them over, and then come up with ways to burn them into the day-to-day procedures of your business. Which is to say, until they become part of your brand.

Identify—As you evaluate each investment in your portfolio, identify which of the obstacles are most likely to get in your way. For projects, the obstacles are unlikely to present much new interference, but as you move into exchange and emergence stage investments the likelihood becomes greater. Exchange efforts challenge the current channels through which you buy and sell, raising the possibility of channel conflict.

Emergence options, by the same token, may set off legal or regulatory warning bells, since they frequently involve several participants in the supply chain (raising the potential for antitrust or unfair trade issues) and expand your buying and selling reach to more global dimensions (demanding an appreciation for local regulations). And the strategy machine as a whole will never run smoothly if your finance and human resource professionals fail to learn the different requirements of later stage investments for budgeting, staffing, management, and financing.

Immunize—For many companies, identifying the obstacles—often by running into them—leads quickly to the end of the investment. "We can't do anything that will bring us into conflict with our channel partners," a senior executive will say, dismissing the idea. Or, the general counsel's office takes the sternest possible view of possible regulatory conflict and demands that you abandon the idea rather than working to craft a solution. Financing, likewise, often creates a hard stop for innovation: "We can't make any

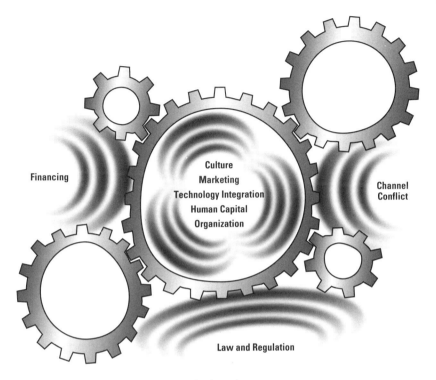

Financing

Culture
Marketing
Technology Integration
Human Capital
Organization

Channel
Conflict

Law and Regulation

Figure 9.1: The Internal and External Obstacles

investments that will dilute quarterly earnings, even if only by one cent, or at least not this quarter" (or this year, or in this particular state of the economy). Even more mundane problems, like inflexible budgeting, project management, and compensation systems, have killed their share of worthwhile initiatives.

You've probably run into roadblocks like these, knee-jerk reactions that are expressed as a final, nonnegotiable rejection of any strategy that challenges current assumptions. They are, in reality, examples of denial, the first stage in Dr. Kübler-Ross' grief process. No problem, internal or external, is as insurmountable as these knee-jerk reactions suggest, especially if all you are proposing to do is experiment. The obstacle is not what is really stopping the process, but rather anxiety that success will alter the day-to-day activities of whoever is complaining.

Immunization requires that you recognize your problem as one of organizational psychology—fear of the unknown. Help those who object to the idea connect the dots and understand what it is they really object to. If they see that change is inevitable, and that the only question is who will benefit from it, naysayers quickly turn into problem-solvers. Company-destroying mistakes become at most minor difficulties that are easily managed, often by the person who first raised the red flag.

Internalize—Obstacles become catalysts when the executive most affected by the investment becomes its chief promoter, what psychologists refer to as internalizing the problem. Using technology to develop a new sales channel is sure to raise organizational, cultural, and channel concerns for the head of sales, concerns she will likely express, at least at first, indirectly and equivocally. Joining an industry consortium to consolidate purchasing, likewise, is guaranteed to evoke a negative response from the general counsel, who may be understandably concerned about antitrust problems. But rather than engage her concerns, she may intentionally bury you under legal terminology, ensuring that there is no further discussion of the problem.

If you take the time to help those raising objections clearly articulate what it is that concerns them, they will often convince themselves that the problem actually poses nothing more than an interesting challenge to their ability to make things happen. To put this in Kuhnian terms, the offending investment may represent a future paradigm shift. Resistance is exaggerated because the initiative is seen as the beginning of the end. By talking it through, the objector is returned to the familiar tools of normal science—just another of the daily crises they manage, business as usual.

Invert—To invert obstacles into catalysts, confront the politics associated with them first, then deal with the actual problem. This is not a job for the faint of heart or the bottom of the organization chart. In many cases, only senior executives can break logjams, and doing so requires unequivocal leadership and a clear articulation of the commitment to the strategy machine. The obstacles are often a handy excuse when the real problem is a lack of strategic ideas in the first place. The more clearly you can articulate the principles of your strategy portfolio, the more obvious how to create catalysts will be.

Each of the obstacles has a natural home in your organization. Law and regulation belongs to the general counsel, finance to the CFO, marketing to the vice president of sales. The transformation from obstacle to catalyst

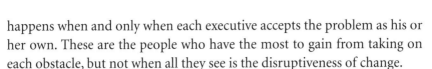

happens when and only when each executive accepts the problem as his or her own. These are the people who have the most to gain from taking on each obstacle, but not when all they see is the disruptiveness of change.

When the owner of the problem willingly accepts responsibility for the investment causing the trouble, he or she will unlock the vaults of invisible capital needed to make the investment a success. If the vice president of sales leads the initiative to develop a new channel, your chances of leveraging existing relationships rather than threatening them goes up dramatically. Having done so once, the solution goes right back into the strategy machine for future use. Obstacles become catalysts when your company invents ways to overcome them that can be applied again the next time they come up.

Motivating the organization to develop new problem-solving skills may take a little brute force. Leadership is essential. If the CEO is committed to the strategy machine, the rest of the organization will quickly put aside the posturing and sabotage that would otherwise choke off its fuel supply. The converse, unfortunately, is also true. A CEO who is skeptical of the process, or merely tolerates it until outside pressure to change eases, will only inspire remarkably innovative new forms of inertia.

The five internal catalysts are described in detail in the following sections.

CATALYST 1: THE ORGANIZATION BAN

The innovator's dilemma, as we saw, is that once a company has established competitive advantage it becomes difficult to experiment with new and radically different goods. As Christensen sees it, managers are understandably afraid to introduce products or services that will cannibalize the existing business. The dilemma is especially acute if new offerings rely on technology that may in its early forms be inferior to what the company developed in a previous revolution.

The problem is real, but the cause is far less dramatic than Christensen suggests. Most managers never have the chance to face the difficult choice of whether or not to cannibalize because their jobs are hard-wired to ensure such decisions never come up. Corporate structure kills most innovation before it poses any risk to existing products. These organizational causes for the innovator's dilemma are unintentional—in fact they are the very features that help keep your regular business operating smoothly:

- **Training**—Managers, especially those whose careers began in the company, are thoroughly indoctrinated in the organization's rules and regulations, the business equivalent of what Thomas Kuhn referred to as normal science. The longer they have been with the company, the more unlikely it is they will be expected or able to think about anything other than business as usual.

- **Compensation**—Performance evaluations, raises, bonuses, and even continued employment are explicitly based on measures of current operations, including revenue targets, expense budgets, and headcount. There is no incentive— and probably a strong disincentive—to spend the company's time or money on new and unproven ideas.

- **Budget**—The budget process, essential for accountability with shareholders, is the leading cause of death for good ideas at many of the companies I have worked with or studied. Capital budgets are generally fixed on an annual or semi-annual basis, and the business case required for approval must show a return on the investment in a few years or less. The highest-potential uses for new information technology, however, cannot promise any return, and surely not in the timeframe of traditional IT projects. Good ideas often come up at inconvenient times and may not live until the next budget cycle. You cannot budget for a revolution.

- **Workload**—Most managers do not schedule time to innovate, nor do they have the free time to spare. Annual retreats to "think outside the box" are a gesture toward innovation, but little more. Breakthrough ideas come, if at all, from outside the company, or during what one client refers to as "after church on Sunday" time. Absent a regular process for challenging assumptions, companies are unlikely to recognize paradigm shifts until it is too late to profit from them.

Obstacle to Catalyst: Build Organizations Appropriate to Each Stage

The solution to the organization obstacle is not to change a successful organization's working structure to suit innovation, but to create parallel organizations that fit the later stages of metamorphosis. Efficiency projects are appropriately left to existing policies and processes. Emergence efforts, where possible, should be developed outside the four walls of the company using corporate venture capital, with each investment tied back to managers whose business is best suited to make use of the venture's products.

In the middle, at the exchange stage, the decision of whether or not to use today's organization may depend on how strong your position is in the existing supply chain. Dominant suppliers are better positioned to impose new processes on customers, particularly customers who buy infrequently, and consequently such suppliers can often develop exchange stage offerings internally. GE's most successful exchange to date, for example, is GE Polymerland, which provides one-stop shopping for a range of industrial products from GE and other major suppliers. In 1988, GE Plastics acquired Polymerland as a specialized distribution channel for smaller customers, but as Polymerland developed into an on-line marketplace, it has become a major sales channel for all GE Plastics customers, generating over $1 billion and representing 25% of total sales for the division in 2000 (GE expects to triple that amount for 2001).

GE's leverage over a large number of infrequent buyers allowed it to develop the exchange channel on its own terms. Polymerland was created for the 80% of smaller customers who represent only 20% of sales, and for them the on-line channel has become the only real way to buy. As the exchange improved, it has drawn in major customers, some of whom find it more convenient to use than buying from GE Plastics salespeople. The strength of Polymerland has helped GE ward off potential threats from startup plastics exchanges as well as industry consortia, which have been unable to achieve liquidity in the face of GE's success. A competitor who offers new products to low-end customers and works its way up the food chain is usually the story of a leader falling victim to the innovator's dilemma, but in this case the market leader used its power to make the transformation itself.

Creating organizations that are appropriate to each stage of metamorphosis is one important step toward inverting the organization obstacle. To make it a true catalyst, tie the efficiency, exchange, and emergence organizations together by creating an Office of Portfolio Management, responsible for reviewing the investments at each stage and ensuring that the different parts of your strategy machine are working well together. The Office of Portfolio Management will ultimately replace what is today the corporate strategy function, headed in larger companies by a senior executive and an internal board of directors made up of the company's executive team. Portfolio Management is the strategy machine's chief engineer. Its goal is to change organizational limits into competitive advantages, helping the machine refine invisible capital to make projects run more smoothly, ventures more relevant, and options more valuable by seeding them into the organization.

Obstacle to Catalyst: Don't Treat Technology as a Crisis

The operation of a strategy machine also requires a significant change in how your company responds to the "discovery" of new technology. When disruption appears on the corporate radar, executives often react as they would to any sudden shift in the market: they create task forces and special teams to eradicate it. Developing an "Internet strategy," as many companies did, treated the technology as a crisis. Often, these ad hoc groups evolved into permanent organizations, responsible for developing and operating the entire range of a company's Internet "offerings," including basic Websites, transactional systems, exchanges, and new technology-enabled products and services.

That approach might be appropriate for an isolated and surprising new development, but it is counterproductive in the world of continuous and even predictable technological change characteristic of the Information Revolution. Having one group that singles out and takes ownership of individual technologies generally leads to an emphasis on the efficiency stage, though technologies like the Internet have valuable applications to all three stages of metamorphosis. Moreover, the ad hoc nature of the response leaves the company without any ability to handle the next wave. There will certainly be a next wave, and another one after that—as any surfer will tell you, waves come in sets. Rather than reacting to technologies when they hit you, a strategy machine anticipates supply chain transformation, and uses whatever new technologies are appropriate for each stage. Lead with the business problem, not the technology it solves.

CATALYST 2: CULTURE SHOCK

The more successful your company has been over time, the more difficult it is to make major changes. Not only do you have organizational obstacles, but you also have a set of beliefs about the organization that raises the

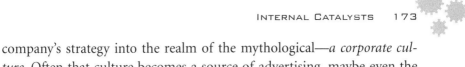

company's strategy into the realm of the mythological—*a corporate culture*. Often that culture becomes a source of advertising, maybe even the company's tagline ("Supermarket to the World," "Think Different," "Fly the Friendly Skies"). Culture can be a valuable information asset, simplifying everything from recruiting to training to marketing, especially when the company practices what it preaches.

Unfortunately, a side effect of a culture that enshrines a company's commitment to the current supply chain is that it adds unbearable inertia when the time comes for major change. Only an outsider can shake loose corporate cultures that venerate stability as strategy. Think of IBM, AT&T, and Procter & Gamble. When market conditions precipitated a paradigm shift, all three companies brought in CEOs with no prior experience in the company. Of the three, only IBM's Lou Gerstner succeeded in turning the company around and keeping his job long enough to see it through.

If your company's culture is built not around history and mythology but around a charismatic leader like a Jack Welch or Warren Buffett, change is as easy or as hard as converting the leader to the new religion. Jack Welch, after watching his family shop through the Internet, ordered every GE business to come up with a plan to put itself out of business using information technology. Buffett, on the other hand, has said that he would flunk any MBA student who even tried to offer an explanation for the market valuation of companies like Yahoo! and eBay. Guess which company's culture would be easier to change.

Obstacle to Catalyst: Cultures That Venerate Change

Not all companies are victims of their corporate culture. Companies built on a tradition of daring innovation, for example, such as Microsoft or Amazon, begin with a culture that is already a catalyst. Such companies welcome technological breakthroughs, and are frequently first in their industries to use them for competitive advantage.

At Southwest Airlines the company culture is committed to offering low fares by keeping internal costs as low as possible. Technology has always been a weapon of choice in meeting that goal. In particular, Southwest was early in allowing customers to make reservations over the Web, using a system that Southwest designed to replace rather than supplement the more expensive telephone and travel agent channels. The airline encouraged customers to make the switch by offering promotional fares available only on-line, and by offering double mileage credit for booking through the Website.

The strategy has worked brilliantly—30% of Southwest's revenue was booked on-line in 2000, saving the company $80 million in reservation costs. Because the airline offers only a handful of fare categories and doesn't assign seats or provide meals, the system is simple and easy to use, another factor in its success. In that regard, Southwest's "no frills" culture not only encouraged the company to develop the system but also helped it to achieve critical mass.

Compare the Southwest system to reservation systems for other carriers, and you can see in stark contrast the difference a culture of innovation can make. Using the United Airlines Website or multicarrier systems like Expedia and Travelocity can be difficult and error-prone, reflecting the complexity of the rest of the airline industry. Trying to appeal to full-fare and bargain travelers at the same time, moreover, the other carriers have sent mixed signals about their commitment to the on-line channel. Unlike Southwest, they cannot afford to alienate travel agents and they are not eager to offend unionized reservation takers. Southwest's system highlights its innovative culture. The conservatism of the other airlines, unfortunately, is also reflected in their on-line services.

Obstacle to Catalyst: Salesperson, Sell Thyself

No matter how hard you try, you cannot hide your culture. Populating the portfolio with good ideas will prove a wasted effort if those ideas conflict with your company's true self. A good idea that fails to take the company's biases and philosophy into consideration—without finding creative ways to turn those biases into support for the initiative—isn't a good idea.

To see why, consider beauty supply retailer Avon. The company has thrived for over a hundred years by sticking to a powerful operating philosophy: direct, door-to-door sales by an army of independent representatives. Avon's culture, however, raises that model to the level of a religion: empowering women to help other women. That's what Avon advertises (most famously in the 1950s with its "Avon Calling" campaign), not the actual products. Even today, the company bills itself as "The Company for Women."

It's hard to argue with success. Despite the phenomenal growth in women working away from home, Avon's revenue has increased for the last 12 years—to over $5 billion in 2001. That year, the independent sales force reached its highest number ever: 3.4 million representatives, nearly all of them women.

CEO Andrea Jung knows, however, that Avon is in need of a serious makeover. Even with millions of sales representatives, the company can only knock on so many doors, and processing orders written out by hand is costly and time-consuming. In practice, many of the representatives produce little revenue—like many direct sales companies, Avon sells 80% of its goods through only 20% of the sales force. New competitors are also on the rise, including significant threats such as mail order and TV shopping and emerging challenges such as on-line retailing.

Given the volume of data it already collects and its worldwide presence, the most promising solution for Avon is the development of a robust information supply chain. Taking and filling orders digitally would reduce the per order cost of millions of transactions, expand Avon's already wide global footprint to countries where selling direct is difficult or illegal, expand the range of goods and services the company can offer, and automate the all-important reordering of cosmetics.

Direct contact between Avon and customers, however, goes against the company's very core, and Jung has learned the hard way just how potent the company's culture can be in blocking innovation. In 1999, in the face of new competition from e-commerce, Avon took the mild step of putting the company's Website address on the catalog. The sales representatives revolted, covering the address with stickers and demanding its removal.

Jung and her team learned their lesson, and are now working to recruit the representatives as partners in forging new information products and services. Representatives can now sign up to become "e-reps" and encourage their customers to place orders through the Avon Website. The e-reps provide product selection, follow-up, and encouragement—all the things they do well today, but on-line. Avon pays their commission on these orders, and at the same time, can continue to develop an on-line channel for customers who do not have a representative.

With 100 years of history, Avon is in for a long transition from obstacle to catalyst. In 2000, only 16,000 sales representatives signed up for the e-rep program, and Jung continues to take heat for creating a competing channel. Her best bet is to hold off trying to sell products until she can first sell the strategy. That will be done the old-fashioned way: one woman at a time.

CATALYST 3: MARKETING THE BIG IDEA

The secret of any good marketing strategy is to sell what you know. If anything, the accelerating pace of the Information Revolution only emphasizes the need to align your marketing strategy with your other information assets. Companies with strong brands know that information technology can do far more than simply repeat the company's advertising campaigns in click-through ads on popular Websites. Brands are a kind of information. In the low-friction environment of the ISC they not only spread faster but also grow in importance—an information asset from which you can create new information goods. Information technology is giving marketers not only new media in which to advertise, but new tools for delivering messages wrapped around the company's products.

Nike, a marketing leader in a variety of media, was initially slow to market on-line. The company today is, after all, a brand first and a set of products (many of them made by other manufacturers) second—sponsoring sporting events and athletes, nurturing a cult of fitness in its showcase Niketown stores, and promoting its lifestyle through powerful self-actualization advertisements. Nike was concerned—as are many companies—about damaging its brand in new media whose characteristics are still unknown. After two years of watching his managers study the Internet, CEO Phil Knight became frustrated, and ordered his managers to follow the company's motto: *Just do it*. Since then, Nike has established itself as one of the leaders in on-line marketing, leveraging its phenomenal brand in new ways.

To see how much is possible, take a few minutes to visit the Nike Website, now the centerpiece of Nike's marketing activities across all media. For summer 2001, the company asked customers to submit their favorite ways to play, and then hosted a film festival showing responses in different cities. Nike offers interactive games that can be downloaded to PDAs, a virtual Niketown, and, of course, a place to buy Nike—not just merchandise, but the Nike religion.

Marketing is the company's best product, and it is demonstrating that expertise even as it explores the potential of new media. Perhaps the most remarkable feature of Nike's digital marketing is the "Nike ID," an interactive design center for customized shoes. With easy-to-use tools, customers create their own pair of Nikes, choosing not only a style and size but six different color accents. Nike provides real-time assistance for customer-

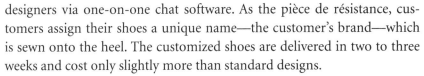

designers via one-on-one chat software. As the pièce de résistance, customers assign their shoes a unique name—the customer's brand—which is sewn onto the heel. The customized shoes are delivered in two to three weeks and cost only slightly more than standard designs.

Nike ID is marketing that promotes the brand as much as it does the products. Helping customers design their own unique shoes reinforces Nike's message to achieve your personal best, and the quick delivery and modest additional charge proves that the company practices what it preaches. Nike has blurred the lines between marketing, product design, and customer service so successfully that all of them leverage the brand even as they add value back, a true strategy machine.

Obstacle to Catalyst: Focus on the Big Picture

Nike's brand is inseparable from what we referred to earlier as the "big idea," but even companies with more modest brands can follow Nike's example when marketing in the new media. Remember that finding your big idea starts by identifying the larger problem customers want to solve when they buy your products or services, then finding ways to deliver the entire solution. Even in traditional media, most advertising goes beyond mere product promotion to sell elements of the big idea by emphasizing values that distinguish you from competitors—perhaps your approach to customer service, product innovation, a predictable experience, or low cost. As transaction costs decline, it is possible to do more than simply point to those values. Now you can use new media to market and deliver them at the same time.

Intuit developed its big idea from a solid base of personal finance and tax software for consumers. The broader context for Intuit customers is the financial life of their households, and Intuit uses its Quicken.com Website to offer an extensive network of products and services in tax, accounting, mortgages, bill payment, brokerages, and financial planning. By populating the new interface with the data that customers have already entered using Intuit's products, Intuit, like Nike, is beginning to forge an ISC that turns its marketing message from a slogan ("Understand our customer's problems and solve them simply") into a product.

For businesses that sell to other companies, marketing can act as a catalyst to create information goods. Business community host Verticalnet began without much credibility in the industries it serves, but through joint ventures and careful cultivation, several of its on-line communities are beginning to achieve critical mass. At GovCon, for example, one of over fifty Verticalnet communities, participants in the government contracting business can post catalogs, follow developments in products, regulations, and other information typical of trade associations and industry publications, and interact with each other in a new medium. If GovCon succeeds, the Website will evolve from observing the market to being the market, delivering value with the information it collects from its members even as it collects more information.

Obstacle to Catalyst: Sell What the Customer Really Wants

A word of caution about marketing: Don't kid yourself. If you market on the basis of advantages you wish you had, or have but know that customers don't really care about, the feedback loop of the ISC will echo back the truth, amplified loud enough for everyone to hear. "A lie can travel halfway around the world," Mark Twain once said, "while the truth is putting on its shoes." Twain's observation is prophetic—in the age of a spreading information network, bad information travels with considerably less friction than good.

A marketing strategy of self-delusion played a major role in the failure of many on-line banking experiments. Most of the on-line banks launched by startups have disappeared, and both Citibank and Bank One have ended their costly and proudly trumpeted on-line ventures, Citi f/i and Wingspan. Wingspan's demise was particularly painful for Bank One, given the $35 million ad campaign that launched the company as a new, virtual bank to compete with traditional branch banks, including Bank One's.

Unfortunately, the marketing campaign not only didn't help Wingspan get off the ground, it was actually part of what sank the company. Wingspan's tag line, "If your bank could start over, this is what it would be," betrayed a truth the company didn't intend to convey. Wingspan was simply a physical bank whose functions were transferred on-line. The traditional products of a commercial bank (checking, savings, loans) were duplicated—nothing more. The real advantage was for Bank One, who hoped to operate Wingspan without expensive branches as a *more profitable* commercial bank. The slogan was literal—Wingspan was, at best, what a bank would be if the bank were the one doing the redesign. For

most consumers, the response to Wingspan's marketing was resounding: Who cares?

What on-line banks still fail to appreciate is that most of their customers don't need the bank redesigned. They don't need the bank at all. Over the last 50 years, much of what banks used to do has migrated to other financial service companies, notably brokerages, insurance companies, and consumer loan specialists. The competitors succeeded not by offering the same products in different packaging but rather by crafting solutions to common problems such as buying a home, planning for retirement, and financing the education of children. Banks rely for income on savings and checking accounts, which were once protected from competition; but these services have become less important parts of their customers' financial lives.

A true redesign would have begun with an appreciation of what customers really want: a financial services solutions provider—an integrated part of the customer's most important life events, rather than a destination. The relationship of most consumers to their bank is already so low on their radar that even a brilliant reconception of the idea is irrelevant, unexciting, and, with only small cost savings over what is today a trivial cost for most customers, uninspiring.

Ironically, branchless banking could have solved a significant problem, but not for the bank's current customers. Banks intentionally price their services to exclude unprofitable low-income families, who are forced to use high-priced currency exchanges to buy money orders, cash checks, pay bills, and borrow against future paychecks. According to the U.S. Department of the Treasury, "10 million American families are not participating in our financial system at even the most basic level. These 10 million families—nearly 85% of who make less than $25,000 annually—lack a bank account."

A lower-cost virtual bank has the potential to greatly expand the customer base, and at a profit, but so far banks have shown no interest. Instead, they have left the field to retailers, including convenience store chain 7-Eleven, which has been testing ATM-like kiosks in their stores which can dispense money orders and cash checks.

If a bank wanted to make itself useful with new technology, it would figure out a way to offer financial services cost-effectively to those they can't serve today. In any case, the bank would not spend $35 million to announce that it had solved its own problem.

CATALYST 4: OF HUMAN CAPITAL

Most companies do not succeed by constant innovation, but rather by superior performance—by business as usual rather than paradigm shifts. Executives are paid to execute, not to destroy. Your information assets might include expertise in many aspects of operating a business, including new product development, but they probably do not include skills in opening new markets, transforming supply chains, or turning products into services using information technology. Few companies can innovate without going outside their organization borders—even high-technology giants like Cisco and Microsoft often acquire rather than develop their newest products. Changing the culture to one that emphasizes innovation will take time, and perhaps new leadership.

In the meantime, don't hit your head against a wall by trying to force managers into the role of entrepreneurs or hiring entrepreneurs and treating them like employees. The wiser course is to outsource as much innovation as possible. Leave the emergence and most of the exchange work to outside partners—venture capitalists, startups, technology companies, consortia, and incubators—while you focus on efficiency projects and portfolio management. Worry about the machine—your partners will help you focus its energy into useful new products.

Most executives are understandably uncomfortable at the prospect of putting their strategic future in the hands of outsiders, and many companies spent the late 1990s engaged in a futile effort to cultivate what Joseph Schumpeter might have called creative self-destruction. Lacking innovation skills internally, they spent a lot of time and money recruiting entrepreneurs and leading edge technical staff to fill the role of "change agents." It was wasted effort, for several reasons:

1. **They could not attract the people they wanted.** Entrepreneurs are risk-takers, and expect their compensation to be tied to success. They prefer a lower wage and partial ownership in their work to a simple salary. Experts in emerging information technologies also tend, to put it as gently as possible, to be strongly individualistic, repelled by large organizations with complex bureaucracies.

2. **Talent was quickly lost to better offers.** Companies that did manage to attract entrepreneurial talent could not hold it for long. When the money flowed, startups could offer better stock options *and* better

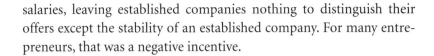

salaries, leaving established companies nothing to distinguish their offers except the stability of an established company. For many entrepreneurs, that was a negative incentive.

3. **Integrating entrepreneurs with the rest of the company proved nearly impossible.** Even without competition from startups, retaining entrepreneurial talent is a significant challenge for public companies. Invariably, employees who think boldly about the Information Revolution are young, inexperienced in corporate behavior, and have different values from employees who have spent entire careers in one company. Efforts to create an environment in which the younger talent felt comfortable failed. In the process, longtime employees grew understandably resentful and demoralized, making the cultural and organizational shifts even harder.

Even service companies with a healthy appreciation for invisible capital, whose cultures emphasize creative thinking, can founder on the human capital obstacle. Disney, for one, failed with uncharacteristic frequency in its efforts to launch on-line initiatives, largely because of a revolving door of leadership. The company lost several directors of its Internet division in quick succession. The heads of its movie studio and cable operations left the company for startups, as did the president of its ABC division.

Why was Disney hit so hard? Aside from the organizational obstacles of any public company, Disney, for one, has a long history of treating creative talent as hired help, with a flat wage structure and little in the way of financial incentives for blockbuster successes. Disney executives were unable to placate entrepreneurs who were frustrated by the company's rigidity. Rather than offer them equity, Disney created an Internet tracking stock, a neither-fish-nor-fowl solution which satisfied no one. In 2001, the company shuttered many of its most expensive experiments (such as Go.com) and absorbed the tracking stock, effectively giving up. The company would have been better served to outsource new media investments, but that too violated the Disney culture. The result: little to show for millions of dollars of investment.

Obstacle to Catalyst: Let Your People Go

Solving the human capital problem will take more than finding partners to provide innovation skills you lack. Sooner or later, to maintain your strategy machine, you must develop those skills internally. The invisible capital engine will function smoothly only if everyone in your company is motivated to contribute to the knowledge base of expertise, relationships, and brand value that is the engine's feedstock. Reorganizing your human capital around their contributions to invisible capital will solve many of the mismatches between portfolio and current operations. The transition, however, is a difficult one to make.

Along the way, you will discover that much of your operating expense goes toward parts of your business for which you have little or no expertise. Any corporate function—purchasing, administration, manufacturing, sales and marketing, or human resources—can be a source of competitive advantage, depending on your industry and strategy. But it is more likely that some of those functions are part of your current operation only because you have never asked yourself whether the market might better manage these activities. If so, you are spending money—perhaps the majority of your budget—operating the business as a commodity that neither uses nor contributes to the invisible capital engine. In the shift to an organization built around the strategy machine, those are precisely the employees who put up the most resistance.

The solution is simple: Get rid of them. Even if they represent a large part of your staff and associated asset base, there may no longer be any need to keep the activities they perform inside your company. Remember that in the transaction cost economics of Ronald Coase, companies perform activities internally only when they can do so more efficiently than the market can. Indeed, according to Coase, companies exist in the first place because their managers know how to execute repeated tasks more efficiently, which is another way of saying that the company has some expertise—even if it is only based on economies of scale—that the market and other companies don't have. If conditions change—if the market or other companies become more efficient—then the only thing keeping an activity in your company is inertia.

Shedding functions that are not central to your strategies may sound impractical, but it is likely that you have been doing so for some time. Information technology disrupts supply chains by making the market more attractive, constantly testing the economic balance between inside and outside activities. If you outsourced your corporate travel function or part of your information technology operations, or downsized your sales staff in favor of independent agents or brokers, you did so because you

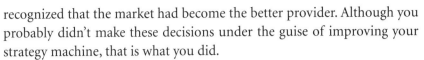

recognized that the market had become the better provider. Although you probably didn't make these decisions under the guise of improving your strategy machine, that is what you did.

As the ISC develops, the flow of information across the supply chain expands. Decisions about what functions to keep inside must be constantly revisited. To take a dramatic example, consider the extraordinary transaction executed in 1999 by systems integrator EDS and telecommunications giant WorldCom. Up until then, EDS had operated a telecommunications network on behalf of its customers, a necessary expense to support their business of running corporate data centers. WorldCom, which found that implementing communications networks for its customers required considerable project management experience, had itself acquired a large consulting firm called Systemhouse, giving itself a captive source of project expertise.

By 1999, however, both companies found that market conditions had changed enough to revisit these assets. EDS didn't need to operate its own communications network, and WorldCom no longer required consultants who were full-time employees. What had once required permanent staff (and the costs associated with their administration) could now, in part because of improvements in information technology, be managed as a series of long-term contracts between two different companies. So the two companies decided to make a trade.

In a transaction valued at $17 billion, WorldCom took over EDS's networking operation, while EDS absorbed the former Systemhouse consultants. Twelve thousand WorldCom employees moved to EDS; 1,000 EDS employees became part of WorldCom. Each year, WorldCom pays EDS $7 billion for computer services and software, and EDS pays $8.5 billion for WorldCom's network services. More important, both companies can focus their attention on fewer activities.

CATALYST 5: INTEGRATING FOR PROFIT

The final internal catalyst involves the difficulty of connecting existing applications and technology platforms with the new components constructed as part of your strategy machine. The other internal catalysts involve problems of organizational sociology, but this last problem appears, at least on the surface, to be purely a technical one. Can you get your systems to talk to each other, your databases to integrate, your business intelligence consolidated and delivered in a useable form throughout your organization and those of your business partners? These are questions of product architecture, technical protocols, and vendor relations, after all, and not of strategy.

In two key respects, however, technology integration has the same impact on the smooth operation of your strategy machine as the other internal catalysts:

- Information systems have steadily moved up the food chain. Stand-alone applications that automate back-office functions such as payroll and accounting have been supplemented by systems that control manufacturing and distribution. Today, most companies have or will develop strategic front-end applications such as customer service and sales management. In many cases these new systems will be used directly by customers, suppliers, and other business partners; some will become embedded components of the products or services you sell and service.

  As applications become strategic rather than purely operational, your ability to implement new strategies is dependent on your ability to modify, adapt, and connect your systems.

- In the course of deploying systems over the last several years, the policies and procedures described earlier as obstacles to innovative change have been immortalized as software code. Even after everyone agrees to a change in organizational policy, implementation often requires a major overhaul of core applications where old assumptions have been hard-wired into every program and database. Opening your systems to customers and suppliers exposes the old assumptions whether you want them seen or not.

  The more your company relies on information assets as a source of future product and service revenue in the emerging supply chain, the more important it becomes to build systems that can be reconfigured and reconnected easily and frequently, not only with your other applications, but with those of your partners, including customers.

Obstacle to Catalyst: Build on a Technical Architecture

The only way to transform your existing technology from an obstacle into a catalyst is to start with a technical architecture. Fortunately, unlike physical buildings, it is possible to impose a new architecture on your existing systems after the fact, and then use the new building code for future systems. Few companies have done this, however. In the rush to respond to the Internet crisis, most companies built temporary patches between old and new applications—connecting a Web-based order entry system for customers to existing inventory and billing systems, for example.

As more features and functions are added to the new systems, patches are placed on top of patches until the architecture is too compromised to take any more changes. Even if the temporary solutions work, the ad hoc approach eventually fails. The more successful your new interfaces are the sooner they will overwhelm the older systems with high transaction volumes. Or perhaps the temporary links will break as you try to integrate the business of a company you acquire or merge with, or as you disconnect another business you have sold.

Eastman Chemicals has carefully avoided both types of failure. Over the last five years, the company completed major shifts in its asset portfolio, acquiring companies, selling off less-strategic divisions and, in 2001, deciding to split the remaining business into two separate public companies. They have been greatly aided in these efforts by a commitment made several years ago to standardize the desktop computing platform and major applications across the company, a decision that extends to each of the companies Eastman acquires.

Like many organizations, Eastman purchased millions of dollars in personal computer and networking hardware and software during the 1980s without a long-term plan for how it would be used. By the early 1990s the company faced difficult problems of integration. Different business units couldn't share data, and even separate departments had their own standards. In 1993, Eastman undertook the aptly named "Project Bulldozer," replacing 15,000 desktop computers with a single hardware and software platform. Though the up-front cost was high and difficult to justify, the effort paid for itself quickly, and the company continues to reap the benefits of their foresight every day. According to E-Business Director Fred Buehler, the company's only regret is that it didn't start earlier.

Integration is essential not only for maximum value from both old and new information technology investments but also because, more than the other internal catalysts, technology integration is the fulcrum on which the successful operation of your strategy machine depends. Do it correctly, and all of your information assets go to work for you. Compromise the architecture, and systems become unmovable objects, holding you back from achieving even a modest return on your project investments.

Obstacle to Catalyst: Use What You Have, Don't Build What You Don't Need

Even as traditional companies can leverage older systems, startups can fail from overdesigning their initial technical architecture. In the grocery delivery business, which promised to put retail stores out of business, heavily capitalized companies such as Webvan and Kozmo sputtered and died under the weight of a technology infrastructure that was built too quickly. Both companies built large and complicated systems that could handle large volumes of orders in several different cities. These were systems neither company would need, even under the most ambitious projections of business, for many years. Rather than saving time and money later, the overdesigned technical environments actually made it harder to service customers and to make refinements to how the delivery business would be run.

The retailers, meanwhile, were leveraging existing investments into a profitable delivery business. The United Kingdom's biggest grocer, Tesco, has succeeded with home delivery through a clever combination of old and new technology. Customers enter orders on-line which are automatically routed to the nearest Tesco store. There, store employees pick the merchandise, aided by special grocery carts that optimize routing through the aisles (the fruits of an earlier set of investments), filling up to six orders at a time. To be cost-effective, deliveries are only permitted within a 25-minute drive from a store, but thanks to Britain's compact geography that distance covers 90% of the population.

Tesco invested only $56 million in its home-delivery venture—a far cry from the billions spent by Webvan—and in 2001 generated delivery revenues of over $400 million. Like Eastman, Tesco's efforts during the previous decade to improve in-store systems had the unexpected dividend of making it cheaper and easier to add the home-delivery business to an existing operation. In early 2002, Tesco began leveraging its home-delivery expertise in a joint venture with U.S. grocery giant Safeway and its home-delivery service, Groceryworks.com. "With Tesco's know-how and Safeway's brand," according to a statement from Tesco, "we have the perfect combination to bring grocery home-shopping to the world's largest market."

10

EXTERNAL CATALYSTS

Overcoming the Outside Obstacles

Your choice is simple. Join us and live in peace or pursue your present course and face obliteration. We shall be waiting for your answer. The decision rests with you.

—Klaatu, *The Day the Earth Stood Still*

[THE MANY VARIETIES OF CHANNEL CONFLICT. THE ACCIDENT-PRONE INTERSECTION OF LAW AND TECHNOLOGY. FINANCING THE REVOLUTION.]

The previous chapter explored the impact on your strategy machine of forces working inside your organization to slow its momentum or, as the Luddites did, break it into pieces. This chapter is concerned with forms of inertia that apply pressure from the outside. Some, like channel conflict and financing, originate from nearby links in the supply chain while others, such as law and regulation, live at the fringes. Both kinds can drain enough energy to stop your transformation. Like the internal obstacles, they must be not only neutralized but reborn as forward momentum.

The same general techniques apply. If you can identify the obstacles before you run into them, determine the true scope of the problems they create, and develop reusable ways to overcome them, the obstacles become effective competitive tools—external catalysts, sending you more quickly on your way.

CATALYST 6: MANAGING CHANNEL CONFLICTS

Channel conflicts are inevitable, and to some extent a natural side effect of every investment in your portfolio. The principal effect of information technology in the Information Revolution is reformulation of the supply chain, and every break in the links creates stress in your relationships with customers, distributors, and suppliers. Efficiency-stage projects, for example, are aimed at identifying and eliminating waste in the flow of goods and services. If that waste represents the profit margin for a channel partner, perhaps a distributor or supplier of materials, it is unlikely that partner will be enthusiastic about helping to implement the new systems. In the emerging supply chain, some of today's participants will be eliminated or replaced by new players. Whenever victims of metamorphosis recognize this, they will use whatever capital they have—visible and invisible—to delay the inevitable.

You may already have experienced significant channel conflicts as a result of investments in new information technology. Perhaps your agents objected to a Website that allowed their customers to interact with you directly, even if it was only to get information about orders placed through the agents. Your suppliers, likewise, may have expressed concern about your participation in electronic exchanges. Offering customers on-line ordering may have led to complaints from your own sales force and store managers that doing so harmed their commissions or their ability to meet budgeted sales targets.

These conflicts are only the beginning of what is to come in the fight for control of the information supply chain. When all the inefficiencies have been squeezed out of today's processes, the new value, new revenue, and new profits will come from turning data into new information goods. As information finds its way into databases that can be turned into business intelligence, conflicts over who owns and controls it will make today's skirmishes seem friendly by comparison. Consumers are already rattling their swords, calling for legislation to limit the collection and use of "private" data.

In the face of all this unpleasantness, your company might be one of many to have adopted a strict rule against any initiative with channel conflict potential. Over the last few years, many of my clients sidelined their most radical experiments in favor of more modest and less threatening efforts. Sidestepping channel conflict, however, is only a temporary solution—and a costly one at that. As you tread gingerly on the toes of your partners, there are others inside and outside your supply chain who have no incentives to protect the current structure. In the days of ready venture capital, dozens of startups were launched with little more business plan than simply to disrupt existing channels of stable (and therefore, it was believed, inefficient) industries, expecting that doing so would turn up hidden value in short order.

As the fortunes of many of these companies fade, their example has inspired more targeted efforts from disadvantaged participants inside the supply chain, encouraging them to break ranks and continue the assault on business as usual. Companies that operate at the commodity end of the value curve, after all, may have little to lose by offending their channel partners, or may have sufficient control over a key link in the chain to dictate when and how metamorphosis will occur.

Someday you will have to accept channel conflict as an unavoidable by-product of your strategy machine in motion. That is the bad news. The good news is that overcoming channel conflict is not as hard as it seems. The key is to control the flow not of products and services but of the information about them, and in particular the information going to and from the consumer. The "last mile" of the information supply chain is the crucial link. If you are the real estate agent with the listing, the credit card company who sends the bill, or the owner of the most-recognized brand (to name three), you are largely free to tinker with new products and services without worrying too much about stepping on the toes of your channel partners. Controlling customer data means controlling the channel. While that control is rarely absolute, the more of it you have, the better.

What if you don't have any control over the information flow? Perhaps you are a manufacturer, a distributor, or a company further up the supply chain with no direct contact with consumers. Channel conflict will be a more acute problem for you, but not a fatal one. Your strategy will be to find out who in your supply chain today is the closest to having control. Then figure out a way in which you can join forces, form a coalition, or pool your resources to improve the ISC and your abilities to profit from it. In short, make a deal.

To do that, you need to determine first who your most promising partners will be; who, in other words, has direct contact with customers and among that group, who does or is best positioned to capture information about their transactions? The answer will depend on how products and services move in your industry today. The consumer's direct point of contact may include agents, service providers, branded suppliers, an internal sales force, or distributors. Each type has a different incentive to work with you, as we will see by looking at each one in turn. Some combination of these participants, though, provides the key to converting channel conflict from an obstacle into a catalyst.

Obstacle to Catalyst: Independent Agents

In industries that outsource sales to independent agents, the agents often form cartels to ensure that key transaction information is not available to alternative providers or, in many cases, to the suppliers of the goods. In residential real estate, for example, commissioned agents are the only ones who know the identities of buyers, sellers, and properties that are for sale. Information technology offers obvious ways to reduce the high transaction costs of buying and selling a home (the agents get as much as 6% of the purchase price), but efforts to employ it are seen as direct threats to commissions and have so far been resisted.

The first wave of Internet startups included many aimed at attacking inefficiencies in the real estate market, with Websites that allowed buyers to apply on-line for mortgages, search properties in various areas, calculate costs associated with home ownership, and arrange for moving services. They all lacked a critical piece of information, however: listings of properties for sale, which were kept in proprietary databases controlled by the National Association of Realtors (NAR), the agents' trade association. Sites were able to show pictures and the addresses of some available properties, but were denied data identifying sellers, forcing buyers and sellers to stay within the existing agent networks.

Some independent brokers broke ranks, however, and began to use the Web to expand their reach. The NAR responded by licensing its data exclusively to one startup, Homestore.com, data it traded for 20% of Homestore's stock. In mid-2001, Homestore was worth over $2 billion, almost all of that reflecting the value of the NAR's exclusive listings. Using Homestore, buyers can query over a million properties in the proprietary listing services, but must still contact a real estate agent to get complete information, notably to find the seller. Even with these limitations, Homestore has a distinct advantage over other real estate startups, who complained about the exclusive arrangement to the U.S. Department of Justice, which began an investigation.

The NAR's goal is to capitalize on its information assets as it continues to protect the existing supply chain, managing the channel conflicts by carefully playing the different participants in their supply chain off each other. The more likely scenario, however, is that pressure will continue to build from consumers, unaffiliated brokers, and regulators to open the system more quickly. It remains to be seen if the realtors will be able to hold the line on commissions much longer.

Obstacle to Catalyst: Service Providers

In industries with high volumes of low-priced transactions, companies that process or clear transactions, claims, or trades may control the information flow. Such information service providers can achieve significant leverage over suppliers and customers through the superior knowledge of price and market conditions their data provides. In the health care industry, for example, health maintenance organizations (HMOs), large insurance companies, and their claims-processing affiliates have used their transactional leverage to reshape the practices of doctors and hospitals—often to the displeasure of health care providers and consumers alike, as calls for a "patients' bill of rights" suggest.

Consider the tragic story of on-line drugstores, many of which failed simply because they underestimated the power of an information service-provider in their supply chain. On the surface, buying prescriptions over the Internet seemed to make tremendous sense. Medication is small and easy to ship. Most prescriptions are refills, requiring little or no consultation with a pharmacist. And consolidation of drug stores in the United States into a few giant chains has led to an in-store experience that is long on waiting and short on interaction with overworked pharmacists. Rising to the opportunity, several well-funded startups, including Drugstore.com and PlanetRx, launched services to fill and refill prescriptions on-line.

Nearly all of these services have since shut down. Why? The problem here was not a bad idea or poor execution, but rather a channel conflict the startups didn't see or resolve quickly enough. Insurance companies pay a portion of 80% of all prescriptions written in the United States, and manage that volume through affiliates called pharmacy benefit managers (PBMs) whose approval is required for the patient to receive coverage. Many of the PBMs, however, owned interests in prescription mail-order companies that saw startups like Drugstore.com and PlanetRx as direct threats. The PBMs simply refused to reimburse orders that went through Websites, effectively cutting them off. Drugstore.com was forced to sell a 25% interest to Rite Aid, a major drugstore chain, not for the synergy of having an established partner but to piggyback off Rite Aid's existing contracts with the PBMs. Drugstore.com, as a result, is still operating, while PlanetRx, which waited longer to find a cartel partner, is gone.

When, as in health care, the information systems of the actual producers are so tightly integrated with those of the information service providers that switching is impractical, producers are unlikely to do much if the service providers decide to extend their reach. But that is now changing. New information technologies using open standards can process more data from more sources at lower costs, setting the stage for conflicts between service providers and the buyers and sellers on either side of their service. When a real alternative exists, buyers and sellers can dare to dream of setting their own rules of engagement rather than having them dictated.

Obstacle to Catalyst: Branded Suppliers

In some industries, channel conflicts emerge when dominant suppliers resist using new channels to sell their products or services, fearing dilution of their brand. Without access to the products consumers want most, of course, the new channels are unlikely to achieve liquidity.

In the multibillion-dollar market for health and beauty aids, brands owned by a few companies, including Estée Lauder, represent the vast majority of all products sold. Lauder alone sells almost half of the high-end cosmetics, through premium brands such as Clinique and Bobbi Brown, which are sold in their own stores or in special in-store boutiques at department stores. Maintaining the prestige of the brand is essential for these producers since the actual formulation of cosmetic products varies little, certainly less than the price difference between high-end and low-end products suggests. As Lauder's Angela Kapp, vice-president of its on-line division, put it in 2000, "Our brand equity is everything."

Cosmetics, like prescription drugs, seemed a natural for on-line purchase, given high repeat sales and the ease of shipping the small but relatively expensive goods. Several startups, including the on-line drugstores as well as beauty sites like Eve, Beauty.com, and BeautyJungle, were launched in 1999 and 2000. Though many of the startups offered innovative features that helped consumers select products and keep track of orders for easy refill—a significant improvement over the retail experience—channel conflict proved decisive. According to BeautyJungle COO Ken Gaebler, despite several meetings with Lauder executives and a partial redesign of his site to separate the company's premium brands from cheaper alternatives, Lauder chose not to sell its products through Beauty-Jungle or any of the other on-line retailers—including sites operated by current retail partners such as Nordstrom's and Macy's.

After the startups had gone, Lauder in late 2001 began to let retail partners sell its products on-line—and relaunched Gloss.com, a Web-based company Lauder had acquired six months earlier. Gloss now sells Lauder products.

Obstacle to Catalyst: External Sales Forces

When new technologies are deployed to improve any part of the sales or marketing process, salespeople who make their money based on private information about customers (including their identities, preferences, and previous transactions) will naturally resist. For many companies, the sales force, even when it is made up of employees rather than contractors or authorized dealers, is a significant source of channel conflict. A sales force compensated by commissions or percentages evaluates change in light of its own interests, not its employer's.

The spread of the global information network has caused particularly acute problems for companies that allocate customers along geographic boundaries, particularly when the regions are small. If new technology means neither customers nor salespeople need to travel to originate or fill orders, the boundaries quickly become a source of increased rather than reduced transaction costs. The problem is worse for what are called "multitiered marketing" companies, where salespeople recruit subordinates and trade small parts of their region in exchange for a share of the commissions on sales by the recruits.

Companies that sell and deliver their respective products door-to-door, including Avon, Tupperware, and the Girl Scouts of America, initially reacted to the availability of the new on-line channel with stunned silence and unconvincing rationales for avoiding it. Tupperware, which sells plastic storage containers at neighborhood "parties," for example, insisted that its customers needed to "hear the burp"; the Girl Scouts argued that learning to sell door-to-door was a valuable end in itself

194 THE STRATEGY MACHINE

for its members (apparently more valuable than learning how to sell on-line).

Of course the real problem is that only salespeople, not customers, care about territory. Customers want the best price or service and they want to shop where and when it is most convenient for them—perhaps at work, late at night, or while traveling. Salespeople can cover only so much ground, and even if current customers do continue buying the old way, increasingly mobile societies with two working adults in each family leave some customers with no way to buy. The obvious solution is selling on-line, but doing so can quickly undermine the commission system.

This conflict between potential new revenue and a long-standing way of doing business led Amway, which sells a variety of home products in a multitiered structure, to look for a compromise. In 1999, it launched Quixtar, which the company called its "biggest change in 40 years." Quixtar is a set of tools to help Amway sales representatives build their own on-line storefronts. Amway itself, however, does not sell directly to the public. So while the geographic restraints have been removed (an Amway representative can direct any customer to his or her Quixtar storefront), the multilevel commission structure is intact. Since this translates to higher prices for customers, just as it does in the traditional channel, it remains to be seen if Amway and others can maintain that inefficiency. If customers are only willing to pay the Amway price because of the personal contact they get, the answer is probably not. Amway and other multitiered marketers will ultimately be forced to create new structures that optimize rather than merely tolerate on-line shopping.

Obstacle to Catalyst: Distributors

For manufacturers with strong brands but no direct sales force, the channel challenge is to find ways to make use of new technology to increase revenue without alienating resellers. The manufacturer may be entirely dependent on a few key distributors for the bulk of its sales, and the distributors may likewise earn most of their income from exclusive arrangements to sell products of a few key suppliers. Manufacturers may want to experiment with new channels that connect them directly with customers, but doing so almost always strains relations with distributors on whom they rely for today's revenues. Tinkering with the balance of power is fraught with danger.

Why not just sell direct? Manufacturers often choose to sell through distributors for complex products, or when customers are physically scattered. A dedicated sales staff selling only your products, in either situation, is an expensive prospect. Manufacturers and distributors will have made substantial investments in their relationships—product training, joint marketing, and integrating information systems—another reason neither is eager to engage channel conflict.

Complex products can be sold on-line by digitizing the expertise of both manufacturer and distributor, making the customer's physical location less of a complication for sellers. As the ISC emerges, channel conflicts with distributors are inevitable. One solution is to use new technologies solely to provide pre- or post-sales information to customers, reducing the workload of the distributors without threatening their income. Appliance manufacturer Whirlpool tried to do just that, developing applications that extended its relationship with consumers (to whom it does not sell directly), including product selection and after-sales service and parts replacement.

The company worked hard, in these delicate first steps in the construction of an ISC, not to offer services or even information that might offend channel partners like Circuit City and Sears, who account for the majority of Whirlpool's sales. (Whirlpool's Website does not sell its own appliances, and says nothing about price.) They hoped that by doing so, the distributors would cooperate in building more robust on-line channels together.

Unfortunately, distributors may have other ideas, a lesson Whirlpool learned the hard way. Circuit City, struggling to improve per-store revenues, suddenly announced in mid-2000 that it was no longer selling large appliances and would turn the floor space over to more profitable electronics. That decision led Whirlpool to cut its revenue estimates for the rest of the year by over a third. More to the point, it had wasted valuable time protecting the flow of information for a partner who was suddenly out of the picture. No more sales and no chance for a better information flow.

So rather than tiptoe around potential conflicts, form alliances with distributors to develop jointly and profit from new channel features made possible by improvements in information technology. A strategy that mixes new channels with retail outlets is essential for durable goods such as furniture and electronics, which are expensive, large, complex, often require service or returns, and which consumers may need to see and feel before purchase. Furniture maker Ethan Allen, for example, sells furniture directly on its Website, but gives its independently owned stores a cut of Web sales in their geographic territory. In exchange, the stores take responsibility for delivery, service, and returns.

Electronics retailer Best Buy implemented a similar feature, integrating a new on-line shopping interface with its store databases to provide consumers with real-time access to store inventory. On-line customers who want to avoid shipping costs can do so by picking up their merchandise at the local outlet, assured that the item will be there waiting for them, already paid for and checked out.

Obstacle to Catalyst: Information-Intensive Industries

As these examples suggest, when supply chains are being transformed the battle line is often drawn over control of transactional information. Not surprisingly, information-intensive industries see the fiercest fighting. Stock trading and insurance, for instance, have already experienced significant carnage, often characterized as a struggle between mature companies (Merrill Lynch and State Farm) and startups (E*Trade and Insweb).

The story is not that simple, however. In these and other information industries, the conflict is also taking place at a deeper, less visible level— who will shape the new, information-rich supply chain, and what will it look like? As these industries enter the emergence stage, the ISC will reward those who add value with more profits and dispose of those who merely heap on transaction costs. In the process, channel conflicts rise and fall, old partners fall out, and odd new alliances may form, sometimes only for a single transaction.

In securities trading, the scorecard so far reads as follows: mutual funds (an information product made by creating winning portfolios for individual investors) are up, trading pits and physical exchanges (with no advantage over electronic alternatives other than tradition) are down. Stockbrokers and analysts took several hits, but are hardly out of the game. Customers have demonstrated that they are willing to pay for superior service and in-depth analysis, but brokers who don't provide any are being exposed, while those who do add value are learning that doing so one-on-one by telephone is neither necessary nor optimal. Stockbrokers, in some sense a creation of the telephone, are slow to adapt to new channels.

Was Merrill Lynch too late to the new channel? Was E*Trade too early? The answer depends on which asset proves to be more valuable—Merrill's existing relationships or E*Trade's ability to add new products and services quickly. Put that way, it's clear that the answer is neither—both assets are necessary, and the sooner traditional brokers get themselves and their clients on-line, the sooner the brokers' invisible capital can be put to profitable use.

To do so quickly, they must navigate the dangerous waters of channel conflict, in this case filled with the brokerage firm's very own sharks. When salespeople are paid in the form of commissions their incentive is not only to pursue customers aggressively but also to hoard them. Hoarding raises the cost of service by making it difficult for the firm to consolidate, digitize, and reuse information in more efficient ways.

With an alternative channel in which customers pull information rather than having it pushed onto them, the nature of the relationship between customer and broker changes. Ultimately, it is a change for the better. Customers take over administrative tasks and read the research themselves, leaving the brokers with the job they claim to have been doing all along—counseling, service, and analysis.

Change will not come, however, without adjusting the way brokers are paid. If they deliver value, pay for value. If they simply deliver transactions and technology provides a lower-cost mechanism for processing transactions, get rid of them. After insisting for a year that it would never do so, Merrill Lynch announced with fanfare in mid-1999 that it would offer on-line trading after all. Brokers responded precisely the wrong way, but in a way entirely consistent with the incentives of commission-based pay. They got mad. "There's a lot of very, very sore egos around here," one anonymous broker told the *Wall Street Journal*. "We have been insulted one too many times. They basically called us dinosaurs."

Some may well be. New channels must be engaged, and not all of that engagement will be pleasant. The alternative is to wait until the new supply chain emerges, then beg for a place at the table.

Insurance is wrestling with a similar problem. In this case, the channel conflict is with agents rather than employees, but that distinction changes little. Over half of all agents are "captive" to the insurance company they represent, meaning they only sell the products of one company.

Unlike the securities industry, information technology in insurance has so far played only a bit part. The information systems of insurance agents are so poor, in fact, that efforts by the carriers to *give* them on-line tools for customer relationship management only made things worse. State Farm, for example, was an early subscriber to Insweb, which launched a pioneering on-line lead-generation service in 1999. Con sumers shopping for insurance go to the Insweb site and complete a detailed on-line interview. Based on their responses, consumers are then directed to agents of subscribing carriers.

Insweb proved popular with insurance customers and generated a large number of qualified leads for State Farm. Despite (or perhaps because of) the success of the service, however, State Farm terminated its relationship with Insweb in 2000. The problem was that State Farm's network of 16,000 agents would not or in some cases could not figure out how to use the leads Insweb sent them. State Farm chose to turn away potential customers rather than risk revolt by forcing change on its captive agents.

Victory for the status quo will prove short-lived. Today there are a staggering 1.8 million insurance agents in the United States, and nearly 10% of the total cost of insurance goes into subsidizing that system— almost $25 billion a year in transaction costs. The inefficiencies of the agent channel are too obvious to list and to attractive to go without repair much longer. If the current batch of on-line efforts all fail, some future combination of software company, startup, breakaway insurers, and enlightened agents will figure out how to use network technologies to benefit customers as well as their own bottom line.

Alliances between small carriers, independent agents, and consumers may also succeed in turning the channel obstacle into a catalyst. If they do, the industry may find itself Napsterized—that is, the victim of a sudden and dramatic reconfiguration of its supply chain. It is not too late for the major carriers to take the lead, but it soon will be.

CATALYST 7: OVERCOMING LAW

Law and regulation are often the weapons of choice during channel conflicts, particularly when dominant players can translate their leverage into restrictive legislation. The influence of law on the smooth operation of your strategy machine, however, goes far beyond channel conflicts. It is a force in its own right, often the most invisible and the most powerful. In the Information Revolution, law is poised to take on a more visible and

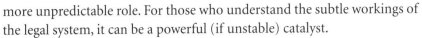

more unpredictable role. For those who understand the subtle workings of the legal system, it can be a powerful (if unstable) catalyst.

I should say from the outset that the infrastructure of law—legislation, regulatory agencies, courts—is essential for the conduct of any business, and that is as true today as it was during the Industrial Revolution. Without the background rules that define property rights the exchange of property would be impossible. Likewise, the cumbersome and expensive process of litigation waiting in the wings to enforce contracts encourages parties to take their commitments seriously. Indeed, the high cost in time and money of litigating may be a good thing—an incentive for buyers and sellers to work out any differences they have using more straightforward techniques. And without governments ready, willing, and able to enforce the rule of law consistently and impartially, there would be no transactions in the first place. You need only look to the struggles of the former Communist countries to establish capitalist economies to see just how much background support such "free" markets really need in order to function at all, let alone efficiently.

Information technology and the volumes of new data it makes available, however, has consistently challenged law's ability to stay current. Legal systems are designed to change slowly but technology changes daily, bringing long-standing legal assumptions into increased conflict with changing environments. Today technology is a hammer pounding away at outdated notions about location (where does an on-line transaction "occur"?), property (who "owns" information?), and national sovereignty (whose law applies on the Web?). In the ongoing conflict between traditional law and Moore's Law, traditional law must adapt. Along the way, expect severe bumps in the road, bumps that can stall your strategy machine. Or, if you are lucky, that of your competitors.

Sometimes the tendency for technology to outdate law quickly has nearly comical consequences. The U.S. Department of Commerce restricts the export of advanced computer technology to unfriendly nations, understandably concerned that technology may be adapted to hostile use. The Department, however, defined "advanced" based on performance, and the constant application of Moore's Law has inadvertently put products on the list that clearly don't belong. In 1999, the Department's guidelines led it to classify the Sony PlayStation II—the toy discussed in Chapter 1—as a "munition" that could not be exported from the United States to China and other countries without per-unit licenses for each sale (remember, Sony has already sold millions). Unable to change its rules quickly enough, the Department could only minimize its embarrassment by granting Sony an exemption.

Law is at its best when promoting and protecting the development of new infrastructure and lawmakers often do their worst harm when they attempt to regulate emerging technologies directly. Before it was clear how virtual exchanges would operate, high-strung regulators were already doubting the legality of intra-industry cooperation and holding hearings on how to regulate them. The U.S. Federal Trade Commission questioned the legality of Covisint, the automobile parts exchange created by the major manufacturers, before Covisint even had a name. After a six-month review, the FTC announced that it would wait until the company adopted its by-laws before making any decision. Meanwhile, the cloud of a federal government review hanging over its head slowed the progress of the company to develop its business plan and hire senior executives.

The existing supply chain, as we have also seen, can use law to slow the progress of new applications made possible by technology. Already in the Information Revolution, this strategy has yielded impressive (if unsustainable) results. One 2001 study from the Progressive Policy Institute estimates that laws restricting Internet sales passed at the behest of retailers cost U.S consumers at least $15 billion a year. Whether a law restricts the practice of telemedicine, of shipping wine across state lines, or of selling contact lenses on-line, industry lobbyists invariably argue that they are bringing lawsuits and drafting new laws to protect consumers from unlicensed or unregulated providers. Naturally there's a grain of truth to that. But often only a grain.

Antitrust, which sunk GE's planned acquisition of Honeywell and which nearly broke up Microsoft, is a key area of conflict, with the potential to seriously gum up your strategy machine. For companies directly involved in emerging technologies, the chasm between antitrust theory and market practice is overwhelming—simply the time a regulatory investigation or approval takes can be enough to sink the viability of an option. Where markets are changing quickly, as in industries where emergence stage activities happen in parallel with the earlier stages, the regulator's traditional tools are of little use. The regulators themselves, including commissioners of the U.S. Federal Communications Commission, have acknowledged that one problem with current merger analysis is that it assumes static markets that rarely stay that way during an investigation.

If nothing else, the extended time (often years) needed to litigate antitrust cases means that markets, competitors, and products will have changed dramatically from the beginning of a lawsuit until its conclusion. From the start of the Microsoft case in 1998 until it was sent back to the trial court in 2001, Microsoft's onetime ally AOL had acquired Netscape (a leading complainant), Linux had gained significant market share as an alternative to Windows, and a booming personal computer market had gone soft. The courts were fashioning remedies for anticompetitive practices that, regardless of their merits at the time, were ancient history.

As this brief survey suggests, a thorough review of the often accident-prone intersection of law and technology would cover an entire book. For now, we will review the three most troubling arenas in which the two are in conflict: *deregulation, globalization,* and the revolution in *intellectual property law.* From these examples we can draw some conclusions on how the impact of law on the operation of your strategy machine can be transformed from a hindrance to a strategic weapon.

The Culture of Regulation

In industries as different as utilities and legal services, companies that operate in highly regulated environments (regardless of whether the regulation is governmental or self-imposed) evolve complex cultures around the rules. The more stable the environment, the less its inhabitants will spend investing in information technology. When deregulation comes, companies in these industries often find themselves ill equipped to take advantage of their newly won freedom and, at the same time, suddenly faced with new competitors who don't share their conservative approach to change.

All industries are regulated to some extent, of course, but often the impact of law on your business strategy is subtle, translated into unconscious assumptions about the market environment. When laws are rewritten or repealed, the assumptions may drop out, leading to sudden and surprising changes in the supply chain. Sometimes the legal change is small, but the ripple effects can be devastating.

In 1996, for example, Congress passed the Health Insurance Portability and Accountability Act (HIPAA). One of HIPAA's modest requirements is that health-care providers develop a common electronic patient record that can be easily transferred along the supply chain from providers to insurers to the patients themselves: the beginnings of a health care ISC. A portable patient record would be a simple extension of the kind of technical architecture a healthy strategy machine requires, but the industry has no such architecture and has done little to prepare for one. Before 1996, there was little incentive for anyone to invest in technology that would collect patient data, let alone share it among industry participants who are often hostile to each other.

Despite objections from the industry to a timetable proposed at the end of the Clinton Administration, U.S. Health and Human Services Secretary Tommy Thompson decided in early 2001 not to back off on either the guidelines or the schedule. The health-care industry now finds itself under the gun to create its ISC or face legal sanctions- -hardly the way anyone would want to execute an innovative new strategy.

Globalization "Gotchas"

Dealing with one government is hard enough, but for many companies the problem is rapidly multiplying. As new communication technologies make it possible to conduct business over longer distances, companies find themselves running afoul of regulations they are completely unaware of and, in the new context of global markets, make little sense to apply. An ISC recognizes no national borders. The more data the better, whether that means more business-to-business buyers and sellers who are visible to each other or more consumers who can buy products—especially information products—through a virtual channel.

European countries have confusing tangles of advertising and trade laws, many passed after World War II to protect local economies as they rebuilt. For U.S. companies just beginning to sell overseas, these laws can be a frightening morass, discouraging what ought to be a straightforward expansion to new markets through a relatively low-cost digital channel. One of my law students wrote a chilling paper in which she took the simplest ad imaginable and demonstrated how just placing it on a Website broke dozens of laws in several European countries.

Much of the problem stems from price controls still in place for many retail products, controls that may have once made sense to protect new or struggling industries, but which now add little more than cost, especially for cross-border transactions. In countries such as Switzerland, where discounting and sales are strictly limited, prices for some goods are so high that Swiss consumers buy them on-line from foreign companies, pay for shipping and customs, and still come out ahead. This end run is technically illegal, but for information-based products like software the ability to download the product without shipping any physical good at all makes international transactions nearly untraceable. Most on-line sellers ignore local restrictions, and governments are either unaware or understaffed to the point of being unable to respond.

The real losers in this regulatory battle are likely to be the local merchants and protected industries, which are spending protected profits to fight change rather than respond. Now, many of the legal oddities are being repealed, not so much for digital trade but to improve the efficiency of the supposedly borderless European market. The EU, for example, has sensibly ruled that the law governing retail transactions is that of the merchant's country, not the customer's, taking most of the local protections out of the equation. This directive actually made a catalyst into an obstacle for local merchants, allowing foreign competitors to bypass the restrictions they are still bound to follow.

There is still far to go. In 2001, Germany began dismantling a crazy-quilt of retail controls—overturning laws that made it illegal to, among other things, give away shopping bags, announce that a small portion of sales will be donated to charity, offer an unconditional guarantee, or advertise a program that offers points for every dollar spent with a credit card. Even with the repeals, however, German markets are still under the control of powerful retailer lobbies. Recently, the German government ordered Wal-Mart to raise prices for basic household goods at its German stores—surely no benefit to consumers.

Information technology is also wreaking havoc with territorial marketing rights, which restrict the countries in which different sellers can offer identical products. Using the Internet, consumers can bypass their local sellers and shop virtually wherever they want. Consumers do so more and more, and not just to get a better price. In 1999, American fans of the Harry Potter books outraged Scholastic Books, the only licensed publisher for the United States, by ordering the British edition of a new installment in the series from Amazon's U.K. Website months before the book was available in the United States. Showing their enthusiasm for global commerce and their disdain for artificial controls, American readers even posted reviews of the unpublished American edition on Amazon's U.S. site which let fellow readers know how easy it was to circumvent the publisher's controlled-release strategy. Amazon refused to cut off sales from the U.K. site to the United States, and Scholastic was forced to speed up its own release.

The Revolution in Intellectual Property Law

No aspect of law is experiencing more conflict than intellectual property (IP) law, which includes copyright, trademark, and patent. Since IP explicitly governs the regulation of information, it is no surprise to find even experts in the field baffled by the almost daily developments that offer new ways of creating, marketing, and distributing information goods. Despite the growing importance of information to the bottom line, only large companies are likely to have one or more members of their legal staff devoted to the company's IP.

Up until recently, that was an appropriate allocation. If your business deals with physical products, after all, there is little need to appreciate the fine points of obscure doctrines of "trade secrets" or "trademark dilution," to name two. I have often heard the CEOs of billion-dollar companies speak authoritatively about copyrighting words or owning ideas, suggesting a nearly complete lack of knowledge about IP (neither is allowed).

Ignorance of IP law is largely harmless, but not for much longer. As revenues become more information dependent, and as new sources of information work their way into the ISC, all executives, regardless of their job description or the nature of their company's products, will require a basic course in information law. This section is merely the introduction to that course.

The most important thing to understand about IP law is that it is concerned with the ownership of invisible capital, which we have seen operates under different economic rules than physical property. It has only been in the last 300 years, in fact, that law has recognized any protection for information products (fortunately for 16th-century author William Shakespeare, who "borrowed" nearly all of his plots from other playwrights). Before that, it was understood that ideas, designs, written works, and songs were free to everyone upon creation, just like the languages in which they were written and the earlier works upon which they were inspired or informed.

It may surprise you to learn that IP law is not designed to reward people for being creative. Rather, its express goal is to maximize the amount of information that is freely available to everyone. How, you may wonder, can laws that grant writers and inventors the right to decide who can copy their work and how they can use it be said to maximize the flow of information? The answer is that IP rights are granted for a *limited* time only; just long enough, in theory, for the creators of valuable new information to recover their costs and make enough profit to encourage them to keep creating. After the time period expires, the information belongs to society—the "public domain"—free to be copied and used by anyone.

IP law, in some sense, began with technology. When England passed the first copyright statute in 1710, Parliament recognized that new printing technologies not only made it easier for information to be spread, but also to be copied, and they feared that if authors could not recover their investment before their work was duplicated, no new works would be produced. Thus copyright (and patent on the same theory) grants a monopoly to authors and inventors during which only those they license can copy "their" information.

That monopoly, however, has limits, both of time and of control. Having purchased the book you are now holding, you are free to resell your copy to whomever you want. You may write a review on Amazon (please do). You may also freely use any of the ideas, concepts, and techniques you like—if I did not think you would, I would not have bothered to write it in the first place. What you cannot do is reprint my exact words and claim them as your own, or make a copy of your copy and sell that at the same or a lower price than what my publisher and I are charging (although after I have been dead for 70 years you are free even to do that—Shakespeare's heirs get nothing no matter how many times *Hamlet* is produced).

The perennial challenge of IP law is to maintain the balance between the value of the incentive and the harm of the monopoly; that is, to give creators enough control to encourage them to produce but not so much that valuable information is kept from the public any longer than is necessary. As new forms of intellectual property are created (in 1710 there was no prerecorded music, software, or movies) the law must determine the extent of the monopoly that should be granted to encourage new classes of creators. Do software programmers need more or less incentive than novelists? Should maps be protected for longer or shorter periods than choreography?

Technology upsets the balance of IP law not only by generating new kinds of intellectual work, but also by undermining assumptions about which costs authors and inventors need to recover in the first place. As new technologies for copying and distributing are invented—photocopiers, low-cost printers, and of course the World Wide Web—the balance for all forms of IP may need adjustment. Printing technology has improved, lowering the cost of production for books, but the Internet makes it easier to copy illegally, which may argue for stronger protection.

Beyond the Internet, in fact, Moore's Law has been systematically lowering many of the costs associated with intellectual property, including research, reproduction, distribution, and marketing. Yet IP lawmakers around the world have been convinced to grant *added* incentives for copyrights, trademarks, and patents—increasing their duration, giving owners more control, and increasing the penalties for unauthorized uses.

Why? When expensive capital investments like printing presses and factories were necessary to distribute information, most authors and inventors had little choice but to sell their rights to publishers and manufacturers who could better bear the risk that the initial investment would never be recovered. As a result, large media companies have amassed huge stockpiles of invisible capital, and they are using their lobbying skills to secure broader rights even as the need for them has largely diminished.

When IP protections are too broad, however, the market eventually forces them back. Even in the first copyright law, judges were given the power to reset prices for books if the copyright holder was found to charge "high and unreasonable" prices. Napster is in some sense a self-help version of that power—a revolt against artificially high CD prices (prices that the FTC has since determined were unlawfully controlled). Software piracy, in a similar vein, may account for as much as 50% of all copies for popular products. The imbalance in today's IP laws will need to be corrected. If it is not, today's minor skirmishes may lead to all-out war between copyright owners and consumers.

Indeed, Stanford Law School Professor Larry Lessig has already declared war. In 2001, a Russian software engineer was indicted under the U.S. Digital Millennium Copyright Act (DMCA), which makes it a crime to circumvent anticopying technology in digital media. Many, like Professor Lessig, believe the DMCA went too far, and that the provisions under which the Russian programmer was charged grant a permanent, unlimited monopoly to authors of digital media (or rather to their publishers). At a rally in support of the programmer, Lessig announced, "This is the beginning of a revolution."

Obstacle to Catalyst: General Techniques

Of all the obstacles to execution, law is perhaps the hardest to convert to a catalyst. It is the most complex, the most dependent on location, and sub-

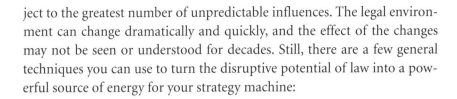

ject to the greatest number of unpredictable influences. The legal environment can change dramatically and quickly, and the effect of the changes may not be seen or understood for decades. Still, there are a few general techniques you can use to turn the disruptive potential of law into a powerful source of energy for your strategy machine:

1. **Be Aware**—To begin with, you must understand that law affects each of your portfolio investments. As you develop the key components of your information supply chain, you are certain to be confronted with difficult and often novel questions of law and regulation. Bring to bear all of your available legal resources. Your company's general counsel is an essential participant in the care and feeding of your strategy portfolio. The more the legal staff understands your goals, objectives, and initiatives, the better they will be able to help you steer clear of legal obstacles or successfully invert those that are unavoidable. In many companies I have worked with, legal counsel is brought in only when something goes wrong. That is a recipe for disaster.

   As you start to buy and sell in more locations, particularly in other countries, you will also need at least passing knowledge of local laws and trade customs. Many companies developed on-line storefronts hoping to increase business in their own country and found almost by chance that they were being contacted by customers and distributors in countries in which they had no previous dealings. If you became a "global company by accident," now is a good time to step back and review your practices for conformity in countries where you have significant new business.

2. **Lobby**—Beyond the specific legal environment for your industry, your lobbying resources should also promote laws that solve broad problems of infrastructure for the emerging ISC. Enacted and pending legislation regarding information privacy can slow by years the progress of building an ISC in your industry. If you and your trade partners engage in the debate understanding what is at stake, it is possible to develop laws that will speed the effort considerably to the benefit of every participant in the supply chain, not least of all consumers.

   In addition to your own legal team, make use of other legal resources at your disposal. Most companies belong to trade associations whose first priority is to monitor relevant developments in law and regulation for their members, and lobby for changes that will improve conditions for the industry as a whole. But many of these groups are unaware of the growing importance of information and information law to the business of their members. Trade associations and lobbyists cannot be effective if they do not understand and share your vision of the emerging supply chain.

3. **Exploit Loopholes**—If your industry is blessed with regulations that protect, at least in part, advantages that work mostly in your favor, do not be ashamed to use those laws as leverage for new initiatives. While you try to build a new channel, for example, enforce protections in place for the old one. Of course you must recognize that many of these protections are entering their last years of service, and at some point may become harmful rather than helpful. But as long as you are aware of their limitations, there is no reason not to make use of them for competitive purposes.

On the other hand, overly aggressive use of legal protections can backfire. Postage meter manufacturer Pitney Bowes enforced its patents to neutralize the threat of new competitors including Stamps.com, which sells postage on-line and prints proof of postage directly on envelopes inserted into a user's personal printer. This in turn led the U.S. Department of Justice to investigate Pitney Bowes for anticompetitive behavior. This was not the first time Pitney Bowes put itself at risk. In 1959, the company was forced to license many of its patents to other meter manufacturers, royalty free, as punishment for anticompetitive behavior. Intellectual property, more than other legal rights, can often turn into a "curse in disguise."

CATALYST 8: FINANCING THE FUTURE

Of all the external catalysts, finance presents the most direct and the most dangerous threats to your strategy machine. To get a sense of why, let me start with the story of a consulting project I was involved with a few years ago.

Our project to review the strategy portfolio of a large hospitality company was going well. The client had made significant investments in new technologies over the previous several years, including a successful on-line reservation system that was already profitable and a sophisticated loyalty program with over 10 million members. The client had also committed

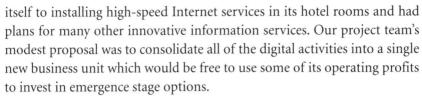

itself to installing high-speed Internet services in its hotel rooms and had plans for many other innovative information services. Our project team's modest proposal was to consolidate all of the digital activities into a single new business unit which would be free to use some of its operating profits to invest in emergence stage options.

At the final presentation to senior management, a brick wall suddenly appeared. The new business unit, we reported, required $4 to $5 million in seed capital, money it would pay back in the first year through contracts to other business units for services already being provided. The company that year reported over $700 million in profits, meaning the money we were asking for represented less than 1% of annual profits. But the company had just completed a series of complex financial transactions to spin-off some of its assets, and neither the chief financial officer nor the chief legal counsel was in the mood to start any new businesses, no matter how little money was at stake. Despite the unquestioned potential of the proposed new unit, the project ended halfway through the meeting.

Though rarely with so much drama, every strategy machine must face the finance hurdle, at roughly the same point in its development—just when you're ready to shift to high gear. Flush from the discovery of a stockpile of invisible capital and the creative potential of the portfolio approach, you may spend a month or two surfacing interesting ideas and classifying them as efficiency-, exchange-, or emergence-stage investments. With a first set of portfolio investments in mind, off you go to propose funding the development of new information goods to the executive team. That is when reality hits: *How are we going to pay for this?*

Even if the initial investment is a tiny fraction of a company's operating budget, as it was for my client, many companies have trouble spending any money on innovation. For most of the portfolio investments, by definition, you cannot confidently predict when or even if they will pay returns, and your company may have no other mechanism for evaluating investments. For public companies, the problem is underscored by the unforgiving capital markets which penalize any expense that reduces earnings per share in the current financial quarter, regardless of whether that expense will generate exceptional returns in the future.

Worse still, during the Internet boom of 1998 and 1999, public companies found themselves competing with technology startups, many of them public companies, who were being evaluated by Wall Street on different criteria. Startups were expected and able to raise money from investors and spend it aggressively to create new markets, giving products and services away for free and advertising obscure offerings on national television. Amazon was famously chided at one point early in its life as a public company for not spending enough money to build its infrastructure and acquire other companies with high-potential technologies.

The run-up in stock prices for early-stage Internet companies gave these companies something even more valuable than the cash raised in their IPOs—their stock. Stock that is doubling every six months (as many did) is a very powerful currency indeed. Stock and stock options were spent wildly, both to acquire other companies and to attract the kind of programming, design, and strategy talent necessary to keep a strategy machine humming. (Yahoo! paid $3.9 billion in stock to acquire free home-page provider Geo-Cities; Internet security firm Verisign traded approximately $19.6 billion worth of its shares for domain-name registry Network Solutions.) When the market was boiling over, Internet companies could even use high stock values to buy companies in the existing supply chain, many of which were suffering from what some analysts called a "stealth" bear market.

Well, that was then, as the saying goes, and this is now. With the market correction of the last few years, many of the startups are gone. Technology companies left standing have likewise had to change their strategy for financing innovation. For the five years ending in 2000, the stock of networking giant Cisco averaged a 100% return every year, allowing the company to acquire rather than build most of its newest products. After buying 23 companies in 2000, Cisco's stock dropped dramatically. During the first half of 2001, Cisco did not acquire any companies.

Readily available capital from the public and private markets has also dried up substantially. Gone are the days when 30-year-old venture capitalist Steve Jurvetson made *200 times* (not 200%) his investment in the free email provider Hotmail when it was sold to Microsoft in 1998 for $400 million. Seed money for the most speculative ventures has likewise slowed considerably, although it is still far higher than it was for much of the 1980s and 1990s.

Obstacle to Catalyst: To Spin or Not to Spin

With the currency of technology ventures severely devalued, non-technology companies are re-evaluating decisions made at the height of the boom to spin out some portfolio ventures into separate public companies. Entities that were taken outside solely to cash in on the public appetite for

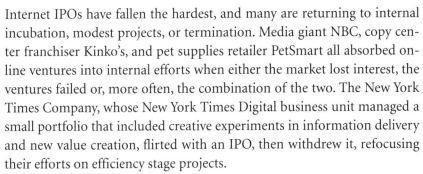

Internet IPOs have fallen the hardest, and many are returning to internal incubation, modest projects, or termination. Media giant NBC, copy center franchiser Kinko's, and pet supplies retailer PetSmart all absorbed on-line ventures into internal efforts when either the market lost interest, the ventures failed or, more often, the combination of the two. The New York Times Company, whose New York Times Digital business unit managed a small portfolio that included creative experiments in information delivery and new value creation, flirted with an IPO, then withdrew it, refocusing their efforts on efficiency stage projects.

Some companies chose an in-between strategy, issuing tracking stocks for their on-line initiatives. Tracking stocks, a virtual grouping of some of a company's assets without formally separating them out in a subsidiary, are a halfway approach, giving companies some currency to compete for employees who might otherwise leave for startups, but not committing the company to taking the ventures outside.

For many, the result was the worst, not the best, of both worlds. The market was often skeptical of the tracking stocks, and the lack of true spin-off meant the smothering corporate bureaucracy was never far away. Disney, as noted earlier, closed its failed Go.com portal in early 2001 and absorbed its on-line ventures tracking stock. Disney's independent projects, including ESPN.com, did better at hiring and retaining entrepreneurial talent without a tracking stock.

How do you decide when to spin-out a promising investment? The answer is simply to manage the strategy portfolio. The decision to spin or not to spin should be made based on the stage of metamorphosis the investment represents:

- **Efficiency**—Efficiency stage projects should never be spun out. They have little of the killer app potential outside investors look for and their need for close integration with the existing business demands that they be kept close to home and under your control. *When it's core, leave it inside.*

- **Exchange**—At the exchange stage, depending on how close the activity is to a core function, either strategy can be appropriate.

- **Emergence**—For investments with the highest risk and longest incubation, leave them outside, and leverage your investment with those of channel partners, venture capitalists, and, when possible, public investors.

These general guidelines do not apply, however, to industries undergoing a rapid transformation, especially one that follows a long period of regulation or otherwise stable relations among supply chain participants. Here emergence-stage activities happen at a rapid pace. If you are now in such an environment, or find yourself in one later, the need to respond quickly will require you to keep emergence investments inside and run them as projects—projects, in this case, on which your future depends. That's what discount broker Charles Schwab did when it realized it was in the middle of a paradigm shift. Transforming the entire company from a traditional discount broker to a virtual asset manager in a matter of months was neither easy nor fun, but it was, as the market now appreciates, vital.

Obstacle to Catalyst: Corporate Venture Capital

To keep your strategy machine firing on all cylinders, you must generate a healthy supply of emergence options and test them in the marketplace. Even if all of your efficiency and exchange investments are kept inside and on your balance sheet, financing the future requires working outside of your traditional budget and organization rules at least some of the time.

The best way to do that, as we have seen, is through corporate venture capital. By investing alongside professional entrepreneurs, your company gains access to skills it may not have and, at the same time, leverages the invisible capital of your brands, relationships, and existing infrastructure. Corporate venture capital, in effect, is virtual research and development. As Visa's Todd Chafee once put it, corporate venture capital "makes all of Silicon Valley our R&D lab."

Since 1996, the numbers of companies that have made venture investments has more than tripled. During the height of the bull market of 1999, in fact, corporate investing accounted for over 15% of all venture funding, representing more than $4 billion in the first three quarters of 1999 alone.

Over the last 20 years, information technology companies have used much of their profits to acquire early-stage companies, operate corporate venture capital funds, and invest in the funds of others. Microsoft, Compaq, Dell, Disney, Lucent, Nortel, Novell, and Sun, for example, are all recent investors with Accel Partners, which manages a wide-ranging portfolio of new communications and software startups. Established technology companies invest with Accel and others in part for the financial rewards but also to extend their own strategy portfolios. Investing in different funds maximizes the potential for early access to companies that may become partners, providers, customers, or possibly subsidiaries.

The choice of Accel as the corporate venture partner of choice is not surprising since the firm has distinguished itself by helping even non-technology companies unlock the value of invisible capital. It was Accel, for instance, that rescued Wal-Mart's stalled efforts to expand its reach on-line (Wal-Mart bought out Accel's share of WalMart.com in mid-2001). In July 2000, Accel also launched eMac Digital with fast-food leader McDonald's, which will develop technologies to improve the company's supply chain. eMac Digital is a separate company with its own capital structure, board of directors, and management team, positioned to benefit from both McDonald's industry experience and Accel's expertise in new technology.

Corporate venture capital delegates much of your emergence stage innovation to professional entrepreneurs, but not all of it. Every manager in your company needs to be alert to the investments you are making and find the early opportunities to exploit the products and services of your virtual R&D lab. Assigning internal champions also gives your company a chance to shape the products it is partially funding around your own strategies.

In particular, the role of your chief financial officer will change substantially as you shift your emergence stage activities toward venture investing. The CFO is a central figure in the operation of your strategy machine, defining criteria for investment, performing due diligence, and measuring the progress of every investment in the portfolio. Some CFOs fit naturally into this new, more strategic role; others require intensive training to develop venturing skills. A few, like Dell Computer's CFO Tom Meredith, ultimately find the venture activities more satisfying than their traditional responsibilities. When Dell decided to expand its venture activities, Meredith left the CFO's office to become the first managing director of Dell Ventures, where he oversaw the investment of $700 million in 90 startup companies.

As with each of the execution obstacles, turning finance into a true catalyst for change requires leadership from the very top. As the company's voice to shareholders and analysts, the CEO is bound to encounter confusion, resistance, and skepticism as company funds, however modest, are spent on speculative investments. The CEO must be comfortable enough with the contents of the strategy portfolio to paint the bigger picture to investors, and do so repeatedly and patiently, buying the company the time it needs to make the transformation to an uncertain future. As Eastman Chemicals' recently retired CEO Earnie Deavenport advises, "You have to be diligent in telling your story, and you have to believe that long-term, the stock market is rational."

In a sense, we end where we began: overcoming obstacles that stand in the way of great inventions. Whether you are trying to build an Information Supply Chain to connect customers with suppliers or, like Ferdinand de Lesseps, a canal to connect East with West, the biggest problems are rarely problems of technology, but of finance, regulation, and most of all conflicts inside and outside your organization. Change, even beneficial change, is hard. It is human nature to resist it, and there is only one technology that can overcome human nature: the technology called leadership.

Most of the examples we have seen were of companies—companies that did or did not rise to the challenge of industry metamorphosis and companies that are now working hard to turn their strategy portfolios into perpetual strategy machines, churning out the new information products and services made possible by the Information Revolution. In all, the strategies, investments, triumphs, and mistakes of over 100 companies have been explored.

In each of those companies, however, the real decisions, good and bad, were made not by machines or markets, but by individuals. As we have seen in these last chapters, this is also where the real changes need to happen. Industry transformation is personal transformation on a grand scale, and your personal transformation is just as dependent on an Information Supply Chain—the one in your head.

To manage your company's portfolio, start by managing your own. Invest in yourself—your skills, your expertise, your personal brand. Build up the value of your own invisible capital, then inspire your colleagues, customers, and business partners to do the same.

In the age of the disposable computer—just as was true in the age of the steam engine—the rest will take care of itself.

ACKNOWLEDGMENTS

My email archive for *The Strategy Machine* includes over 1,000 messages, many from clients and colleagues, as well as readers of my monthly column in the now-defunct magazine *The Industry Standard,* who gave generously of their time to enlighten, correct, or simply to disagree with me. I cannot thank them all, but suffice it to say the book you have just read benefited enormously from their collaboration.

I owe particular thanks to Luke Mitchell, who as my editor at *The Industry Standard* made me rewrite my columns until I was ready to kill him, but always, in retrospect, just the right number of times. He played a similar role with this manuscript. My gratitude as well to former *Standard* editors Mickey Butts and Jonathan Weber, and to the organizers, speakers and attendees of Net Returns 2000, whose agenda formed this book's earliest outline.

For helpful suggestions and guidance on the manuscript, my thanks to Richard A. Posner, John Donohue, David Johnson, David Reed, and Peter Christy. My thanks as well to the many people who took the time to review and correct my comments about their companies and strategies, including Kevin Ashton, Hank Barry, Alex Moissis, Gaurav Dhillon, Phiroz Darukhanavala, Peer Munck, Erwin Martinez, Ken Gaebler, Dick Costolo, John Malloy, Dave Kellogg, David Simon, and Andy Lippman.

At Eastman Chemical Company, I am particularly grateful to Fred Buehler, Mark Klopp, and Roger Mowen and also Regg Bonnevie, Earnie Deavenport, Brian Ferguson and Raj Mehta. Jerry Schlather tracked down and verified several elusive pieces of Eastman data. Adrian Slywotzky and Heidi Mason, my fellow members on the Eastman Board of Advisors, were regular sources of great ideas, many of which I have freely appropriated.

Thanks also to Hal Varian, Seth Godin, Geoffrey Moore, Don Tap-scott, Kevin Maney, and Bob Gardner. For research assistance, my thanks to John Castro. Nancy Bacal kept my pen moving, no matter what.

At HarperBusiness, I have had the guidance and support of too many people to name, but I must single out Carie Freimuth, Joe Veltre, Lisa Berkowitz, Adrian Zackheim, and Sarah Beam.

For support of every imaginable kind, my deepest thanks go to my partner Richard Bessman, without whom nothing is possible.

CRITICAL READING

A Brief Bibliography

Charles Francis Adams, Jr., and Henry Adams, *Chapters of Erie* (Great Seal Books 1956)

Henry Adams, *The Education of Henry Adams* (Houghton Mifflin Company 1973)

C. Gordon Bell, *High Tech Ventures* (Addison-Wesley 1991)

Melville M. Bigelow, Editor, *Centralization and the Law* (Little Brown 1906)

Frederick P. Brooks, Jr., *The Mythical Man-Month* (Addison-Wesley 1982)

James Burke, *Connections* (Little, Brown and Company 1978)

———. *The Pinball Effect* (Little Brown and Company 1996)

Clayton M. Christensen, *The Innovator's Dilemma* (Harvard Business School Press 1997)

Ronald H. Coase, *The Firm, the Market and the Law* (The University of Chicago Press 1998)

———. *Essays on Economics and Economists* (The University of Chicago Press 1994)

Paul David, "Productivity growth prospects and the new economy" *European Investment Bank Papers,* Vol. 6, p. 56 (2001)

———. "The Dynamo and the Computer: An Historical Perspective on the Modern Productivity Paradox," *American Economic Review,* Vol. 8, p. 355–61 (1990)

Larry Downes and Chunka Mui, *Unleashing the Killer App: Digital Strategies for Market Dominance* (Harvard Business School Press 1998)

Peter F. Drucker, *Post-Capitalist Society* (HarperBusiness 1993)

———. "Beyond the Information Revolution," *Atlantic Monthly* (October, 1999)

Amy Friedlander, *Natural Monopoly and Universal Service* (Corporation for National Research Initiatives 1995)

————. *Emerging Infrastructures: The Growth of Railroads* (Corporation for National Research Initiatives 1995)

————. *Power and Light* (Corporation for National Research Initiatives 1996)

————. *"In God We Trust" All Others Pay Cash* (Corporation for National Research Initiatives 1996)

George Gilder, *Telecosm* (Free Press 2000)

Gary Hamel and C. K. Prahalad, *Competing for the Future* (Harvard Business School Press 1994)

Franz Kafka, *The Metamorphosis,* translated by Willa and Edwin Muir (Schocken Books 1948)

Randy Komisar, *The Monk and the Riddle* (Harvard Business School Press 2000)

Elisabeth Kübler-Ross, *On Death and Dying* (Touchstone 1997)

Thomas S. Kuhn, *The Structure of Scientific Revolutions* (The University of Chicago Press 1966)

Lawrence Lessig, *Code and Other Laws of Cyberspace* (Basic Books 1999)

Bernard Liautaud, *E-Business Intelligence* (McGraw-Hill 2001)

Henry Mintzberg, *The Rise and Fall of Strategic Planning* (Free Press 1994)

Geoffrey A. Moore, *Living on the Fault Line* (HarperBusiness 2000)

————. *Crossing the Chasm* (HarperBusiness 1991)

Nicholas Negroponte, *Being Digital* (Vintage Books 1996)

Tom Peters, *The Circle of Innovation* (Vintage Books 1999)

Michael E. Porter, *Competitive Advantage* (Free Press 1980)

————. *"What Is Strategy?" Harvard Business Review* (November-December, 1996)

————. *"Strategy and the Internet," Harvard Business Review* (March, 2001)

Richard A. Posner, *Overcoming Law* (Harvard University Press 1995)

David P. Reed, *"The Law of the Pack," Harvard Business Review* (February, 2001)

Hugh Joseph Schonfield, *The Suez Canal in Peace and War, 1869–1969* (University of Miami Press 1969)

Carl Shapiro and Hal R. Varian, *Information Rules* (Harvard Business School Press 1999)

Robert J. Shiller, *Irrational Exuberance* (Broadway Books 2000)

Adrian J. Slywotzky and David J. Morrison, *How Digital Is Your Business?* (Crown 2000)

Tom Standage, *The Victorian Internet* (Walker Publishing Company 1998)

George J. Stigler, *The Structure of Industry* (The University of Chicago Press 1968)

Don Tapscott et al., *Digital Capital* (Harvard Business School Press 2000)

Frederick Winslow Taylor, *Principles of Scientific Management* (W.W. Norton and Company 1967)

Alvin Toffler, *Future Shock* (Bantam Books 1991)

Frederick Jackson Turner, *The Frontier in American History* (Dover 1996)

Max Weber, *The Protestant Ethic and the Spirit of Capitalism* (Charles Scribner's Sons 1958)

Lynn White, Jr., *Medieval Technology and Social Change* (Oxford University Press 1964)

Oliver E. Williamson, *Markets and Hierarchies* (Free Press 1975)

INDEX